CONTENTS

Contents

III RELATIONSHIPS OUTSIDE THE SCHOOL

Preface

The second edition of this book maintains the high standard of the first edition and incorporates revisions as a result of recent legislation. The whole thrust of the Education Reform Act will place a greater emphasis upon the management role of Heads and Deputies in Primary Schools. This book will continue to be invaluble to those Heads and Deputies in the coming years.

D.M. Hart, OBE
General Secretary
The National Association of Head Teachers
Haywards Heath
West Sussex

Acknowledgements

The author and publishers wish to thank the Education Department of Dorset County Council for permission to reproduce an extract from the Dorset LEA Rural Schools submission on page 281.

Introduction

During recent years, as never before, there has been considerable pressure on headteachers to manage their schools more efficiently. Some headteachers have said that they have always been conscious of their managerial role and have always sought to improve their organisational skills. Some heads have misunderstood calls on them to improve these skills, unsure of how learning about management will make them better headteachers. Whatever our preconceptions, we all believe that it is the role of the headteacher to provide the most stimulating enrivonment possible for the children within the school. Management is the organisation of that enrivonment, and headteachers need to take management development seriously if they are seeking to improve the quality of teaching and learning in their schools.

This book tries to identify some of the key areas in which development is presently taking place. It is written by practitioners, most chapters by headteachers, but some by Inspectors/Advisers with responsibilities in primary education. Only three chapters have been written by people from outside this group, two contributors (Derek Esp and Michael Brunt) being LEA administrators having considerable experience within the primary sector, and one (Barbara Bullivant) is one of the best known authorities in the country in her particular field, that of governing bodies, and her views are greatly respected by all those practitioners who meet her.

With this array of authors, there should not be the 'credibility gap' often found between the writers and readers of books for Primary educators.

Most books on school management are written by one person. The writer may be very knowledgeable, but cannot possibly be an expert in every facet of the subject. Consequently, the books are often very basic, and of use only to 'new' headteachers. By using a team of writers with such wide experience in the management of primary education, it has been possible in this book to explore important topics in some depth.

It is usual for books on school management to be sequential – it is necessary to read earlier parts of the book to understand later parts. Each chapter in this book is self-contained, and they can be read in any order. No chapter is too long not to be read in one sitting, and most end with a booklist for the interested reader to follow up particularly interesting ideas.

It is often difficult for books on educational issues to deal with *current* topics because of the timescale between conception and publication. Because this book was written by a team of twenty-one writers it was conceived and brought to publication within a very short time. We have therefore been able to tackle issues that are *important now*.

This book is intended to inform *and* to change practice. Many of the chapters give practical ideas for readers to use in their own schools. It is not intended to be an 'academic' work, to be used mainly by teachers following courses in 'educational management', but a book to be read by all those involved in the management of primary schools as part of their normal professional reading. It should be of particular interest to headteachers, aspiring headteachers, Inspectors/Advisers and administrators with responsibilities within the primary phase.

Ian Craig

PART I PROFESSIONALISM

1 Appraisal – The system in one primary school

Ian Sandbrook

Introduction

Time – before school: As I approach the office I notice Miss A hovering; she has seen a job advertised and has come to talk about her prospects. I am surprised . . .

Time – two minutes before school starts: I meet Mrs B on the stairs; she is worried about Jason. A few sentences make it clear that she is worried about more than just Jason . . .

Time – morning break: Mr C corners me in the staffroom to call into question our new handwriting policy, agreed (so I thought) by the full staff only two weeks ago . . .

Time – end of break: Miss D, hiding behind a large pile of new library books, passes me in the corridor, we exchange a smile – I don't seem to have seen much of her recently . . .

Time – just after break: I find a large requisition for art materials on my desk awaiting signature. Miss E has once again canvassed the whole staff most efficiently . . .

I am sure you will recognise this pattern. These rushed encounters, exposing a mixture of surprises, inadequate consensus, uneven and inequitable contact, neglect, isolation and people taken for granted, hardly add up to good management. I knew as much when I discovered a booklet by Warwick (1983). He argues that we all need to know to whom and for whom we are responsible (position), about what we have done and are going to do (performance), and how our functions fit in to the school's development and in to our own career (potential).

Subsequent reading has shown me that appraisal, as a consistent procedure for evaluation, has other purposes too. On an excellent course entitled *The Effective Manager* (formidable title!), run by the Open University, I learned about the 'control loop'. This is the cycle by which the management of an enterprise proceeds: firstly standards must be set; secondly performance must be measured; thirdly the performance must be compared with the standards; fourthly corrective action might be needed (either to revise the standards or improve the performance). This cycle needs to be sustained and revitalised in all its stages; appraisal is a means of doing so.

I had not been conscious of another important element in the notion of appraisal until the DES started to advocate its inclusion in the contract negotiations of 1985. In many situations, particularly in industry, appraisal is inextricably bound up with reward. The Suffolk Education Department study (1985) funded by the DES discusses this very fully. Reward is not a function of the system of appraisal I shall describe. It is a person-centred approach, heavily dependant on trust, which tries to escape hierarchy as far as possible. Even so, I would concede that its effect has been greater because it has been carried out in a headteacher – assistant teacher context. This context cannot avoid some element of 'brownie-points', a kind of reward but if the process were to be used to assess incremental bonus entitlement, its value as a motivator and facilitator of performance and growth would be seriously reduced.

Since I originally wrote this chapter in 1986, the national context for appraisal has changed. It was included as an element in the 1987 Teachers' Pay and Conditions Act, and after six local education authorities have completed pilot appraisal schemes, it will be implemented across the country over three years, starting in the autumn of 1989. I have not changed my description of the appraisal system at Rosendale Junior School because to do so would be to undermine the essentially organic approach I was then describing. At the end of the chapter, I make comment on some of the aspects of the system which I might now approach differently, partly in response to the pilot schemes, partly in the light of my subsequent experience. The signs are that the DES regulations will contain many of the characteristics of the scheme I describe.

The context

Rosendale Junior School is a 3-form entry school. It has twelve classes with twelve full-time teachers and a roll of approximately 295. There are six post-holders besides the deputy headteacher. It was early in my fourth year of headship that I began to recognise that 'management' is central to headship and not something slightly unmentionable done by 'people in commerce'. The step into appraisal would not have been as logical as it seemed to be if one or two other steps had not been taken first. Cliché though it may be, the idea of 'growth' had always been central to my philosophy and had started to permeate through the staff. I had also begun to emerge from the insecurity of the early days of headship which can so easily preclude delegation and the trust that goes with it. There was some climate of understanding whereby criticism could be seen as constructive and a distinction could be made between the personal and the professional. I do not mean to open up an awkward debate about this much abused, over-used and often inappropriate word 'professional'. I merely mean that the teachers could accept that a dialogue about their performance and potential should take place in the context of the children's needs and the school's enterprise, and need only move into the personal context (the teacher's or mine) as far as we feel safe to go.

Beyond this climate of trust and growth, quite a considerable momentum of change had been established, in curriculum, ethos, teaching style and school organisation. This momentum had been facilitated in part by self-evaluation, both on a school level, using in particular the ILEA document, *Keeping the School Under Review* (1982), and on an individual teacher level, using the Open University's *Curriculum in Action* (1980) materials. We had used these materials to underpin a school-focussed inservice training project two years previously; its 'six questions' provide a most effective model for self-evaluation, for the observation that should precede an appraisal interview, and, to some extent, for the appraisal interview itself. Here they are (a little simplified):

1 What did the pupils actually do?
2 What were they learning?
3 How worthwhile was it?
4 What did I (the teacher) do?
5 What did I (the teacher) learn?
6 What do I (the teacher) intend to do now?

When I describe the appraisal process in detail, it will become clear that observation of the teacher in the classroom is important. The DES Suffolk LEA investigation (1985) identifies this part of appraisal as essential. I do not totally agree, since it would be possible for an outsider to conduct an appraisal interview and for it still to be productive. Even so, the process is enriched if the appraiser knows the context in which the teacher works and can challenge the teacher's perceptions of what is happening there. Furthermore, in so far as the teacher is seeking validation for his/her practice, the appraiser can offer more if he has seen the performance in question. Certainly, if the appraisal is seen as a management tool rather than a support mechanism (which it also is), then observation in the classroom becomes necessary.

Our scheme was much easier to implement because the practice of 'coaching' already existed. This is the 'working alongside' method of training, where the teacher benefits from the prompts and stimulating questions of a colleague. Teachers at Rosendale were already comfortable (on the whole) with my presence or that of a colleague in their classrooms. Considerable mutual learning takes place when teachers visit each other.

Getting started

So there was a readiness when I started to signal the idea of appraisal to the staff in the late Autumn of 1983. There were the beginnings of a person-centred culture, a climate of trust and growth, a momentum of change, an understanding of self-evaluation and a practice of coaching. I have emphasised the context of this innovation because I do not feel that change can take place successfully if it is not in some way organic, growing out of what is already there. This is, perhaps, the danger of a top-down, imposed scheme.

I explored the idea with most of the staff individually, looking for possible resistance, finding out who would be enthusiastic, talking it through with the isolated teacher, the anxious teacher, the confident teacher, the taken-for-granted teacher. I finally put the idea formally to the whole staff at the end of a staff meeting just before Christmas 1983, explaining that I wanted to make sure that each teacher had a fair chance to discuss all aspects of his/her performance and potential. I followed this up with a short explanation of what I was proposing in the first weekly staff bulletin of the next term. I explained the purposes as follows:

For you it will ensure:
   – an opportunity to share in the discussion of central aims
   – a clear understanding of the responsibilities you hold
   – knowledge that your abilities are known, appreciated and will be used
   – knowledge that no aspect of your performance need be hidden

- knowledge that practical help can be negotiated to identify and overcome weaknesses
- the opportunity to discuss the future
- assistance in achieving your goals and ambitions

For the school it will ensure:
- overall aims are understood by all
- we are moving towards achieving those aims (or we find out if we aren't!)
- no doubt exists regarding areas of responsibility
- changes can be made in the light of changing needs
- potential is recognised and developed
- there is an equality of treatment between staff

(These purposes were drawn almost verbatim for the booklet by Warwick [1983])

I went on to explain the frequency, the confidentiality, the recording and the need for an agenda, emphasising that I wanted the interviews to be 'positive, productive, constructive and supportive' and that I would still be available for 'the little chats that take place all the time'.

Two weeks later the proposal was discussed in the staff meeting. There was considerable anxiety, particularly about the confidentiality of the notes taken and the prospect of the actual interview, but several of the teachers seemed already to have made up their minds to give it a try and began themselves to advocate its potential benefits. I had deliberately given the introduction of the idea a lot of time to germinate and I was pleased that several had reached a point where they had their own image of how it could be valuable. The notion of ownership is important in implementing change; the innovator often needs to become anonymous as quickly as possible, particularly if it is the head.

The confidentiality was emphasised, the scheme was to be voluntary and I ventured that I'd seek appraisal from our local inspector so that the risk involved (there was a lot) was shared. One of the teachers offered to go first and the scheme was almost ready to go.

Two weeks later I included in the weekly bulletin a ten-question prompt sheet which I proposed as an agenda for the appraisal interview:

Appraisal questions

1 How have you performed as classteacher/postholder?
2 What are the barriers to more effective performance?

3 What has gone particularly well?
4 What has gone rather less well?
5 How do you feel about your job?
6 What do you like particularly?
7 What do you dislike particularly?
8 Is there any uncertainty or ambivalence?
9 What help do you need from me or from courses?
10 What are your career ambitions?

In March 1984, the first appraisal interview took place.

The Process

Making the appointment

In the first cycle, I took the teachers in the order in which they offered themselves and then asked those who had not if they wanted to have an appraisal interview. In the end, all the teachers had an appraisal; the teachers who went first seemed to pass on a positive feeling to the others.

In the second cycle, I fitted in the teachers in the same month as they had been appraised the previous year. There is a slight problem with new teachers. I spend more time with them anyway, but I feel that a formal appraisal should not come too soon. As a result there are more appraisals in the summer, particularly as teachers leaving have asked for a 'final' interview before they leave.

When I set up the appointment I give the teacher a new copy of the ten-question prompt sheet and, in the second cycle, I have also given a copy of the classteacher prompt sheet and, where appropriate, the postholder prompt sheet, of which more below. I explain that I shall be visiting them more often in the two weeks leading up to the interview. None of the appraisal appointments has been broken.

Observation

I have tried to spend the equivalent of half a day in each classroom during the two weeks prior to the appraisal interview. This has usually been in four blocks of half an hour or so. In the cases where I have not managed this I have found the quality of the appraisal has suffered as a result. I do visit all classes regularly throughout the year but I find that the special visits are helpful because I deliberately set out to test the impressions and assumptions I have of that teacher's practice. It is easy to build up an impression which is not strictly accurate or which is only inferred from another context, it is also easy to retain an impression which was once true but is no longer so.

For my observation I use the six 'Curriculum in Action' questions and also, in my second cycle, the classteacher prompt sheet: ·

Classteacher Prompt Sheet
  – Classroom environment
  – Preparation and planning
  – Organisation and management
  – Relationships
  – Special needs
  – Content and curriculum
  – Teaching style

I do not carry these sheets about or make notes in the classroom. I remind myself of the points beforehand and make notes afterwards if appropriate.

Preparation

For the very first appraisal interview, the teacher had pages of closely-written responses to the ten questions. Since then I have made it clear that the questions and prompts are to help us focus before and when we meet and that extensive written preparation is not expected. Even so, a majority of teachers have come with a short list of points they want to discuss and this has certainly helped.

My preparation is a sifting of data. It is not my intention to deliver a report on the teacher. I want the teacher to report on his or herself, but I do usually find that there are a few specific questions I want to ask. If I am not happy with several aspects of a teacher's performance, I try to identify the three most important questions I would like to raise; more than three seem to lead to overload. I commit these points and questions to memory although usually the teacher brings them up first anyway.

On the day before the appointed day I confirm the time with the teacher, making sure that a full ninety minutes will be available. I also enquire if the teacher is happy to come to my room. All of the interviews except one have taken place in my room, the exception took place in the classroom. It is important to be aware that territory could be a problem and may need to be negotiated.

The appraisals have all lasted for at least an hour and a half, most for about two hours. In almost every case the postholders have needed a second session, arranged at the end of the first session, so that we have discussed the class teaching and career in one session and the post of responsibility at the next. The second round appraisals have tended to be a little shorter.

Uninterrupted time is important. It is hard to restart after an interruption, I switch the phone over and put a notice on the door.

The seating needs to be comfortable, on the same level, and with no barriers between. I have two easy chairs which I place at an angle to each other. It can alter a dialogue decisively to put one person above the other or to 'protect' the exchange with a desk or a table. At the same time, sitting directly facing one another can be intimidating.

I usually suggest a cup of tea before we begin. This takes us both to the staffroom to make it and enables us to enter the room together to sit down and start, at least going part of the way towards neutralising the territory.

Agendas

In the first year of the scheme, the ten-question prompt sheet provided the agenda for the appraisal interview, supported in the case of postholders by that person's contribution to the annual review for the governors. However, it became clear that the question 'How have you performed as a class-teacher?' is so unspecific that I was using my own hidden agenda to open up the discussion. I had made (and forgotten) a commitment to job descriptions in the original proposal for the scheme, something along these lines was clearly necessary. This is where the seven-point class-teacher prompt sheet came in.

At the same time, postholders were asking for a framework for their reports to the governors and there were other pressures pointing towards job descriptions. A small working party decided to evolve a universal job description that would fit all designations.

Post of responsibility: job description
1 Knowledge of designated area:
  – What steps have you taken to refresh or extend your knowledge of the principles and practices in your specialist field during the past year?

2 Scheme of work:
  – Do you have a clear up-to-date understanding of the curriculum content of your specialist field?
  – Is it written down?
  – Is it sequentially organised to provide a coherent progression through the school?
  – Does it take account of infant and secondary continuity?

3 Resources:
 – Are the necessary resources available?
 – Are they well distributed?
 – Are they adequately maintained?
 – Is there any avoidable extravagance?

4 Leadership and Management:
 – Are your colleagues fully aware of the scheme of work and the philosophy behind it?
 – Do they see the implications in terms of methods and organisation?
 – Is there agreement about the presentation of work?
 – Is there an approach to assessment and recording to ensure a real progression in the children's learning?
 – Is there a consensus about standards?
 – Are you receptive to your colleagues' different styles?
 – Can you see what further support is required by way of workshops, discussion, with whole staff, year teams or individuals?

5 Integration:
 – Do class projects sufficiently reflect your area of responsibility?
 – Do you feel confident of the balance of your specialist field within the curriculum as a whole?
 – Have you explored the overlaps between your area and those of other postholders?

6 Special need/equal opportunities:
 – Is the scheme of work flexible to the needs of children of all abilities?
 – Are your colleagues confident in the diagnosis of children's difficulties?
 – Do your colleagues have the strategies to support and stretch children?
 – Does the scheme of work and the teaching approach of your colleagues give equal access to boys and girls, whatever their ethnic or class grouping?

7 Extra-curricular co-ordination:
 – Are you aware of all the activities that take place outside of school time in your specialist area?
 – Are such activities well coordinated and consistent one with another and with the curricular provision?

8 Review:
 – Is the development in your curriculum area monitored?

- Is it recorded?
- Have you been appraised in the past year?
- Do you feel adequately supported?

This has proved effective as an agenda for the postholder part of the appraisal in the second cycle of the scheme. I would wish to point out that it lacks a proper reference to the community or parents, a serious omission.

Starting off

I have usually explained that I shall be noting down the salient points of our discussion as we go along before suggesting that it might be best to start off positively by looking at question three from the ten-question sheet. 'What has gone particularly well?' This has always worked, though with several teachers the idea of admitting success has not been easy to pursue, but then a humourous reference to modesty, or a reference to something I know has gone well has broken the ice. Once the wheels are in motion, it has not been difficult to range across the ten questions, incorporating the other agenda sheets as appropriate.

Skills

Control or release?
The skills that I have found helpful to the process all operate within a context of 'release'. There are some in the world of education who work from the principle that 'people need to know their place'. I am not one of those people. When I used the notion of the 'control loop' earlier, I did not wish to imply a hierarchial or repressive view of the world, merely that, as a headteacher, I have vested in me the responsibility to ensure that the school has purpose and that it is organised effectively to fulfil that purpose. The aim is to release potential within the boundaries of the school community as a joint enterprise. The children need and will need to create their own society, not succumb to it, though that creativity will need to deal with the constraints that history has placed in their way. Appraisal is also about releasing potential, although I may have my own views of the particular means and of the school community and its purpose. The focus is on the teacher and his/her perceptions; (s)he needs to feel his/her own sense of power, though (s)he may also feel mine. So, this is a dialogue, tipped in his/her favour, not a briefing, tipped in mine.

Open questions
Throughout the discussion and especially at the beginning, the teacher needs to be encouraged, given permission, to 'open up'. Questions that have a range of responses are helpful and allow the teacher to feel his/her way onto the more uneven ground. Later on, the question can be used to steer the teacher into an area that I want to refer to; it is far less threatening than a bald statement of criticism, for example: 'how do you feel about doing drama with your class?' as opposed to 'you don't do enough drama.'

Active listening
It helps the teacher to feel valued if what (s)he is saying is obviously being heard. Re-stating his/her comments from time to time, seeking clarification on points of detail, letting go of one's own agenda, frequently renewing eye contact, and acknowledging the risk that has gone into a particular comment all work to take the discussion deeper.

Summarising
A specific aspect of active listening is summarising. I find that doing this fairly frequently creates natural breaks for me to jot down a key word or two. Summarising also helps to point up any particular problem which is going to require a search for strategies and solutions. It also provides a chance to change direction – I find that time passes very quickly; one has to be aware of that.

Overload
I have discovered after one or two appraisals that the teacher had come out feeling swamped; this despite my best efforts to limit my own contribution! The range of the agenda is such that overload is an obvious hazard but then the opposite can also be true; one teacher came back and asked if we could have another go!

Levelling
I would commend to anyone the ideas of 'transactional analysis' (Thomas Harris' book, *'I'm O. K., You're O. K.'* (1973) provides an easy-to-read introduction). The appraisal interview will not work if the appraiser makes the teacher feel like a naughty child or vice-versa; nor will it work if the conversation is played like a game, just for fun; nor will it work if a conspiracy is established whereby both the appraiser and the appraisee talk about the real teacher as if (s)he were someone else (these three examples equate to the parent-child, child-child, and parent-parent transactions). What is needed is a level adult-to-adult discussion in which emotive or manipulative devices are absent. That is not to say that straight-

talking need be brutally frank – it is part of levelling to acknowedge feelings to check out if something might be painful, to accept praise. If one of the parties takes to blaming, either the other or some 'them', then the discussion is losing its way. It is better to keep the dialogue in the first person (not pedantically), so that it does not become abstract or theoretical and begin to avoid what can be done concretely by the two people present. 'Avoiding' can be achieved by changing the subject to sidestep a difficult issue, or by saying 'I cannot' when what is really meant is 'I prefer not to'. Furthermore, if a point has to be made it has to be made; it won't be if it is wrapped up in a lot of placating. There is a way of softening the blow by saying 'I have the impression that . . .' rather than 'you are . . .', but if a blunt statement is made and then half-retracted out of fear for the other's reactions it will lose its point. So, no blaming, no avoiding, no generalising and no placating; blaming is especially dangerous.

Stretch and support
This valuable session needs to be rigorous if it is not to be a waste of time. The best teacher still needs goals to aim for to provide motivation. There must be a feeling that the core of the appraisal operates around and just beyond the teacher's threshold of learning. The best sessions have operated at my threshold too. If this stretching is taking place there needs to be a strong sense of support, an acknowledgement that risks are being asked for or taken. This support needs to be part of the emerging contract: 'Over the next few months, you are going to try this and I am going to support you by doing that.'

Two-way
This idea of contract is part of the fundamental quality of negotiation that permeates the interview. There is always the intrusion of role – I am the headteacher and somehow that is always there – but nevertheless the teacher is the powerful subject of the appraisal; it is his/her job that is under discussion. It is important that the dialogue provides opportunities for him/her to question how I function and to give me feedback, particularly in so far as my performance affects his/hers. This can be quite uncomfortable, but I have learned a lot about myself which has been very helpful, and, after all, the discomfort is the same discomfort as the teacher has to feel.

Ownership
In a report on a teacher that is written for a third party, my view is offered as my view, to be accepted or rejected. In the appraisal

there is no third party and my view is only valuable if it is accepted by the teacher. I have found that my opinion is better heard if it is in reaction, either as a confirmation or a questioning, to something the teacher has already said. As a discussion of performance, past present and future, the appraisal will lead in one of two directions: validation or problem-solving. In validation, I find that my offering something that I approve of is usually greeted by an embarrassed half-rejection, whereas a confirmation of something the teacher has already claimed some satisfaction for is better received. Alternatively I may question the 'achievement' by asking for clarification or offering an alternative view for the teacher to test it against.

Problem-solving
In this aspect of appraisal it is important for the teacher to be the person who states the problem and for him/her to be saying it as 'I' ('I find science difficult') not as 'you' ('so you think I don't do enough science'). When it comes to solutions, the teacher must look for them; I can offer suggestions in response to that. The teacher then needs to evaluate the range of solutions to find the one that suits him/her. I can venture my views on how well it might work, but ultimately (s)he is the one who will have to put it into action. On several occasions, to acknowledge the problem has been as far as the interview has reached. The agreement has been to explore solutions and I have offered the support of release so that she can go and observe how colleagues have solved the problem.

I have noticed that, when two teachers (or two headteachers!) start to talk about their work, there is a tendency to 'celebrate' the problem ('isn't it awful . . . '). It is easy for this to creep into the appraisal but it is not productive and negates the power we have to move towards solutions. There are, it is true, some problems (constraints) that we have to live with, but even here there will be strategies which make such endurance easier to bear. 'I feel much better now I've got that off my chest' may be a valid part of the discussion, but 'I know what I am (you are) going to do about it' is better.

Documentation

One or two of the teachers have noted things down as we have gone along. I try to record all the topics we cover, the particular positive achievements (validation), the strategies agreed (problem-solving) and the tasks to be done by both of us.

I expand these notes, taken mostly in the form of key-words, into a form which can be followed by the teacher. We each have a copy. I always ask the teacher if they represent our discussion accurately and as yet no-one has disagreed with them. These notes are confidential to me and the teacher in question and are then available as part of the agenda for the next appraisal interview.

Whilst I have shown my copies of the notes to no-one, I have referred to them when I have been called on to write a reference, though, in any case, all references in our authority (ILEA) are open to the teacher. I do know that some of the teachers have shown their copy to a colleague.

Outcomes

How effective has appraisal been?
The purposes which were circulated to the staff at the launch of the scheme have been well satisfied. I have found that the cycle of setting standards, monitoring standards and reviewing standards and performance (the control loop) has been more effectively managed. Furthermore, all of the conditions which helped the scheme's implementation (trust, growth, change, coaching, self-evaluation and the person-centred culture) have been developed to a higher level through the scheme itself. Perhaps appraisal could be used to establish these conditions, perhaps it needs these conditions before it can function usefully – a chicken and egg situation?

I cannot itemise the benefits the scheme has brought to individual teachers without breaking confidentiality, but there would be countless examples of how all the points on the classteacher prompt sheet and postholder job description have been moved forward. I can be more forthcoming about how it has changed my own performance: I have had to 'let go' of much more in genuine delegation; I have realised how important it is for change to come from the teachers and not from me – and it does come! I have become very conscious of 'crowding' in the school week and have had to look again and again at priorities and at balance, particularly the balance between events and process in the school year. I have, I feel, become more accepting – accepting that the teacher's way may be better than the one I had in mind, that different teachers are in the job for different reasons, that we all move at a different pace. When I was appraised by our local Inspector I found the experience rather like stopping to look at a map after trying to cross a moor without one; I was able to see how far I'd come, where I'd taken a wrong turning, what I could now do to get back on course. I also felt as if I'd been 'given permission' to stop and realised that I had been running somewhat breathlessly as if that would somehow make up for my doubts about where I had been going.

The teachers have all been happy to come back for the second cycle and there seems to be a view common to all of them that the experience makes them feel valued and valuable. It is a block of time, in some cases as much as four hours (spread over two sessions) which is just for them, or so they experience it. I experience it as time for me and for the school too – it would appear that we are all winners.

Several of the interviews have led directly to curriculum development or innovation. It is significant that one of these came from a teacher who had always been rather isolated; the existence of an agreed scheme led to a quality of interview which would have been hard to set up had it not been everyone doing it.

One particular problem has emerged from the appraisals. Several of the teachers perceive other colleagues as star performers and so belittle themselves. Two of the staff included me as a 'disabling' force. The appraisals have presented an opportunity to tackle this very real difficulty, both in terms of supporting the 'disabled' as they find confidence, power and assertiveness, and in terms of helping the 'disablers' to recognise and notice how, when and why this happens. It has been important for me to discover that if I am tempted to rescue someone, I run the risk of reinforcing that person's self-image as a victim, powerless not powerful.

Developments

Job descriptions

Both the classteacher prompt sheet and the postholder job description came out of the first cycle of the scheme.

Co-appraisal

When the scheme started I suggested that it might help if teachers deliberately paired up to co-appraise each other in the two terms of the year that did not contain the main interview. This suggestion has not been taken up as such though the year-group teams (three teachers each) have discussed particular aspects of each other's appraisals. Very recently we have started a school-focussed inservice training project entitled 'Meeting Individual Needs' and the teachers have paired up to observe particular children in each other's classrooms, again using the six questions from 'Curriculum in Action'. The feedback from these observations will be close to co-appraisal.

Given the level of stress and the state of morale amongst teachers, there is a good case to be made out for 'supervision' as used by social workers.

Children appraising

Some teachers have realised that the appraisal model can be used with children. They have established a pattern of 'conferences' (tutorials) with the children, usually once per half-term, backed up by a record book in which the child reviews her week, including feedback on her teacher's performance, and the teacher writes a reply. It would appear that both the teachers and the children are finding this rewarding.

And finally . . .

There have been several references to power in my description of our faltering steps into appraisal. The further the scheme has gone the more critical I feel this aspect to be. The impression that has been given of appraisal in the debate on teacher's contracts is of a process by which teachers are held accountable for their performance. Of course we are all accountable, above all to our clients the children and, indirectly to their parents. But the unique and thrilling task of fostering the growth of children, enabling them to discover, control and direct their power, is not achieved by teachers who are denied their own power. Teachers have also to discover, control and direct their power, we all do, and it is a process that is never complete. In appraisal I too have power and my role as a headteacher may give me more; I must be careful not to manipulate. Ultimately power can be used to create or to destroy; the correct moral choice is, perhaps, obvious, but is that the choice we always make?

Subsequent thoughts

Shortly after I wrote this description, I moved from Rosendale into the ILEA Inspectorate, and subsequently into the Hampshire Education Advisory Service.

My successor at Rosendale has continued to operate the appraisal scheme. As the pace of change has accelerated, she has found a need for more frequent interviews, with a more limited focus, and, because of limits on time, with less observation, but with a negotiated focus. She has also found that the agendas which I evolved with the staff have needed simplification so that she now works to the following items:

- positive feedback from the observation
- things that are going well
- things that are not going so well
- what is needed for professional development
- how she (as headteacher) is, or is not, supporting the teacher

She has developed the idea of the documentation of the appraisal interview as a contract by arranging that the notes be signed by her and the appraiser. She finds that each interview needs about one and a half hours, for which she arranges cover for the last half hour of the day, incorporating the remaining hour into directed time. The frequency with which she is conducting appraisal, and the heavy investment of time, demonstrate the priority she places on appraisal as a management tool. She also sees appraisal as an effective way of offering systematic support to her staff at a time of rapid change.

As an inspector and adviser, I have conducted a number of appraisal interviews with headteachers, following an in-depth look at the school and at the work of the headteacher. I have used the same basic format and the headteachers concerned claim to have valued the sessions highly, particularly as 'time for them'. Several of these headteachers have successfully implemented an appraisal scheme in their own schools.

In some of the schools I currently work with, the idea of self-evaluation and review is well established. In these schools, the appraisal interview becomes an opportunity to test, or triangulate, the perceptions of the teacher which have been formulated beforehand. Ironically, this is close to the practice of the first appraisal interview I ever conducted, when the teacher arrived with his own written answers to the 'ten questions'. There is considerable advantage in this approach. The ownership of the appraisee over his/her evaluation is established before the appraisal interview, when the view of the appraisee can be more directly offered as evidence from observation which confirms, contradicts, or qualifies the appraisee's view.

A further attraction of this modification to the scheme I evolved in my own school is that it relates closely to the use of a 'critical friend' or 'response partner' in action research. Action research is the identification by a practitioner of a gap between what is happening and what (s)he would like to happen, followed by the implementation of a deliberate change, followed by an evaluation of the effectiveness of that change. The use of a second pair of eyes to provide a reference point in this process is invaluable. I would identify action research as one of the most effective tools available for professional development. Although it is more focussed than appraisal, the two approaches have much in common and can obviously feed off each other.

In 1986, we were still talking of post-holders. Since the implementation of the teachers' contract in 1987, every teacher has some responsibility for curriculum coordination. This means that the process I have described for post-holders will need to be applied to everyone. Unfortunately this adds significantly to the time budget which has proved to be one of the main complications of the national pilot schemes. I established an annual pattern, which I had hoped would be supplemented by peer appraisal. My successor has found that more frequent interviews are useful. There are suggestions from the pilot schemes that a full appraisal will only be feasible every three years. I do not see this as supporting appraisal as a tool either for management or for staff development. For those who recognise the value of appraisal, time can be found, particularly if the scheme is voluntary. But if there is to be a compulsory scheme, there should be time allocated, and paid for, to implement it. The issue of non-contract time in the primary school has been kept in the background for too long; it is time to address it head on.

There are other issues surrounding a national scheme which will need to be resolved. The governors are now more fully involved in the school and will want to play their part in the monitoring of staff development; the assessment of the National Curriculum may well be used as evidence in the appraisal process; the appraisal of headteachers reveals the difficulties of identifying their effective line managers; open enrolment introduces a competitive element into the picture which could complicate the solution of peer appraisal for headteachers; and there remains a lingering doubt about whether the political will for appraisal is inspired by good management practice in support of staff development or is driven by a desire to root out alleged incompetence.

It is a pity that the notion of 'appraisal' carries such a range of connotations. The honest truth of it is that many schools already have structures to support self-evaluation and staff development. The scheme I have described is an attempt to put the informal sharing of feedback about performance, position and potential on a more organised and equitable footing. There are few schools where the volume of such informal evaluation is not already substantial enough for the shift to 'appraisal' to be relatively straightforward. We need now to demystify it and look for a simple process which enables professional judgement to be shared in the interests of supporting each other systematically, equitably, and openly as we do our level best for the learners in our care.

References

Harris, T A (1973), *I'm O. K., You're O. K.,* Pan
ILEA (1982), *Keeping the School Under Review*
Open University (1980), *Curriculum in Action*
Open University (1983), *The Effective Manager*
Suffolk Education Department (1985), *Those Having Torches*
Warwick, D (1983), *Staff Appraisal*, Education for Industrial Society.

Further Reading

Suffolk Education Department (1987), *In the Light of Torches*
Turner, G & Clift, P (1985), *A First Review and Register of School and College Based Teacher Appraisal Schemes*, Open University Press.
Turner, G & Clift, P (1989), *Studies in Teacher Appraisal*, Falmer
Wragg, E C (1987), *Teacher Appraisal – a practical guide*, Macmillan

2 Preparing job descriptions: the head's role

Ciaran Clerkin

Job Description: The Curriculum Coordinator

In consultation with the headteacher, the curriculum coordinator is responsible for:

Overall curriculum management
1 Identifying and determining overall aims and objectives in the subject in accordance with the requirements of the National Curriculum.
2 Determining a curriculum within the subject area relevant to the abilities and needs of all pupils, including those with Special Educational Needs.
3 Organising curricular activities across the school and liaising with feeder schools.
4 Evaluating standards of learning in accordance with National Curriculum directives.
5 Compiling information on achievement and making this available for parents, governors and appropriate external groups.
6 Allocation and supervision of resources necessary for implementing the curriculum.

Leadership and human relations
1 Arranging staff development and support within the curriculum area.
2 Motivating pupils and staff by personal influence and concern for individuals.
3 Helping to solve problems and resolve conflict by using skills of arbitration, negotiation, reconciliation.
4 Helping to establish effective channels of communication within the school.

External accountability

1 Involving parents in school activities connected with the curriculum area and explaining aims, methods of working and assessment procedures.

2 Reporting to parents, governors and inspectors on overall policy as well as assessment results.

3 Helping to represent the school to the local community through displays and exhibitions of work.

4 Liaising with other schools and groups representing an interest in the curriculum area.

This is a job description for a curriculum coordinator. Although it is not an exemplar, it represents an attempt to provide a written account of the person's job, its component tasks and the circumstances in which it is performed. In this chapter I propose to consider the issues arising from the description in relation to the head's managerial responsibility. Having briefly discussed the role of the primary head at present, I shall then comment on preparing a job description using the headings cited as a framework.

For reasons of space, however, I shall refer mainly to job descriptions for those with specific responsibility for one area of the National Curriculum. In doing so, I recognise that there is a danger of overlooking the boundary and possible overlap between jobs and across curriculum areas unless there is regular discussion between the head and others about common objectives.

Job descriptions for those with responsibility for managing the curriculum are a relatively modern development. Prior to the imposition of the School Teachers' Pay and Conditions Document (1988), it was frequently assumed that because people with responsibility knew what their job entailed there was no need to write it down. Indeed, some took the view that it might be counterproductive to engage in an exercise carrying overtones of time-and-motion studies and job-analysis techniques more akin to industry than to education! Others were often wary of identifying teachers' duties too precisely for fear of being unable to alter them at a later stage.

While the Pay and Conditions Document is a comprehensive charter, its main focus is on the *contractual* obligations of staff. It came about mainly because of the widespread industrial action during the mid 1980s. Ideas about accountability coupled with a much greater emphasis on corporate management were, however, already gaining ground in many LEAs since the late 1970s. The Primary Survey (1978) stressed the necessity of clarifying the obligations of teachers. In this document HM Inspectors concluded that 'Heads need, *in consultation with those concerned*, to make quite clear the responsibilities of individual teachers.' (My italics).

The quotation clearly implies that HM Inspectors regard this as a 'shared' responsibility rather than a function of the power used by one individual by virtue of position within the school. It is noteworthy also that their remark comes at the end of a section dealing with *training* as well as 'making the best use of teachers.' There are important implications in the statement to be considered not only concerning the school as an organisation but also the professional development of staff within it.

In the post ERA age, I believe it is more important than ever that all teachers, including the head, should have specific job descriptions related to their individual schools. They should ideally be drawn up in consultation with the school governors who now have a significant role to play not only in determining the curriculum but also in the financial management of the school.

The role of the head

Without doubt the role of the head has changed significantly in the last decade. As Morgan, Hall and Mackay (1983) pointed out, various factors brought about this change, including the development of new power bases within the school coupled with the increasing demands for accountability already referred to. Consequently, the authors argued, heads could no longer promote their policies without contest or impose their values without bargaining and compromise. Clearly the head's traditional role has been modified from determining policy to leading the policy formation process. As a result, leadership is now more concerned with a dialogue focusing on the teacher's and governors' view as well as the head's. A collegial strategy, therefore, based on open negotiations is likely to be the most effective means at present of securing the enthusiastic commitment of staff in the preparation of job descriptions.

The organisation

The organisation in which the head and others work is a dynamic one where individuals are constantly modifying responses to situations, both internal and external. In such circumstances, people have to respond to a range of events occurring in a context of political, social and economic constraints. So, at best a job description can only offer a single snapshot at a particular time in an organisation's history. Moreover, as Gray (1981) argues, most descriptions 'are in reality "notional" structures in that they are a simplified example of what is desired'. He claims that because human behaviour never totally conforms to desired behaviour we must be 'exceedingly cautious' in distinguishing between what is sought and what actually occurs.

It is axiomatic, therefore, that specific job descriptions for individual teachers are less useful as instruments for *controlling* behaviour than *offering a framework* for staff to develop their own strengths for the good of the school. Besides, they should be sufficiently flexible to enable teachers to modify or alter their responsibilities in relation to fresh demands. But this does not mean descriptions should offer unattainable goals or raise expectations beyond what can be achieved, particularly at a time of contraction in the profession.

Preparing the job description

The initiative for preparing a job description may stem from a variety of reasons. At worst, it could be a vague list of duties hastily assembled in preparation for a forthcoming interview. Or it might be put together by a long-serving teacher making way for a new one, in which case intuitive familiarity could blur perception so that it becomes hard to describe the job accurately. Finally, the head could set up the exercise in consultation with others as a means of involving staff more fully or making more effective what they are doing in school in relation to the responsibilities and obligations of the National Curriculum.

How useful a job description is as a practical instrument will depend largely on who made it and how it was made. Other important factors will be the time and other resources available, the experience of the holder and the actual responsibilities agreed. Although the head and the person in the post will normally be the main contributors, it is important to involve individuals and groups in the role-set with whom the teacher must relate to implement the policy. It should be remembered, of course, that *every* job description has its limitations. While it provides a framework for action, a description does not offer guidance on *how* major tasks should be carried out. From the initial preparation stage, therefore, the head ought to stress the need for review and renegotiation when interpretations of a person's role appear to be at variance with what was originally intended.

With *new* appointments, the process ought to begin well before the interview. A concise job description provides a means of enabling potential candidates to assess their suitability for the post. Besides, it can be a relevant point of departure at the interview and an aide in establishing the worth of a candidate in relation to the school's needs. As well as the details contained in the *Pay and Conditions* document, both Bullock (DES, 1975) and Cockcroft (DES, 1982) provide useful guidance in establishing a framework.

The generic example cited at the beginning, adapted from Morgan et al (1983) focuses on the *three* basic elements in need of analysis in preparing a job description:

- overall curriculum management
- leadership and human relations
- external accountability

Curriculum Management

Identifying aims

The key factor in the preparation of a job description is the identification of aims and objectives in the subject area. It is likely that a clear statement of overall aims, such as the one contained in the Warnock Report (DES 1978) will already have been formulated to enable staff to agree together in broad terms what they are doing for all pupils.

When these fundamental perceptions have been established, the head and the coordinator can work together on drawing up more specific aims to be tackled within an agreed period. Although there is no longer any shortage of guidance for undertaking the task in various National Curriculum publications, constant consultation with the other staff and governors is important.

Successful management is the art of the possible. Once the aims related to the job description have been agreed and others have been informed of these, considerable skill and judgement will be needed to recognise where the possibilities lie in determining the curriculum and creating situations where the aspirations in the description can become realities. Complex management skills are involved in the process, for the opening up of curriculum issues can often be an uncomfortable process, threatening individual prestige and personal security. Consequently, close attention must be paid to developing effective relationships and sound communication. This will be referred to in the next section.

Curricular continuity

Most people would agree that education should be envisaged as a coherent whole and that the transition between stages should be as smooth as possible. In the past, however, as Dean (1980) has indicated, this was a concept to which the profession paid only 'lip service'. HMI noted in their Primary Survey that the 'importance of continuity in the curriculum of the schools was largely over-looked'. The document *A View of the Curriculum* (DES, 1980) also argued for more thought to be given to curricular continuity across the sectors. It stressed:

that between primary schools and the schools which receive their pupils there needs to be not only communication about individuals but also consultation about aspects of the curriculum.

With the introduction of the National Curriculum many of the problems regarding continuity are being overcome. But if this aspect of the curriculum coordinator's job description is to be more than just rhetoric, certain considerations need to be taken into account by the head and written into the job description. In the first place, adequate cover to underpin teacher release needs to be organised. This may be achieved in a variety of ways depending on the school's internal policies and the degree of support provided by the LEA.

One option may be to use part of the school's INSET budget to enable the coordinator to work alongside other staff and offer them professional support. Another solution may be for the head to have a regular teaching commitment, thus freeing another member of staff. Whatever arrangement is made, it should not be at the expense of the children's learning nor the effective management of the school. It is essential too that both teaching and non-teaching staff are consulted in advance and their cooperation secured. This helps to keep interruptions to a minimum while ensuring that proper communication is maintained with parents and external agencies in the absence of a senior teacher from normal duties.

The head and the coordinator need to reach agreement about training and inservice support with regard to curricular continuity and decide upon an appropriate time-scale for this activity. The competencies demanded include:

- interpersonal skills
- subject knowledge across the curriculum
- sensitivity to traditions and power positions in other institutions

At the time of preparing the job description, the teacher and the head may find it useful as well to draw up together a framework establishing the kind of liaison which already exists or ought to be developed between infant, junior and post-primary schools in the locality.

Evaluation and review

As the general topic of appraisal has already been dealt with in another chapter, I propose to look briefly here at *evaluation* and *review* of both children's work and teacher performance in relation to the preparation of job descriptions.

Since the introduction of the National Curriculum together with current procedures for assessment, these processes are now coming to be regarded as managerial tasks not only within schools but across cluster groups of schools as well. Consequently there are important implications for both the curriculum postholder and the head.

Much will depend on the degree of trust already existing between staff as well as their willingness to discuss classroom work in an open manner. If evaluation is to be considered as a relevant part of the job description, it is vital that opportunities to visit other classes and schools to discuss the work are provided on a regular basis. Clearly, skill and sensitivity as well as training in the process of observation and interviewing are required.

In *Quality in Schools* (DES, 1985) HMI mention the value of a 'state of readiness' when introducing an individual scheme. For those including evaluation in the job description for the first time, 'pre-evaluation' activities which introduce some of the concepts and attitudes could be examined by the head and the postholder. The stages agreed as a result could then be presented to others for discussion and subsequently included as an appendix to the job description, perhaps with a date for review recorded. The appendix should emphasise the *supportive* nature of this part of the job description as well as the evaluative one. Moreover, attention should be focused on the direct effect of ensuing activities on *pupils' learning*.

Resources

The allocation of proper resources to deliver the curriculum must be considered carefully within the context of Local Financial Management if the description is to have any relevance. The head, working in conjunction with governors, must take a lead in determining financial priorities and creating opportunities for discussion with the post holder about forward planning and budgeting in relation to the overall curriculum for the school.

It is the coordinator's responsibility to look at priorities for additional resourcing in relation to the planned programme as well as any national or local developments which are envisaged. Other staff need to be consulted and the way in which materials are cared for in individual classrooms should be carefully monitored. An efficient system of 'booking' for expensive equipment is necessary as well as a timetable which ensures materials in short supply are circulated fairly.

Inevitably each LEA and individual school will regard certain subjects or activities as being more prestigious than others at any particular time. This may sometimes lead to a feeling within the school that some curriculum areas are treated more generously than others. My own experience, however, suggests that a coordinator who takes the trouble to submit a well prepared brief, supported by accurate costings, is unlikely to go empty-handed when funds are being allocated. It is worth remembering too that careful management of resources together with regular feedback on their use increases the chances of favourable consideration when additional finance is being distributed!

Leadership and Human Relations

The second element in the job description reminds us that the role is concerned not only with tasks and objective but also with people. As a member of the management team, the curriculum coordinator is responsible for getting others moving – or keeping them moving – in the desired direction. The subject of this motivating activity includes pupils as well as individual and team members of staff.

How senior teachers lead develops an atmosphere in the school which helps to operate the mechanism for the achievement of goals. A lot will depend upon the overall ethos together with the head's leadership style which sets the tone vis-a-vis such things as communication, style of management and oversight of work. However, leadership of the kind mentioned earlier in the chapter cannot be confined to the head alone. On the contrary, there is a variety of leadership functions throughout the school to be shared by others, especially senior staff.

Although leadership duties cannot always be readily itemised, discussion about the job description should focus on the coordinator's role in acting as a stabilising force within the school, clarifying aims and objectives as well as providing encouragement for others. From time to time, it will be necessary also for the post-holder to engage in 'productive conflict'. As far as the *resolution* of problems within the school is concerned, there needs to be agreement between the head and the coordinator, with decisions conveyed to staff on the limits of authority in relation to delegated duties.

In recent years there have been major changes in the way the curriculum is organised, many of them imposed from the centre. There will, however, always be a need for schools to be ready to adapt and review in the light of new circumstances. *Initiating change* rather than just reacting to it requires insight together with the capacity to find solutions to difficulties and win acceptance of these by others. Hence the willingness to persuade colleagues to accept new ideas positively, including those who may be lukewarm about innovation, is an important consideration for the coordinator.

Waters has noted (1983) that the *manner* in which responsibility is carried out is of crucial importance. The author argues that:

> while most people will expect the coordinator to exercise responsibilities . . . (with) an air of authority . . . an autocratic style will be met by resistance and may indeed be counterproductive.

Consequently, the coordinator needs to regard the leadership aspect of the job description as a two-way process, paying careful attention to the attitudes and feelings of colleagues. To quote Waters again:

> putting together the situation as it is, the wishes of the head and staff as it might be, and the faith of the post holder in what it could be, a task and role can be negotiated and finally established.

External Accountability

Accountability in education has been defined 'as a means of maintaining or improving the level of public confidence in the education system' (Barton et al., 1980). Although its origins are frequently attributed to events in the 1970s, especially the William Tyndale affair, many activities associated with accountability were present long before these dramatic occurrences. But in the 1990s the framework is more explicit and priorities for schools have been clarified considerably by the National Curriculum Council.

Trends such as falling rolls and freer parental choice have for some time underlined the necessity for schools to be more conscious of their corporate image. The introduction of Local Financial Management of schools together with the requirement for schools to publish their assessment results so that parents and the wider public can make informed judgements about the school, means that marketing the school and managing its reputation is now a key task.

The need to define this aspect of the curriculum coordinator's role in the job description arises, firstly, because others now have a legal right to know what goes on inside schools. Moreover, effective communication coupled with clear understanding can be a positive influence in improving learning attitudes and relationships among pupils. Finally, experience clearly shows that a school's efforts are more likely to win tangible support from governors as well as the wider community, including enhanced resourcing, when respect for the output of the organisation is high.

The issue of marketing the school is discussed more fully in another chapter. However, for the purposes of preparing a job description, the head and the coordinator should consider effective ways of publicising the school's strengths and achievements. This does not, of course, mean sweeping weaknesses under the carpet but rather making sure that shortcomings are identified and where possible a strategy towards eliminating them agreed and conveyed to those with a right to know.

Most day-to-day transactions between parents and teachers with regard to accountability are informal and cannot easily be separated into tasks and commitments. In preparing the job description, however, the head and the coordinator should try to ensure that certain practices are enshrined in school policy.

Parents' entitlement to detailed results of assessment in simple and clear language is the key element in the process. Regular communication on pupils' progress with class teachers is obviously necessary as well as the opportunity to visit other classrooms at appropriate times. In view of the coordinator's wider responsibility for progress in an individual subject, it is also necessary for *parents* to know how to make contact when a particular concern arises. Naturally, the headteacher will usually wish to be involved in the process when parents require further clarification or wishes to make an official complaint in accordance with the terms of the Education Reform Act (1988).

As well as encouraging a general atmosphere of openness and enquiry, the coordinator will also have a significant contribution to make by organising systematic arrangements to explain not only to parents but governors and external groups the school's programme of work for the curriculum area as well as the assessment results achieved by pupils. Where modifications or disapplications have been made for pupils with Special Educational Needs, the coordinator will also have a responsibility along with the headteacher to ensure that accurate information is once again provided for parents and governors.

An account of curriculum development together with reports on general standards of performance can also be furnished in various informal ways, including talks to governors, discussion evenings for parents, news bulletins, class magazines and displays of work.

Summary and Conclusions

To sum up, the contents of the job description should be concise
and straightforward, covering the job title, organisational relations
(to whom and for whom the curriculum coordinator is responsible
and others with whom the teacher must liaise) as well as a general
statement of the tasks to be performed, as outlined in the introduction. Once agreement has been reached on the contents, the document should be circulated to those entitled to see it.

My analysis indicates that a job description is not merely intended
to prescribe minimum requirements or reduce opportunities for
initiative. On the contrary, it seeks to promote a firmer realisation
of the responsibilities involved in a teacher's work, leading to higher
standards of professionalism in the school. Moreover, the aim is to
extend not only the coordinator's role but that of others with whom
the teacher must interact so that the purposes of the organisation
can be fulfilled more completely.

Throughout the chapter I highlight the fact that leadership is
exercised through a variety of formal and informal channels. It
involves persuasion and influence to link and reconcile the often
disparate objective of the wider school community. Because
schools are dynamic, the job description is frequently concerned
with *change* in the system. But, as Paisey (1984) points out, leadership should also be identified with routine maintenance of
initiatives:

> the working life of most people (in school) today, in spite of the uncer-
> tainties and complexities which abound, consists essentially of steady
> application, a good deal of repetition and attempts to make existing
> relationships work well.

Given the diverse set of duties portrayed in the job description,
the management of *time* is an important consideration. Organising
administrative tasks as well as class teaching presupposes careful
forward planning. Nevertheless, even the most efficient teacher is
likely to experience stress occasionally because of discontinuity in
the work pattern. The pressure of a host of minor matters which
sometimes prevent attention being given to more professional concerns can be a source of frustration. Besides, the teacher may lack
the confidence to accept the less pleasant aspects of the role such
as resolving conflict or the supervision and correction of others.

The ensuing anxiety could be detrimental to overall effectiveness
and job satisfaction unless it is recognised and the support to cope
with it is provided. Both the head and colleagues who appreciate
the specific circumstances of the school can exercise an important
counselling role here, especially with new appointees. Discussion

and training in style and approach as well as assistance with inter-personal skills may be needed. A good way for the coordinator to tackle unfamiliar elements of the job description may be through 'bridging delegation' – working alongside another person and examining together the methods employed afterwards.

In determining the best use of time, the coordinator needs to be clear about priorities and relate activities to these. Discussion on how to *create* time can in itself often enable individuals to define more clearly how they propose to tackle their duties. The crucial decision is between what is urgent and what is important. Within the 'important' category, the coordinator and the head need to think about the short-term and long-term. For both it can be helpful to negotiate intermediate stages in the job description (with 'do by' dates) which others are aware of.

The tasks set out in a job description of the kind referred to in this analysis entail the obligation that those in managerial roles support the job-holder in undertaking allocated duties. There are plenty of messages in HMI surveys and elsewhere in the literature suggesting that coordinators require time *during the school day* to enable them to carry out their duties effectively. The consequences for senior management, particularly the arrangement of suitable cover, must therefore be considered carefully.

The delegation of responsibility cited at the beginning clearly implies an increase in decisions which can be made without referral. Consequently, good communication and trust as well as an accept-ance by others that mistakes will be made occasionally is important. Inevitably, some aspects of management are interrelated and the head must recognise this in assigning job descriptions. The precise cut-off point at which one job ends and another begins is often hard to specify. Furthermore, as roles are constantly developing, descriptions soon become outdated so that review is necessary from time to time. As circumstances change, certain functions within the school may become obsolete with the result that people may need to be informed of redefined duties and where possible involved in the development of new approaches.

Finally, we must not assume that just because a job description has been constructed and the managerial recommendations above have been acted upon, all will be well. It has to be remembered too that the occupant of the role is by nature functionally imperfect. But, to end on a positive note, people have capacities for develop-ment together with the resilience to face new challenges which far exceed any limitations or specifications we may define for them. For the true leader, like Wordsworth's 'Happy Warrior',

Looks forward, persevering to the last
From well to better, daily self-surpast!

References

Barton, J, Becher, T, Canning, T, Eraut, M and Knight, J (1980), 'Account-ability in Education', in Bush, T, Glatter, R, Goodey, J and Riches, C (Eds) *Approaches to School Management*, Harper and Row.

Dean, J (1980), 'Continuity' in Richards, C (Ed) *Primary Education: Issues for the Eighties*, Black.

DES (1975) *A Language for Life* (The Bullock Report), HMSO.

DES (1978a) *Primary Education in England – a Survey by HM Inspectors*, HMSO.

DES (1978b) *Special Educational Needs* (The Warnock Report), HMSO.

DES (1980) *A View of the Curriculum*, HMSO.

DES (1982) *Mathematics Counts* (The Cockcroft Report) HMSO.

DES (1985a) *Curriculum Matters*, HMSO.

DES (1985b) *Quality in Schools – Evaluation and Appraisal*, HMSO.

DES (1988) *School Teachers' Pay and Conditions Document*, HMSO.

Gray, H (1981), 'The Relationship Between Organisation and Management in Schools' in *School Organisation*, Vol. 1, No. 2.

Morgan, C Hall, V and Mackay, H (1983) *The Selection of Secondary School Headteachers*, Open University Press.

Paisey, A (1984)'Trends in Educational Leadership and Thought', in Har-ling, P (Ed) *New Directions in Educational Leadership*, Falmer.

Waters, D (1983) *Responsibility and Promotion in the Primary School*, Heinnemann.

3 The headteacher's role in the development of staff

Ann Mason

The perceptions I hold of the headteacher's role in staff development are based upon my particular concept of headship. To my mind a headteacher has never been simply a manager or an administrator who keeps the institution running. It has always been far more complex than that. For me it had to include the concept of leadership, with all that that implies about innovation, and the professional development of staff and self. Thus when faced with the Education Reform Act in all its vastness I am not daunted. I discover that much of my everyday practice has now become enshrined in law and that now I have authoritative backing for many things I do as a matter of course. The role of headship has never been a simplistic one and the new responsibilities only make it all the more fascinating.

Since the 1950s research has been undertaken in America, Japan and the UK into leadership styles. Much of this work has explored the relationship between the leader's style and the success of the institution. I, as a headteacher, am concerned for the success of my particular institution and my understanding of 'success' in this context is to do with the personal fulfilment of all those in the school. I look for children who enjoy being at school, who succeed in learning across the curriculum and who can achieve external norms where possible. I look for staff who are competent, confident and committed and who continually grow in their understanding of their craft.

There are indicators in research from which one can learn. Gross and Herriott (1965) found a positive connection between what was called EPL (Extended Professional Leadership) on the one hand,

and high staff morale, high professional performance by staff and high level of pupil learning on the other. Halpin (1966) cited two leader behaviours, 'initiating structure' and 'consideration'. He went on to ask teachers to rate their heads on 4 point scales which related to the organisational climate and the head's part in it. Paisey (1980) talked of a 'two-factor theory'. The factors were to do with managing either 'product' or 'persons'. He went on to suggest that 'a simultaneous emphasis to both may be given'. One very much gets the impression from this article that he feels this is the way forward. Blanchard and Hersey (1982) working at the Ohio State University School of Management have produced a model based upon Halpin's two leader behaviours. They state that the 'successful leader must facilitate toward both task achievement and people management'. Earlier, Misumi and Tasaki (1965) working in industry had discovered that highest output accorded with the highest blend of these same two parts of the leader's role.

These conclusions have for some time now been increasingly supported by research being done in British schools, Hughes (1976) said that heads fulfilled their task by providing this duel function, supervision of professional staff and organisational leadership which those professionals would accept. He went on to say that if the emphasis was upon leadership and encouragement of colleagues then the head's contribution could be invaluable in enabling the combined expertise of staff to be mobilised for the achievement of agreed . . . objectives.' This was stated in another way by Razzel (1979) who said that it is the 'concentration of decision-making in the hands of the headteacher which prevents the development and emergence of professionalism in so many schools'. Similar ideas have been put forward by many others; Hoyle (1986), Burnham (1969), DES (1977), Nicholls (1983) and Mortimore (1986) for instance.

It should be said here that the view of headship I hold is not one which has been commonly held by colleagues in the past. It is one which I arrived at slowly, through experience, rather than one which I took with me into the role ready made. What is true is that I have always had a healthy respect for reliable, significant research and have tried to understand its import for practice. However, on becoming a head I was unaware of the existence of such research relating to headship. As time passed it became quite clear that the only way forward for the children was via the staff. The amount of 'teaching' heads do, as distinct from child minding, is insignificant, and with the new demands of ERA this is likely to be marginalised even more. It is the staff who are with the children, trying to put into practice what heads, LEA and now central government demand. It became obvious that whole school development as an on-going part of the school life was the only sensible approach.

Thus, for the sake of the children, we began the staff development described in the remainder of this short article. Our attitudes and policies are now commonplace, indeed are the law of the land; five professional inservice days per year are no longer a surprise. Regular staff meetings too are now very ordinary. For my staff, past and present, ERA has brought no dramatic change in staff development. What it has done is to make quite clear to Governors and parents alike that this is a key area in the school (ILEA 1989) and that teachers are truly professional people, a recognition that is long overdue.

The head

I propose to deal first with the general ways in which the head influences staff development, as a fellow professional: as exemplar, initiator, facilitator and counsellor.

Exemplar

As teachers are exemplars of attitude, behaviour and commitment to children, so are heads to staff. Those who show appreciation of what staff do, who 'notice' things, build up the confidence of teachers and make them feel valued. Those who hold a positive attitude to their job, are not 'burnt out', who are still excited by its challenge, are likely to inspire staff. Enthusiasm is catching! Those who have high expectations of staff are likely to see high achievement from staff and pupils. Those who are approachable, whose doors are open, are likely to foster trust and confidence and are often able to prevent destructive tensions arising. Those who show respect for human dignity of child or adult, and who are consistent in their approach to people earn the respect of their staff and are more likely to be listened to and imitated.

How heads actually behave is vital. One's attitude may say one thing but one's deeds may say quite another. Consistency is also important. If one says that the environment is important for children's learning, then it follows that the environment around the head's room should be attractive, well thought out and conducive to work. The head's room can be somewhere where good work is promoted and where work that has taken real effort receives acknowledgement. The head can be, and often is, the first on site and the last off. Teaching demands more than a bell to bell commitment, maybe even more than 1265 hours! (DES, 1987) and heads are often the prime exemplar of this time commitment. Staff are more likely to value promptness and regular attendance if they see such things in the head. Equally vital I feel is the behaviour of the head regarding regular reading and further study. Simply because one has achieved the status of headteacher it does not mean that one knows it all. It is essential to keep one's mind alert and alive, to be always reading, thinking and discussing new ideas and methods.

The head is also exemplar of community involvement. The more the head can relate the school and the community to each other the more both sides will be able to understand each other and work together for the children. Alongside this information-giving behaviour I put a willingness on the part of the head to be the 'blame-taker', the one who helps the staff to confront unpleasant-ness, be it from colleagues, parents or children. I realise that this is probably not what most heads do. I worked for a time in one school where the teachers were never involved in helping to sort out problems involving parents. The head always did it and I, as a teacher, learnt nothing from such exchanges. I therefore now believe that to include the staff in any discussions that impinge upon their work assists them in their own professional growth.

Initiator

In all schools the head has ultimate responsibility. However, many ideas people have, however much they want to initiate, it is the head whose interest and support puts the seal of success upon that innovation, (Nicholls 1983). However much people wish to take responsibility they can only do it if the head is prepared to delegate it to them, (Razzel 1979). Delegation is to me therefore the key issue in innovation. Too often one hears of staff being given a role to play but being totally powerless to fulfil that role because the head holds the pursestrings or has to approve all decisions. Real delegation is trusting people to do the job well and giving them all the backup they need to do it. It means leaving them alone while they do it in the knowledge that you will pick up the pieces if they fail. The ability to delegate and to facilitate the development of dependable self-reliant staff is itself dependent on the ability to make correct judgements about people, about who is ready for that sort of responsibility and who is not. Blanchard and Hersey (1982) call this 'situational leadership' and I believe it is an art all of its own.

The same can be said of consultation. The staff may set up consultations with each other but it appears to be effective only if the head has some involvement, be it purely minimal. Consultation is also valid only if the decisions of those who are consulted are actually listened to and acted upon. If people feel they are being consulted to keep them happy but the real decision has already been made elsewhere they will not want any part in it. Consultation is something that heads can develop either by their presence, their support in person or in kind, their response, or by simply facilitating it in some way in the first place. The head is also the prime initiator of ideas and inservice training. Obviously ideas are not the prerequisite of the head. However, if the head has ideas about the way to do or to organise something they are much more likely to be able to disseminate those ideas and put them into practice than are the other staff. Staff seem to expect the head to have ideas. They do accept that the head has legal authority to make decisions on many matters, so the groundwork is done. If those ideas are communicated in an acceptable fashion much can happen. The provision of on-site inservice training is another way in for the head. We all have the power to allow or disallow course attendance, but we also have the power, if we wish to use it, to so organise the school that staff can receive INSET in school time, in addition to the statutory days we all now have. If we do this it can be balanced to meet the needs of the individual teacher and the school and there is some control over the input. There is also much more control over the output in that the whole staff can be reskilled in something and can therefore work in a coordinated way.

Facilitator

It seems appropriate here to discuss further the role of the head as facilitator of in-school-time INSET. The head has to make decisions about freeing experts to coordinate training, freeing other staff to cover for each other, 'doubling up' for story time etc. Consultants from outside can be invited in to work with teachers, in class or out, to extend their knowledge and expertise. Funds may be released or even obtained by the head. I see no reason to be proud of a large bank balance. We are given what money we have to spend upon facilitating children's learning. We are not over resourced and we need every penny. If there is no more money, and more is needed, there are many ways of raising it, not only by jumble sales, 'sponsoring' or through the PTA (if one has such a thing). There are many firms who will assist if someone is prepared to spend time making contacts and writing letters. Let me give an example. I spent one evening at a community function where I met an executive of a large multi-national company. He became interested in the school and offered help. Since that initial contact the school has received grants totalling many hundreds of pounds towards computers, books, travel for a twinning project and for a new environmental garden. Some firms have mountains of excellent quality paper and files which can be collected, free. Schools can also receive funding from local charities to pay artists and poets to be in residence in the school.

Counsellor

Finally heads have a role as counsellor to staff that is ignored at their peril. Assessment of staff, appraisal, is already on the threshold. For some staffs this will be traumatic. For others it will simply be a regularising of an already essential part of that staff's development programme, head included. How can one write references for staff if one does not know them as full rounded people, if one does not know how they will react in any given situation, if one has no idea of their hopes for the future? I have long been committed to staff appraisal interviews, which includes my own. I always try to spend time in each class with the teacher before we meet for the actual formal interview. I need to know how they feel about what they do, how I can help them improve, how I can support more effectively. Alongside appraisal goes a willingness and an ability to be used as confidant/counsellor when necessary. The head is obviously not the best person in some senses to do this because it means that teachers show their weaknesses to their assessor. Yet still the aim should be that when necessary staff do feel able to come to the head.

Staff

Probationers

For those in their first year of teaching life can be full of tension and fear. Some authorities have an induction programme, others do not. My view is that probationers who are released for induction, or whose school has its own induction programme, never forget it. They develop a feeling of belonging, of being a wanted member of a supportive team. The feedback for all which results is positive and longlasting.

Apart from induction what else can be done to assist new teachers? First, schools need to appoint a forward-looking, approachable and competant teacher as teacher-tutor. I realise that this may sometimes pose problems! It then follows that teacher-tutor and probationer must be enabled to spend time together, in both classrooms, as a regular commitment. They must also be given time to discuss their perceptions of what they have seen. Secondly, probationers need to visit other schools, to see good practice and bad, in order to be able to put their school and their teaching into some sort of focus and perspective. Thirdly, they must be part of all school-based inservice. Fourthly, they need to know that the head is concerned to support and develop them too. To this end I try to spend regular time in probationers' classrooms and also to meet them weekly to discuss what I see happening. Finally, probationers must be faced with their professionalism from day one. They are full members of a team and must be encouraged to make their specific contribution. Gone forever I hope are the days when one of my former staff (a probationer at her first staff meeting) dared to speak and was shouted down by the head. 'Shut up! You count for nothing here. You cannot possibly have anything to say that would interest us.'

Main scale teachers

Many of the staff in our schools will be fairly low on the main salary scale, sometimes with no likelihood or intention of ever moving from the classroom. Staff development for such people must include involving them in consultation that is meaningful, giving them a value and a place. It must include regular meetings, so structured that all have a chance to speak and to lead. Everyone has a specialism and this must be used. Encouraging staff to share expertise with each other leads to personal and professional growth. Regular inservice training, in school time and out, is essential and has already been discussed. Visiting each others classes and working together as a whole school on a theme, discovering how each person tackled it with their differing age groups of children, both gives insights and throws up new ideas. A staff which shares will grow in mutual understanding and cohesiveness. Encouraging people to take responsibility for something, however small, paid or unpaid, communicates the head's trust and confidence in them. This is true whether it be ordering the TV pamphlets, seeing to the nature study equipment or even organising the daffodil competition or the sponsored swim. All have a place and each small task can be a stepping stone toward someone's maturity.

Most essential of all, as is now recognised by most thinking teachers, are regular appraisal interviews for each member of the team. I have already referred to this too but it seems important enough to expand a little on it here. Areas covered can be the actual practice of teaching as observed, personal and career prospects and what action is needed to achieve these. My experience has been that action taken by staff as a direct result of these interviews has resulted in noticeable professional development. Here are two examples. Julie expressed interest in finding out more about English as a Second Language, (ESL). After discussion about the relevance of different courses, she applied for and was accepted on the one of her choice. She is now part of a specialist ESL team in Staffordshire. Barbara was concerned she had no specialism. As a result of the appraisal she decided to read up on Special Needs, particularly on ways of coping with behaviour disturbance for which she seemed to have a flair. She took on private study with the Open University and is now a Deputy in another school who can hold her own with anyone in this specialised field.

I, for one, look forward to the time when such staff appraisal is a regular part of the working year. It can only be of benefit to us all.

Incentive allowance holders

Senior staff in primary schools are very important. They carry, or should carry, an enormous burden of responsibility. My experience suggests that they are usually willing to carry that responsibility, particularly if they feel supported and sustained by the head. I do realise that there are still some staff holding allowances which they all but inherited as a reward for staying put! Such people can be difficult to motivate and well nigh impossible to move or change. However, I firmly believe in never giving up. The most unlikely people have changed, given the right lead and the right context. I hold that if one has high expectations of all and makes one's point of view quite clear, then, slowly, most people can be moved along. Sometimes people are difficult and stuck in a rut because no one has had the courage to try to help them move. We do bear great responsibilities as heads and stirring up settled waters frequently seems the last thing one should do. 'Keeping the lid on the ashbin', as one colleague described it, seems easier. Yet is it really? Is it really easier to work day in day out with dissatisfied, bored and often unhappy staff? Perhaps it is actually easier, in the long run, to face up to the need for change.

Senior staff, as well as having curriculum responsibility and usu-ally a class also have a part to play in the overall management of the school. Firstly, they all have an advisory function within the school, sharing expertise and skilling those who are less skilled. This is obviously achieved most simply via staff meetings and work-shops but it can be done without them if the will is there. Secondly, they need to be allowed to develop their particular area within the school, prepare discussion documents and take real responsibility. Thirdly, they need to be part of the policy making process, when there is a decision to make all senior staff meet and the situation is put before them. Everyone has an equal say and is of equal value. The debate is always centred upon what is best for the children and usually a consensus can be found. Finally, senior staff can be encouraged to do things that are more usually the sole prerogative of the head or deputy. By that I mean things like admitting children, writing letters to parents on the head's behalf, checking on staff presence each morning, 'phoning for supply teachers and organising temporary cover, and handling the money attached to their curriculum area and having to account for it. As a result of this policy it is possible to virtually detach oneself from the crisis management of the school, thus making time to be in class with probationers and others who need your help.

Deputy head

The only way to use a deputy in a professional way is as the senior member of the team; Burnham (1964), Clerkin (1985), Coulson (1974), Coulson and Cox (1975), Razzel (1979). This most important area of staff development is dealt with elsewhere in the book so I shall be brief.

Head and Deputy need to be in constant communication. A system must be evolved whereby they do meet regularly and frequently. If the deputy has a full-time class commitment that is more difficult, but there is always before and after school and during any breaks, and there is also the possibility of another colleague doubling up once a week to allow this to happen. The head opening up his/her room fully to the deputy is another facilitator. Heads need to use the skills and knowledge of their deputies who are often the most experienced and most knowledgeable people on the site. We lose touch with them at our peril and to our own detriment.

Deputies should be able and willing, at any moment, to take over headship responsibilities. As heads, we should know that the person we have chosen or inherited has had sufficient training from us to allow them to do just that. This takes confidence however, for one risks the deputy being better at the job then one is oneself. Arranging for the deputy to assist writing the report to Governors and to actually attend in the head's place by arrangement is one sure way of showing confidence and trust, and developing skills. Another would be to share all major assemblies, for doing things jointly is a learning process.

The role of the deputy is well documented as probably the most conflict-filled in the whole of education. As heads we have all once been in that unenviable position. It is up to us not to repeat our predecessor's mistakes.

Support staff

In my LEA heads have always had a large proportion of their monies to spend as they and the staff deem fit. This means that money has been available to buy in extra support staff, untrained people who work alongside teaching staff in class or are extra supervisors at lunchtime. These people are invaluable, and, with training, become effective partners with the teaching staff in all areas of school life.

Regular support staff meetings have proved effective in terms of their development. They are keen to do more for the children and they wish to do it in the right way. I have therefore held sessions on Breakthrough to Literacy, batik, tie-dye, hearing children read, paired reading, developing mathematical thinking, etc. These staff also have joint inservice training with teaching staff on occasion and have taken a full part in developing school policies.

The position of untrained people in the school can be difficult. It is the head's place to make sure they are all given sufficient training to enable them to do their job effectively. Only when this happens do these people feel confident to deal well with children, and only then do the children respect them. This is particularly so of dinner supervisors. They have a far higher child/adult ratio than do teaching staff, they work in the unstructured situation of the playground, yet no training is given. I therefore usually set up training sessions for such people. We cover topics such as playground games, techniques for diffusing confrontations, methods of crowd control and behaviour modification. The difference six such sessions make to attitude and approach, to say nothing of confidence, is quite striking.

Conclusion

During the writing of this chapter two issues have emerged for me and I would like to share them with you. The first is that everything that has been said about the development of staff seems to be echoing all that I believe about good practice generally. All the ways in which teachers support, encourage and develop their children, both personally and academically, seem to be exactly those ways in which the head can support, encourage and develop staff. We are all learning every moment of our lives. Unfortunately, in the past, once having attained qualified teacher status those who are our superiors have usually left us to sink or swim, to pick up new knowledge and learn to cope as best we can. It has all been totally haphazard and has resulted in a great waste of human resources and much heartache. Staff development programmes could have prevented much of that.

Secondly, it seems likely that when staff are being supported in the ways suggested they can begin to grow and are more and more able to take on real responsibility. It then becomes possible for the head to be free of the nuts and bolts of daily management of the school. Instead, as the good teacher creates space in which to see individual children, the head finds he/she has created space to be the leader, the innovator, the agent of change. Heads cease to be the plumbers mending the burst pipes. They are instead the architect of the new vessel and its chief navigator.

Schools built on these principles can become positive extensions of initial training and when that happens the staff feel they are on the move and the head's major battle is won. As Peter Mortimore's Junior School Project puts it, the head and teachers have a consistent philosophy and that makes for an effective school. Perhaps then it is time for you, as head, to start looking around for your next drawing board.

References

Blanchard, K and Hersey, P (1982) *The Management of Organisational Behaviour*, Prentice Hall.

Burnham, P (1964), 'The Deputy Head', reproduced in Allen B (1968) *Headship in the 1970s* Blackwell.

Burnham, P (1969) 'Role Theory and Educational Administrations,' in Baron, G and Taylor, W (Eds) *Educational Administration and the Social Sciences* Athlone Press.

Clerkin, C (1985), 'School Based Training for Deputy Heads and its Relationship to the Task of Primary School Management,' in *Educational Management and Administration*, Vol. 13 No. 1.

Coulson, A A and Cox, M (1975) 'What do Deputies do?', in *Education 3–13*, Vol 3 No. 2.

DES (1977), *Ten Good Schools*, HMSO.

DES (1987), *Teacher's Pay and Conditions of Service*, HMSO.

Gross, N and Herriott, R E (1965), *Staff Leadership in Public Schools – A Sociological Enquiry*, Wiley.

Halpin, A W (1966), *Theory and Research in Administration*, Macmillan.

Hoyle, E (1968), 'The Head as Innovator', in Allen, B (Ed) *Headship in the 1970s*, Blackwell.

Hughes, M (1976), 'The Professional as Administrator – The Case of the Secondary School Head', in Peters, R S (Ed) *The Role of the Head*, RKP.

ILEA (1989) *ILEA News* 11.1.89. ILEA.
Misumi, J and Tasaki, T (1965), 'A Study of the Effectiveness of Supervisory Patterns in a Japanese Hierarchical Organisation', in *Japanese Psychological Research* Vol 7 No. 4.
Mortimore, P (1986), *The Junior School Project*, ILEA.
Nicholls, A (1983) *Managing Educational Innovations*, ULP.
Paisey, A (1980), 'The Question of Style in Educational Management', in *Educational Administration* Vol 9 No 2.
Razzel, A (1979), 'Teacher Participation in School Decision-making', in *Education 3–13* Vol 7 No 2.
Watts, J (1976), 'Sharing it out – The Role of the Head in Participatory Government', in Paters R S (Ed) *The Role of the Head*, RKP.

4 Corporate decision-making versus headteacher autonomy: A question of style

Eric Spear

I once rang a colleague, the head of a large secondary school. 'Is Mr X available?' I asked the secretary who took the call. 'No, I'm afraid not', she replied, 'he's busy dictating.' For one fleeting moment my imagination toyed with the ambiguity. It conjured a vision of Mr X, enthroned on the stage of the assembly hall, issuing edicts like bolts of lightning which were received by suppliant minions scurrying forth to deliver them to subservient staff in every corner of the school.

It is the image of the headteacher assiduously cultivated by fiction and one which persists in the minds of many unassociated with schools. Indeed, there are, no doubt, weary headteachers everywhere to whom the role, so described, would come as a welcome relief from the reality which is so different from this fictional image.

One of the problems of headship, especially a new one, is that everyone will have his different expectation of the way you should play the role and will try to impose that view upon you by the way he treats you. It takes time and practice to develop the style which best suits your personality and beliefs. To begin with you inherit the role of your predecessor but, like a second-hand suit, it only fits where it touches. Nevertheless, there will be those who insist that you wear it whilst there may be others who will want you in teeshirt and jeans!

Whatever style you adopt you must bear in mind that many of the models of yesteryear are unlikely to serve the needs of tomorrow. In the days of the Elementary Board Schools, forerunners of today's county primary schools, and well beyond, the headteacher personified the school and was perceived to be personally controlling all that went on within it. It is probably still true that headteachers are seen as having a close identity with their schools but there is a well developed and growing awareness, both within schools and in society generally, not only that the head does not control all the forces acting upon the school or within it, but a feeling that the headteacher should not have this monopoly over the school's destiny. The authoritarian model of the headteacher worked in the past because it was a reflection of a more authoritarian society than exists today.

Certainly today's curriculum is no longer regarded merely as a static, knowledge based timetable of subjects despite forebodings over the introduction of the National Curriculum. Though much of the National Curriculum is described in terms of knowledge to be gained it also recognises those other dimensions to do with attitudes and empathy and leaves the organisation and process of teaching in the hands of the teacher. In particular, it recognises the cross curricular nature of much primary school work. It is conceived in social and moral as well as in academic terms. The curriculum is seen as needing to be dynamic, changing in response to, even in anticipation of, changes in society and of being adaptable to the needs of the individual. The number of different people to whom the school is accountable and the range of institutions with which it must maintain 'diplomatic relations' is enormously increased.

The 1988 Education Reform Act gave greater emphasis to the role and responsibilities of governors and it is likely that, in the future, governing bodies will play a more active part in the management and policy making of schools. The head stands, in many ways, in relation to his governors as his elementary school predecessors did to their school boards and will do so even more if his school opts out of LEA control. It thus becomes necessary for heads to exercise their managerial role 'upwards' in advising and guiding the governors, as well as 'downwards' in leading the staff.

All heads, through participation in the work of their governing bodies, already have some knowledge of what corporate decision-making involves. You only have to imagine how you would feel if you were now treated by governing bodies as heads were once treated in some instances in the past. 'Old timers' remember being summoned to the 'office' to sit outside the meeting until summoned to present their report and then being dismissed so that the meeting could continue to make judgements about and decisions on 'their' schools. Such a procedure strikes as inconceivable today, yet some-times headteachers are guilty of treating their staff in the same way. The complexity of this model of a school places great strains on the structure of its organisation. It bears particularly heavily on the autocratic headteacher, not only because he becomes burdened with more and more complicated and important decisions at a faster and faster rate, but because he has to persuade his staff to accept these decisions and to adapt themselves to the necessary changes. He cannot command these changes in the sense of issuing edicts to be obeyed. His staff, educated as autonomous pro-fessionals, operating in a society whose climate has shifted away from authoritarianism towards participation, will resent such a man-agement style and will tend to subvert proposals for change by, at best, simply going through the motions of conformity while ignoring the spirit of the proposals. Now that the imposition of a national curriculum and assessment procedures by central government has occurred, some of that professional autonomy has been eroded. This makes it even more important that headteachers should give the fullest recognition to the value of what professional autonomy is left if active participation in implementing innovation is to be promoted.

Authority, responsibility and leadership

By virtue of his office the headteacher is set in authority over the rest of the staff but it is obvious that this fact alone will not empower the head to gain acceptance of and compliance with new ideas. The exercise of authority has been described and analysed in vari-ous ways but a simple model suffices to explain the derivation of different types of authority.

1 Bureaucratic authority derives from a person's position. You have the authority of your title, 'headteacher', and everyone will expect you to exercise this authority though, as we have already seen, everyone will not agree on how it should be used. Your position will be underpinned by the often separately described, but closely related, legal authority which is supported by the law, rules and regulations. You start out with this authority as a 'given' when you are appointed head.

2 Professional authority derives from your command of the pro-fessional skills, knowledge and understanding of the job that your subordinates are doing. Your length and variety of experience enhances this type of authority, though it can count against you if you are seen to be relying upon distantly past experience and

have not obviously kept in touch with recent developments. All heads should possess this type of authority. It is the type of authority which you can acquire by study and training.

3 Charismatic authority derives from personal charm and magnetism which most are tempted to think they have but which few actually possess. It is, therefore, risky to rely on this type of authority alone, though as an additional element to support the other types of authority it is a bonus. Alas, it is difficult to teach and difficult to learn so not much use as an element of inservice training or in staff development programmes. It is no substitute for professional authority as easily charmed appointing bodies have sometimes discovered, too late! You have to recognise that there may be informal staff leaders who possess greater charismatic authority than you as head anyway, so that reliance on this type of authority may lead to your being out-manoeuvred by a member of staff.

The present day head has to recognise that he is not just a more highly qualified and experienced teacher than the rest of the staff (not always true nowadays anyway) but that he is a leader who must inspire professional respect and loyalty. He is also a manager – a manager of people. It is a well rehearsed aphorism that 'management is getting things done through other people', and the success of a school depends, to a very large extent, on the head doing just that.

Motivating people to give of their best is the major task confronting all managers. It is not simply a question of offering 'bribes', even in situations where the manager has command of resources financially to reward effort. This news will come as a relief to headteachers because they do not have that type of power anyway.

Students of management are always made aware of the work of two writers in this field, McGregor and Herzberg, whose theories crystallise much thinking on the subject of the motivation and management of people.

McGregor's Theory X and Theory Y sum up two extreme views about the nature of people in organisations.

Theory X states that the average person is lazy and does as little work as possible, prefers to be led and lacks ambition, puts personal needs before organisational needs, dislikes change and is gullible and easily manipulated.

Theory Y states that people are not by nature passive or resistant to organisational needs but only become so in response to the way they are treated by the organisation. People have the capacity for hard work on behalf of the organisation, for ambition and personal and professional development and it is management's job to create the circumstances where these potentialities can be realised. Individuals can gain personal satisfaction through the fulfilling of institutional goals.

It is obvious that these propositions are extremes and that many people's make-up contains elements of both. Your own philosophy will need to take account of the fact that these characterisations are 'ideal types'. You will have to make up your own mind towards which you most incline because that will powerfully influence the way you choose to manage people.

If you largely subscribe to Theory X you are likely to believe in an autocratic view of headship where you make all the important decisions for people and persuade them, either by reward or threat of punishment to do what you see as being in the best interests of the school irrespective of the views or personal needs of individual teachers.

Theory Y protagonists are more likely to see their headship role in terms of satisfying the individual, professional needs of the staff thus motivating the staff to serve the needs of the school.

What are these needs which will motivate staff? More importantly, what is it which demotivates them? The second theorist known to all students of management is Herzberg who proposed that there are two distinct facets of organisation which reflect those factors in the institution which act as 'motivators', or satisfiers and those dissatisfiers which Herzberg refers to as 'hygiene factors'.

Herzberg says that those things which give rise to most dissatisfaction among workers are policies and administration, supervision, working conditions, interpersonal relations, money, status and security. The motivators are achievement, recognition, challenging work, increased responsibility, growth and development.

Herzberg points out that it is not enough simply to remove causes of dissatisfaction, such as improving working conditions and paying people more money. People need to be more positively motivated by the job itself, by the nature of the work and the sense of responsibility and achievement it offers. Most teachers will, at least, agree that the nature of their job is a major source of satisfaction and motivation, but they may be surprised that money itself is not a motivator. The lack of money may be a demotivator but paying people more money doesn't necessarily increase their motivation. Studies have shown that when asked what is important to them about their jobs, what they find most satisfying, people generally do not give a high priority to financial reward. They are more concerned with achieving success, experiencing a sense of professional fulfilment and having their achievements recognised by others.

All of this has obvious lessons for the headteacher in his management of staff in schools. In brief it means sharing the management of the school with the rest of the staff and offering them genuine opportunities to participate in decision-making.

The head has a duty, not only to the long term image and success of his school, nor only to the short-term goals for the education of the transient child population. He has, also, a responsibility towards promoting the professional growth of his staff, both as regards their present effectiveness as classroom teachers and their potential within and beyond the school.

The style of management the head teacher adopts, therefore, needs to take account of these factors and he must have regard to such issues as how decisions are to be taken and by whom, for making decisions is only half the job, the other half is getting them effectively implemented. The method by which decisions are arrived at has a direct bearing on how, and even whether, they are given practical effect at the 'chalk face'.

Autocrat or democrat?

It is too simplistic to suggest that all we need is a good dose of democracy to replace the autocracy of the head and all will be well. It depends on how democracy is interpreted for one thing. Does it mean everyone being equally involved in every decision? Such an approach to problem solving would be extremeley time-consuming, inefficient and not guaranteed to come up with the best solution anyway. Everyone knows the old saying that a camel is the result of a horse having been designed by a committee! If you consulted everyone before taking any decisions staff could well become annoyed by your apparent inability to make up your mind about anything.

On the other hand even a benevolent dictator can't always get things right and people who feel that they can never really influence the courses of events tend to become passive and resigned, hardly what a school needs in these demanding times. Outright autocracy leads to resentment and an unwillingness to exercise initiative on the part of subordinates. They in turn will always 'play safe' rather than take risks by behaving imaginatively or exploring new ideas. The autocratic head who manages to impose uniformity and conformity on his staff is not only minimising the potential of his most expensive and adapatable resource, his staff, he is also fooling himself. For who really believes that people can be moulded into identikit look-alikes. A head may, by exercising his bureaucratic authority, achieve uniformity and conformity in the superficial and most trivial aspects of school life, but those which are fundamental to a school's purpose are not susceptible to change by directive. To achieve a concensus view on the philosophy of the curriculum, for example, requires much patient debate and mutual exploration. It also requires great leadership skills.

The fact is that the head is not just a manager, a term which smacks of coping with the routine of everyday decision-making, he is the leader of the school, a term which perhaps conjures up more of a vision of someone positively shaping the organisation, showing others the way, and encouraging them to follow where he is going. The difference between the autocratic head and one who engages his staff in corporate decision-making is the difference between driving and leading. By corporate decision-making I mean involving others on the staff in making decisions either as a group or individually both with the head, and, sometimes, in his absence. The difference between autocracy and corporate decision-taking reflects the difference between the role of a master and the role of a manager.

One point has to be clearly established at the outset. Legally the headteacher is responsible for the internal management, organisation and conduct of the school. No staff group can assume that responsibility will or can indemnify the head against the consequences of their decisions. To that extent the decision-taking capacity of other members of staff is circumscribed. That does not mean, however, that the head should always take all the decisions alone. There is a difference, not merely a semantic one, between decision-making and decision-taking. Making a decision involves all those factors which contribute to arriving at a proposal for action. The agreement to give effect to the proposal is decision-taking. The former allows much scope for all staff members to subscribe their views. The latter is ultimately the province of the head or those to whom he chooses to delegate that authority. There will be some decisions on which he will always have to have the final say. There will be others where this is unnecessary, even undesirable. It all depends on the type of decision being made.

The decisions that are made in a school may be broadly characterised as those of principle and those of practice.

Decisions of principle lay down the ground rules. They establish, if an organisation is to be coherent, standards and beliefs which inform all other decisions. Decisions of principle embody the philosophy of the school. An example of this type of decision would be either to stream or teach mixed ability. Vertical grouping might be another, though it must be recognised that practical considerations may sometimes make such decisions as the latter unavoidable, regardless of principles.

Decisions of practice, on the other hand, are lower level, though nonetheless important for they may more immediately and practically effect what goes on in the school on a day-to-day basis.

There are different levels of decisions of practice including those which have such a long term effect that they set precedents which can become principles. The decision to use this rather than that textbook or the decision to use one or other published reading or maths schemes may begin by being a practical decision but its long term influence may be more akin to a policy decision because the philosophy of the authors will permeate the thinking of the users.

Other practical decisions will be less far reaching in their consequences and may set no precedents for the future. The decision to line up children in the playground at the end of break rather than let them walk in informally may reflect the philosophy and ethos of the school but it is a decision that can easily and quickly be changed if there are practical reasons for doing so.

In the foregoing examples, such decisions affect everyone in the school. It would be unwise, therefore, for one person to take these decisions without reference to the views of those who have to implement them. Plainly if people can understand the reasoning behind a decision and can be persuaded of the benefits it will bring they are more likely to make a sincere attempt to implement it. But what if they understand the reasoning but disagree with it?

This is a real dilemma for the head who believes sincerely that he has a good idea which will benefit all in the organisation if only they will give it a try. Should he impose the decision in the belief that once people have been forced to do something the self-evidence of its virtue will become apparent? While there is some virtue in this view it is a dangerous philosophy to rely upon wholesale. Nevertheless a strong positive leader should not shrink from giving a lead at times, even when all about him doubt the course he has set. You need to be an experienced and confident head to do this though and very sure you are right.

Perhaps it is better to reserve this approach for the less important and reversible decisions. For example, you want an established member of staff to try teaching an age group different from that she is normally used to taking. You may be able, by exercise of authority, to make the change in the hope that by the end of the year she will have been converted by the experience. On the other hand, there is always the danger that she will have her worst fears confirmed. At least you can then return her to her previous age group. You need to know your individual staff members really well as personalities before employing this tactic.

If you cannot persuade your staff of the value and benefits of a change you propose and you don't know them individually well enough to forecast that they will be converted by the practice, even if the theory doesn't appeal, then maybe it is the wrong moment to insist upon or to impose the change. A half-hearted or hostile implementation of an idea will condemn it to failure. I recall an exercise in staff profiling on a course where someone wrote of a teacher, 'Miss X is always ready to try out new ideas and determined to make them fail'. Presumably Miss X had been on the receiving end of a large number of imposed decisions in the formulation of which she had played no part.

Sometimes there simply isn't time to do anything other than take the decision yourself. Where it seems to make no real difference to anyone else except you then it is quite legitimate to take the decision yourself anyway. Sometimes, though, there may have to be a decision which affects everyone but which has to be made on the spot without reference to anyone else. A decision to evacuate the school building after a bomb-threat 'phone call, or to close the school because the water supply has been frozen up, are two dramatic, but not unusual, examples. Both have happened to me recently. These are leadership decisions and are taken in the full knowledge that you are entirely responsible for the consequences and that you may have to justify the decisions after the event, when hindsight will be available to those who judge you. Sometimes these decisions turn out to be wrong, but, as long as they were responsibly taken on the best evidence available at the time, no reasonable person can justify criticising you.

On the other hand there will be times when other views can be solicited before you make a decision which will, nevertheless once made, still be your responsibility. The decision to regard the bomb threat 'phone call as a hoax and to reenter the building could be one of these. It would be taken after consultation with the rest of the staff and after advice from the police, but it would still be your decision.

Fortunately most instant decisions are not as momentous as these. It may just be a matter of, with both of you with diaries in your hands at that moment, making a date for the school photographer to call. Such arrangements will be made with due regard to known calendar and timetable commitments and subject to revision if it turns out to be really inconvenient for the rest of the staff. For this reason such arrangements should be made sufficiently far ahead of the date to allow changes to be made and for the staff to be given plenty of notice of the event. A date set for next term would be a reasonable on the spot agreement in these terms, a date set for next week would not.

Generally speaking if people can know what options are being considered before a decision is made the more likely they are to accept a decision than if they only hear about the decision after it has been taken. Hearing about the options beforehand implies, of course, that people will have an opportunity to make their views known and will expect to have them taken into account, so that there is a real opportunity to modify or change the final decision.

The main difference between the teaching staff and the head is that they do not have the authority to 'tell' the head to adopt an idea, they have to 'sell' it to him. The wise head will also sell rather than tell when it comes to implementing his own ideas.

It is not always wise to enter into a debate with a very firm commitment to one particular solution to a problem. Sometimes this amounts to prejudging a situation before all the evidence has been heard. A wise head will prepare himself by thinking through all the alternatives he can think of in advance of a staff meeting called to make a decision on some matter, but he may not have thought of some of the alternatives of which others have thought. Keeping an open mind and not closing one's options too early is the sign of a wise negotiator.

Delegation

Another general principle in decision-making is that, ideally, decisions should be taken by those closest to the level of implementation. Decisions about classroom practices, for example, should be made with the fullest contribution possible from classroom teachers because it is at their level that the immediate and practical consequences will be daily felt, not in the head's office. Delegation may be to an individual or a group but it must be clear to all concerned at the outset what is being delegated, to whom and within what confines decisions are to be made.

Decisions on curriculum matters are probably those which require the most complete staff involvement if they are to be successfully implemented. Such decisions cannot usually be taken quickly and require lengthy and skilled negotiation and periodic review. This type of decision-making process can be frustrating for the impatient but the alternative of an imposed scheme of work is, as experience has often shown in the past, largely an exercise in self-deception, for if people are not committed to a procedure they may present the outward signs of conformity but will remodel the spirit of it to suit their own beliefs and practice. The study of curriculum innovation has taught that much to its investigators as the Schools' Council's experience has shown.

True delegation is not just giving a job to someone or to a group, all the decisions and procedures having been minutely worked out beforehand. There would be little point in that. It would be offering very little responsibility to the delegate and wouldn't have off-loaded much of the work from the delegator. Of course it is often easier to do things oneself than to get someone else to do it. It is often necessary to do things oneself if one wants things done in a particular way, but the question then has to be asked, 'Even if this is an excellent way of doing something is it the only excellent way?' A harder question to face is, 'Even though my way may produce the best result in terms of the specified task, will there be additional incidental benefits to be gained by allowing someone else to apply their own, second best solution, which will more than compensate for the effects of a less than perfect conclusion to the task?' Teachers make these decisions every day in the interests of their pupils' education. In art and craft work, for example, is the production of a prespecified artefact a more important consideration than the pupil's exploration of his own ideas and his experience of handling tools and materials, even if in the latter case nothing concrete is produced at the end? It is a matter for judgement when the one course is more appropriate than the other.

The manager has to balance the value of the immediate task being done in a specific way against the long term growth and development of the staff and the organisation as a whole. People only learn to do things well by doing them, sometimes doing them not so well to begin with. They cannot learn everything by simply watching someone else do it well, though they can learn much from others' experience and mistakes. All heads know that, however many course and lectures about headship they attended before they became heads, there was nothing like the real thing for promoting rapid and effective learning. The same principle applies lower down the management chain.

If you really want something done your way then don't delegate the job. It is very demotivating to be delegated to perform a task and then to feel that the delegator wants to operate the delegatee by remote control. It insinuates a lack of trust and confidence by the manager in that staff member.

Staff participation – the pros and cons weighed up

It is perhaps, appropriate at this point to summarise the arguments for and against autocracy and 'corporacy' in school management.

Autocratic management depends upon the will of one person, the headteacher. The effective exercise of autocracy will lead to swift decisions and consistent decisions being taken by the person who is, after all, supposed to be the senior person paid for taking responsibility for everything to do with the school.

The problems with autocracy are that the person exercising it has to be infallible, will need to spend an inordinate amount of time and effort persuading people to implement decisions in exactly the way they were intended to work and will almost always upset someone every time a decision is made. The autocratic head has also to contend with a general move, in society at large, away from authoritarian to participative practices and a teacher force which is more professionally aware of the forces which interact to promote healthy management structures in schools.

The headteacher who promotes corporate decision-making in schools is delegating some of his authority to others lower down the management chain. This ensures that teachers understand the reasons for decisions and by being involved in making them become more committed to them and their implementation. It increases their interest in and satisfaction with their job and motivates them more surely than old-fashioned 'carrot and stick' methods.

The problems with the corporate approach to decision-making are all soluble but need to be recognised in advance so that the advantages are not lost through failure to avoid the potential pitfalls.

Firstly, not every staff member is immediately ready to assume full-blooded participation in the decision-making processes in the school. Those who have previously been used to an autocratic regime will not necessarily welcome the increased involvement and greater responsibility that is implied by a corporate approach to decision-making. Corporate decision-making is not a more permissive form of management. It actually requires people to work harder than they were expected to do under an autocracy. This will quickly become obvious to those who become involved in corporate decision-making and it may not, at first sight, seem much of an incentive to some members of staff. Handled with patience and sensitivity, however, people will begin to appreciate that the personal benefits which accrue will more than compensate for the extra work and responsibility.

Teachers unused to participating in decision-making and with little experience of shouldering real managerial responsibility will need training for their new role. To begin with it may be difficult to get decisions made at all, and meetings will tend to be long, argumentative, and inconclusive. This can be frustrating for all concerned but it can be a valuable self-learning process for the staff and one which it is often necessary to go through before progress can be made. Skilled chairmanship by the head will be particularly necessary at this stage. It is probably better to concentrate on simple relatively unimportant problems at this learning stage. Strangely it is the apparently simple decisions which often generate the longest debate and the strongest opinions. Perhaps that is because, in these matters, everyone feels sufficiently confident to express an opinion.

Be aware that there will be many areas where staff may not have an opinion and will feel insecure being placed in a position where they have to help to make decisions without feeling that they understand the issues involved. This is the time when they will look to the head for leadership and it will be his task to demonstrate his command of the pros and cons to assist and guide the uncertain towards making an informed choice.

Group problem solving is slower than individuals making decisions but it should lead to a richer solution which has been formed by the collective thinking of several minds. Because all those minds have contributed to the solution they will have a better understanding of the problem and a more ready acceptance of the actions decided upon.

Finally, be aware that often opinion is not unanimous about a particular course of action or a particular decision. You must decide at the outset how conflict is to be avoided even though agreement may not be total. You may decide that a majority vote is the best way of resolving a deadlock, but this can be divisive and leave a sometimes substantial minority disgruntled. Consensus decisions, on the other hand, may end up as compromises which do not entirely satisfy anyone. With practice groups get better at making decisions and learn that every member may find himself in a minority at times but that he must sometimes be prepared to 'go along' with decisions for the good of the group and for the achievement of a decision. Good advanced groundwork by the head amongst individual members is an important way of avoiding open public conflict in a large meeting. People may often be prepared to speak more frankly in very small groups of two or three and also are often more tolerant of opposing views. If some of the difficulties can be faced and argued through before a large meeting this will speed the decision-making of the meeting itself. The ideal number for good decision-making is probably four or five, the maximum number ten or a dozen. Primary school teachers will recognise that the majority of primary school staffs will fall within these limits and so have something going for them to begin with. Larger primary school staffs must decide how they are going to be divided up for the concentrated 'committee work' which goes into decision-making before its conclusions are presented for public affirmation by the whole staff.

The most important decision, however, is made by one person, the headteacher. The decision is to eschew autocracy and embrace corporate decision-making. You can't ask a committee to decide that for you!

Further Reading

Everard, K B and Morris, G (1985), *Effective School Management*, Harper and Row.

Glatter, R et al (Eds) (1988), *Understanding School Management*, O U Press.

Handy, C (1976), *Understanding Organisations*, Penguin.

Handy, C (1984), *Taken for Granted: Understanding Schools as Organisations*, Longman/Schools Council.

5 Using time efficiently

Ian Craig

Teachers tend to be less 'system-conscious' than those in many other professions. But successful management in a school as in any other enterprise involves using every available support system to the full, in order to save time for the tasks which really matter and which cannot be left to subordinates. (Richardson, 1984).

We are constantly being bombarded with directives and recommendations to manage our schools more efficiently. The realisation that efficient school management is an essential element of an effective education system has within the last few years led to considerable pressures being exerted on headteachers.

Within our education system the burden of managing personal boundaries and time rests with the individual headteacher. It is only by the systematic management of that time that headteachers will achieve their full potential and thus manage their schools more effectively.

In this chapter primary headteachers will be introduced to *some* of the techniques that can be used to improve the management of their most important and costly resource, their own time. An improvement in time efficiency, saving even one hour in a week on administrative tasks, would ensure that this additional time could be spent on planned, high-value activities. This chapter, by its nature, cannot hope to cover the whole subject of 'time management', and inevitably some important aspects of the subject have been missed out due to lack of space. The interested reader can make use of the bibliography to read wider on the subject if (s)he desires to do so.

Most writers in this field of management suggest that before any important steps can be taken to control time, an analysis needs to be made of how time is being spent at present, Ferner (1980) lists three stages that need to be worked through:

- Keep a log of where time goes,
- Analyse your key problems.
- Find solutions.

All headteachers are used to the practice of setting curriculum objectives, in principle if not in practice, first setting broad aims and then analysing the stages needing to be gone through to get to them. How many headteachers look at their own work pattern to try to analyse it with a view to improving their own efficiency? Inefficient use of time by the headteacher tends to signpost general ineffective management, so analysing how one should change management patterns is an activity that can ultimately lead to enormous benefits for the whole school organisation.

There is little published research suggesting how Primary headteachers actually spend their time. Clerkin (1985) and Harvey (1986) give us some good recent data, but Cook and Mack (1971) provide us with perhaps the most interesting information which is as relevant today as when it was written. All the evidence suggests that there is never enough time in the day for the Primary headteacher to tackle all the tasks that (s)he wishes.

What is obvious is that much of the headteacher's time is taken up with activities that are non-productive, or of 'low value', and if this time could be identified and cut down, or even eliminated altogether, more hours would be available for the more important tasks. Using a very simple analysis the average Primary headteacher is being paid in excess of £90 for each working day, and that results in a cost to the organisation of approximately £15 for every hour that children are on the site. It is not unusual for a headteacher to spend an hour or more in any particular day engaged in 'low value' tasks, often ones that could be carried out by others much less qualified, enabling him or her to spend this time on other tasks that are of much greater importance to the school. But some headteachers appear to find it hard to delegate even the simplest task.

The problem of time management is not confined to education. McConalogue (1984) reports that 'in a recent survey of managers in industry more than 80 per cent considered time as a problem for them', and that 'there are always complicated choices to make between alternative uses of time'. Time spent on tasks is even more complicated by the fact that it is often fragmented. Minzberg (1973) found that 'half the things a manager does takes less than nine minutes duration', and this must be as true for 'managers' in education as for those in industry.

But how do we assess what is important, and how do we know

how we are spending our time? Harling (1981) and others have provided useful checklists that headteachers could use to ask themselves 'how well am I functioning relative to these criteria?' Using such lists, headteachers should be able to produce their own management objectives, tailored for themselves and for their own schools.

Assuming that you *are* aware of your priorities, how do you adjust your pattern of work to make more time available for them? The first step, as Ferner (1980) suggests, is to analyse how you spend a typical day at present, and the most effective, and probably the easiest way to gain a realistic picture of a typical day is to keep a 'time log'.

The time log

The 'time log' is as useful as you are prepared to make it. It can contain little information recorded over a short period of time (perhaps a week) or a great deal of information recorded over a longer period of time. At the outset the task seems a daunting one, but after the first day or two recording becomes almost automatic and not nearly the chore that it first appears.

Figure 5.1 – Time log record sheet 1

Activity start time	Activity
8.20	Arrived at school – talked to deputy
8.33	Caretaker took me to see broken windows
8.46	Saw Mrs Rose about Jane's swimming
8.54	Saw Mrs James re Jane Rose's swimming
9.05	Assembly
9.25	Post
9.32	Telephoned Divisional Office re staffing
9.44	Saw Darren Andrews about his maths
9.52	

Keeping a log on which you write down your activities as *they happen* is of necessity going to be very difficult, as often the log is going to be left for an hour whilst you deal with a crisis, and written up in retrospect. It is quite likely that within any one hour period you could be engaged in any number of activites, and with the best will in the world it may be impossible to record accurately. A detailed log requires constant recording, and should note the *exact* time when each new activity is begun. If kept rigorously for any prolonged period (eg a week or more) this method could become disruptive.

If well kept it does give a great deal of information that can be used for time analysis. This technique should not be disregarded without some consideration. Figure 5.1 reproduces a sample record sheet for this activity.

If such a log is kept for a period of perhaps a week, times which have been spent on each activity can be totalled to provide a 'picture' of relative time use.

An alternative, and much simpler system, is one in which broad categories are used, and are ticked each time you become engaged in that particular kind of task (Figure 5.2).

The disadvantage with this system is that it does not record the amount of time taken over each task. It only tells you the *number of times* a particular kind of activity is undertaken during the sampling period. Although it does not give accurately timed information, the categories can be predetermined, so that the kind of information you require is recorded. For instance, categories such as staff,

Figure 5.2 – Time log record sheet 2

Category	Activity	Total
Talking to children)	✓✓ ✓✓ ✓✓ ✓✓✓✓✓ ✓✓ ✓✓ ✓✓	18
Talking to staff	✓✓✓ ✓✓✓✓ ✓✓✓✓✓✓ ✓✓ ✓✓ ✓✓ ✓✓	21
Reading information	✓ ✓✓✓ ✓✓✓ ✓✓	9

children, parents, officers, governors could be listed if you wanted to sample *who* you communicated with each day, and how often. Categories such as office, classroom, staffroom would tell you *where* you spent proportions of your day.

An accurate *and* relatively simple technique involves the regular sampling of activities every hour throughout the day. If this process is repeated over a number of days a very useful picture of the daily pattern can be built up with very little disruption to work.

Ideally, each sample should be randomised, but pressure of work would make this difficult, so I suggest that the process is rationalised. It is at this point that a certain amount of time spent planning is essential if the task itself is not to be too onerous. The first requirement is a table of random numbers from 1 to 60 (representing each minute in an hour). If a published table of numbers is used (Fisher, 1965 for instance), then only the numbers ending in 01 to 60 would be used. If a published table is not available it does not need much ingenuity to work out ways of generating one.

The number of days to be sampled is of course the decision of the headteacher who is using the technique, but I have found that a sample of ten to twenty working days (two or four full school weeks) is an acceptable period – long enough to provide a good sample of activities to analyse, but not too long to make it a wearisome chore. Before starting it is *essential* to determine the number of days and to prepare record sheets in advance. This forward planning pays dividends later.

When planning your record sheets, begin with your base time, which should be at least a quarter of an hour before you usually arrive at school to allow for possible early arrivals during the sampling. Try to set your base time at a convenient computational point, such as on the hour, or on the half hour. If you usually arrive at school between 8.15 and 8.25, set your base time at 8.00. For each record sheet take a random number from your list and add it to the base time in minutes. For example, if the random number for that sheet is 17, then the first time that an activity is to be sampled on that particular day is 8.17. Samples would then be taken at one hour intervals for the rest of that day. A simple record sheet for that day is produced here as an example (Figure 5.3).

Like the majority of headteachers, you will find great difficulty separating the lunch break from the rest of your day, so I suggest that you continue sampling through this period. Although tasks may differ through this time from the rest of the day, they will be no less important to your work profile when you analyse your data.

On your record sheets, allow for sampling times well beyond the time that you usually leave school to return home. You should make sure that a prepared space is always available if you are

Figure 5.3 – Time log record sheet 3

Date: Monday 21 March 8.00 + 17 = 8.17	
8.17	—
9.17	In Assembly
10.17	Talking to Ed. Psych. on phone
11.17	In class 3 looking at work
12.17	Eating lunch
1.17	Reading report from Social Services
2.17	Mending duplicator
3.17	At field with 2nd year for games

detained at school beyond your normal departure time. It does not matter if a sample is not taken because you arrived at school after the first sample time or if you left school early that particular day. It is the most complete picture of your activities that you are trying to obtain. You should also consider continuing sampling after you leave school if you are still working on school related activities – it is for you to decide what information you wish to gain from your sampling. You may of course *only* wish to analyse your use of time whilst at school. You should certainly consider continuing sampling if you return to school for an evening meeting.

There are a number of prompts that you can use to remind you to write down your activity each hour. Perhaps the easiest to use are alarm wristwatches or small travel alarms. Your first action each morning, preferably before you arrive at school, is to set your first sample time on your alarm. When it sounds, immediately record your activity and re-programme one hour later. Re-programming takes a matter of seconds. The alarm should be small enough for you to carry it with you *at all times* during the day, but it may of course be that your sample record sheet is not always to hand when the alarm sounds, as it may be difficult to carry this everywhere with you. It is essential that you note down your activity immediately on whatever paper is to hand, and transfer the note to your record sheet as soon as possible thereafter. Apart from one or two surprised reactions from staff and pupils at the 'alarm' times at the beginning of the exercise, there are really no other problems to overcome.

If you manage to sample for twenty working days, at the end of the exercise you will have approximately two hundred individual samples, and they will be as detailed as you will wish them to be. The information collected will provide you with an excellent picture of your typical working day. You will then be able to analyse how much time you spend on certain activities as compared to others. The analysis can be carried out in different ways to extract different information. The same set of data can be examined to find out how you spend your day (talking, writing, reading etc.) or *with whom* or *where* you spend it. Repeated at intervals, this information can help you set and review your own personal management objectives, so that you can improve your own performance.

Perhaps the most valuable use of this technique is to compare how your *actual* use of time relates to how you think you *should* be spending it. It is useful, perhaps before you attempt to keep a 'time log' for the first time, to try to write down as percentages the proportions of time that you would ideally give to each of your various tasks. When you come to analyse your 'log', you can also express the activities you recorded as percentages of your whole time. You will then be able to compare your actual use of time with your ideal figures. How do the two sets compare? Concentrating on the one or two activities that show the greatest differences, what steps can you take to change your work priorities and pattern to close the gaps?

After the first attempt at sampling it may of course be necessary to redraft your ideal time-plan. You may have missed significant tasks off the first list that were highlighted by the 'log' and that you now wish to include. You may now realise that you were totally unrealistic in your percentage allocation for certain activities when comparing this with what you actually do. The log may make you review their importance.

With the second attempt the ideal time-plan becomes much more of a tool, and the second time-log begins to give you information as to whether or not you are achieving time management objectives by reducing discrepancies between ideal and actual percentages. It may be appropriate at this point to consider changing the tasks on which you intend to concentrate your efforts. If it is to be of real use, the time-log should be repeated at regular intervals to monitor progress. Frequent use and analysis will develop competence and confidence in this management skill.

The time-log forms the basis of a rescheduling strategy enabling the headteacher to make decisions to improve a very valuable and expensive resource, his or her own time. Everard and Morris (1985) say 'it is very easy to be busy doing the wrong thing'. They go on to suggest that 'those colleagues who are perpetually racing against time are seldom the most effective'. Headteachers are well known for their lack of planning – they tend to manage by moving from one crisis to another. However, having begun to think about this issue by using a time-log, it is then a small step to move on to other techniques, to spend more time on *planned* activities, and to establish priorities, giving them allocated times within the working day.

McConalogue (1984) lists as 'the four top secrets of good time management':

- Establishing goals and priorities,
- Making time to do planning.
- Delegating unnecessary work.
- Allocating and scheduling time to important and priority activities.

It is these 'secrets' that we shall examine in the remainder of this chapter.

Establishing goals and priorities

Much has been said in recent years about the importance of 'knowing where you are going'. It is essential for all *schools* to establish goals for which to aim, and to review these at regular intervals, and this aspect of school management is dealt with elsewhere in this book. It is equally important for headteachers to establish their personal priorities for action, which although they should not contradict the goals of the organisation, may not necessarily be exactly the same. It is important too that these are reviewed regularly. To help focus my thoughts, I find it useful to keep a list readily available on which I have written the various 'areas' over which I have influence in my work, eg:

- Staff
- Curriculum
- Children
- Plant and Resources
- Community
- LEA and Governors
- Monitoring and Evaluation

This list is taken from Harling (1981), and is a useful starting point. Your list may not be exactly the same, but you will probably end up with one that is very similar. If it is going to be useful as a management tool, it should not contain more than six or seven 'areas'; if you get more, examine the list to try to combine similar headings together. You should then ask yourself 'How can I improve my *personal* contribution to the school in each of these areas?' Your answers should enable you to produce at least one, but not more than two short term objectives for each heading. Your objectives, like all good objectives, should be time-bounded, ensuring that they are achievable within a specified period of time. These objectives should be regularly reviewed, and action taken to achieve them should be noted on the 'to do' list, and in the 'action diary' as necessary (these two tools will be discussed later in this chapter). When an objective under any one of these headings is achieved, it should be replaced with another, always ensuring that you are considering all aspects of your role. Below is reproduced an example of a personal objectives 'prompt' sheet which should have enough spaces on it to incorporate each of the headings on your list, and have space on it to allow for new objectives to be added to replace those that have been achieved (Figure 5.4).

Figure 5.4 – Objectives prompt sheet

Areas of responsibility	Personal improvement objectives	Tick when achieved
Staff	By end of term to have introduced the revised system for - - - - - that we agreed at the staff meeting of 21 March.	
Curriculum	By half term to have worked alongside each teacher for at least half a day, introducing a 'technology' aspect into their project work to help them realise how exciting it is.	
Children	To spend one lunchtime each week sitting with children and	

Making time to do planning

Many managers say that they do not have time to plan their work
– it takes too long. In fact, the reverse is true. Time spent planning
work is repaid many times in greater efficiency and time saved
later.

Headteachers should plan to have a regular quiet period each
day, preferably as early as possible in the school day, when they
should only be disturbed for important matters. It is surprising how
much time is wasted each day by unimportant interruptions, and it
is possible that this 'quiet period' could lead the way towards
consideration of how these disturbances can be eliminated at other
times during the day. Care must be taken, of course, to make it
known that those disturbances that you consider essential to your
work are *not* eliminated during this time. This period can then be
used as 'thinking time' when, amongst other things, you can plan
the rest of your day. Even if your plans go awry because of crises,
priority tasks for the day have been placed at the front of your
mind. If it is possible, you should not allow yourself to be timetabled
at the beginning of the day to allow for this planning time to be
taken then. Ferner (1980) says that:

> 'the purpose of daily planning is to allow you to see what has been
> done and what is still to be done while not forgetting smaller but
> important tasks. Daily planning is one of your strongest allies in getting
> control over your time rather than letting events and people and crises
> control you.'

It is interesting to note here that Richardson (1984) tells us that
'most experts advise five to ten minutes per hour of complete
mental and physical relaxation' if a manager is to work effectively.
I do not know many headteachers who are able to heed that advice.

Delegating unnecessary work

It should go without saying that delegation is essential, and some
headteachers find this very difficult. Most headteachers still feel that
their place is essentially in the classroom, and although there are
many good reasons why regular classroom experience is important,
the head should remember that teaching is *not* his or her prime
function – it is the management of the school. It is very easy for
the headteacher to become overburdened with teaching at the
expense of other duties – some headteachers even pride themselves on the fact that they spend all their session time teaching.
This self-indulgence (as it most often is) cannot be beneficial to the

school as a whole. All tasks should be regularly examined to identify those that can be delegated, or shortened, or even eliminated altogether. This is another important reason for the time-log analysis to be repeated at intervals.

Allocating and scheduling time

The action diary, the 'to do' list and the working timetable combine together as tools to enable the headteacher to schedule time more efficiently.

The action diary

The action diary is a development of the traditional desk diary probably in use in every school in the country, where appointments are written in by the headteacher and the school secretary. With a line ruled vertically down the centre of each page, the usual 'week to a view' diary can be adapted quite easily to provide a useful time-management tool. To the left of the line the diary can be used in the traditional way for appointments etc. To the right of the line the diary is used to note required actions.

The first task *always* on beginning a new diary is to insert a sheet into the pages beginning each month, and using last year's diary to assist you, note down at the beginning of appropriate months events that are likely to occur (sports, concerts etc). This will not commit you so far ahead to specific dates, but it is sensible forward planning to enable you to anticipate and not forget. A simple task, but one that is done surprisingly little.

On the right hand side of each page of the diary, 'do by' dates are noted down. Whenever a project is planned, however grand or however small, the dates should be written into the diary by which time each action comprising the project should be completed. For small projects it might be sufficient to note down a single 'do by' date, but for larger projects it should be possible to break them down into parts and give each section a 'do by' date of its own. Large projects are much easier to accomplish when broken down into smaller parts. It is important for longer projects that need this sort of breakdown, to be looked at for constituent parts *before* noting down the end date, and planning time must be given for this analysis. Project planning techniques justify a complete book of their own, but there is neither time nor space in this chapter to examine these in detail. If the reader is interested, there are many avenues here to explore further, from very simple plans discussed by Everard (1985) to more complex techniques such as

critical path analysis for educational applications see OU course
E221 Unit 15 (1974) and Snape (1971).

The 'to do' list

Short term priorities should be noted down on a 'to do' list which
needs to be nothing more than the page of a small notebook kept
specially for the task. Tasks that must be completed in the short
term are listed, and the list is added to when appropriate. It is often
suggested that as items are added to the 'to do' list, they are coded
to indicate the degree of priority to be given to them. Whenever
the list is redrafted, the items are then reconsidered for their priority
ratings, and reallocated as necessary. For this activity it is advan-
tageous to have pre-printed sheets to use, similar to that illustrated
below (Figure 5.5).

This kind of list is suitable for those headteachers who can
manage to begin each day with a planning session. If you can keep
your list short, you may not find it necessary to prioritise it in this

Figure 5.5 – 'To do' priority sheet

Date	Tick when completed
HIGH PRIORITY: do today	
MEDIUM PRIORITY: do this week	
LOW PRIORITY: do soon	

way. You may find it useful each time to look at the list as a whole, and to review it in your mind. Items which may not have been a priority when they were added to the list, may become a priority after a day or two. I do find it useful to date each task when I add it to the list, and to time bound my action if appropriate by allocating a date by which the task should have been acted upon. *Always* give yourself a specific deadline rather than 'as soon as possible' – an important tip to remember when you are delegating tasks too; 'as soon as possible' may be in a month's time to someone, and that is probably not what you have in mind. Setting specific deadlines wherever possible avoids procrastination.

As time becomes available, the most important task on the list is acted upon and crossed off. It is not necessary to redraft the list each day – you will however find that after several days the crossings out become so considerable that you are forced to redraft on a clean page. The list does need to be in a prominent place, and looked at *at least* at the beginning of every day, but preferably, if it is to be a useful tool throughout each day. It needs to be *one* consolidated list, not a collection of scraps of paper.

These lists provide a daily sense of purpose and also a sense of achievement to see what has been done. Try to concentrate on one thing at a time from your list. Mackenzie (1975) says that one of the most important time savers is to 'handle a task only once. When you pick it up dispose of it'. Otherwise the task can take at least twice as long, as you must 're-tune' to it, and review your progress so far, every time that you go back to it.

Almost everyone realises the value of such lists and probably most people have used them when faced with an unusual or complex problem. But how many headteachers use them daily as a matter of course? Lakein (1973) says that:

> most people in business know about 'to do' lists, but while lower level employees and less successful managers tend not to use them, very successful people invariably rely on them.

The working timetable

This is simply a blank timetable sheet for one week which is kept in a prominent place on the headteacher's desk. Each week usually on Friday afternoon, the appointments diary for the next week is scanned, and all appointments and other commitments (teaching obligations etc.) are recorded on it in the appropriate places. The action diary is also scanned for the next two or three weeks, estimates of time needed to complete tasks by 'do by' dates are made, and time is allocated on the timetable to complete these tasks. It is important that allocated times are placed well in advance of the 'do by' date, so that if a crisis occurs and the task cannot be completed at the scheduled time, extra time is available and the activity can be immediately rescheduled. To allow for this, all spaces on the timetable should not be 'booked' in advance. It is important to leave spaces each day if possible to allow for unforeseen circumstances. Forward planning in this way does in fact help you if a crisis situation arises. If the spaces are not filled, either from moved activities from earlier parts of the timetable or by last minute appointments, then the time can be used to carry out tasks from the 'to do' lists.

Conclusion

If you are to be considered a good manager, you must be organised. The techniques discussed in this chapter do not provide an exhaustive list of time management strategies, but by using just these few ideas you can be certain that you will be operating more efficiently than before. There are many more techniques that I would like to have mentioned had I the space, but these must be left to another time, perhaps another book. I must however make one final suggestion. Great emphasis has been given in this chapter on the noting down of plans of action. It is imperative that ideas are noted as soon as they are thought of, and this is usually an easy task to accomplish. Many headteachers do however drive to and from school each day, and it is during these times, when minds are preparing for and winding down from the onslaught of the day, that many ideas come to mind and cannot be noted down immediately. It is a useful investment to provide yourself with a micro tape-recorder/dictating machine to keep in your car to record your ideas as they occur to you. If they are not noted immediately, they tend to be forgotten. As soon as you are able to do so, transcribe these recordings onto the relevant list or diary.

In his book on Primary school management, Waters (1979) offers this advice to headteachers. He reproduces a tract written by one John Ford in the year 1733:

> Undertake no more than you can manage.
> Perform with delight and a kind of unweariness.
> Be watchful over strangers.
> Trust not to memory, but immediately make entries in proper books.
> At proper times inspect your affairs.
> He who observes the rules laid down will be likely to thrive
> and prosper in the world.

What better way to conclude this chapter!

References

Clerkin, C (1985) 'What do Primary School Heads actually do all day', in *School Organisation*, Vol 5 No. 4.

Cook, A and Mack, H (1971) *The Headteacher's Role*, Macmillan/Schools Council.

Everard, K B and Morris, G (1985) *Effective School Management* Harper and Row.

Ferner, J D (1980) *Successful Time Management*, Wiley.

Fisher, G H (1965) *The New Form Statistical Tables*, ULP.

Harling, P (1981) 'Primary School Headship: Towards a Job Specification' in *School Organisation*, Vol 1 No 1.

Harvey, C W (1986) 'How Primary Heads Spend Their Time', in *Educational Management and Administration* Vol 14 No 1.

Lakein, A (1973) *How to Get Control of your Time and your Life*, Wyden.

Mckenzie, R A (1975) *The Time Trap: How to get More Done in Less Time*, McGraw-Hill.

McConalogue, T (1984) 'Developing the Skill of Time Management', in *Leadership and Organisation Journal*, Vol 5 No 1.

Mintzberg, A (1973) *The Nature of Managerial Work*, Harper and Row.

Open University (1974) E221 *Decision Making in British Educational Systems, Unit 15, Introduction to Planning and Decision Models*.

Richardson, N (1984) *The Effective Use of Time*, Education for Industrial Society.

Snape, P (1971) 'A Management to School Leadership', in *Journal of The Association of Education Committees*, December 1971.

Waters, D (1979) *Management and Headship in the Primary School*, Ward Lock.

Further Reading

Arnold, R (1988) 'Making the best use of teacher time' in Craig I (Ed) *Managing the Primary Classroom*, Longman.

Garratt, S (1985) *Manage Your Time*, Fontana.

Haynes, M E (1987) *Make Every Minute Count*, Kogan Page.

6 School-centred financial management

Audrey Stenner

Independent schools have a long history of financial autonomy, but those in the maintained sector have no such tradition and primary schools in particular have not been encouraged to believe them selves capable of self-management in financial terms. The level of authority vested in a primary head has not been in any way matched by a comparable degree of financial responsibility and his/her role in that respect has been restricted to the administration of the capitation allowance – which represents only a tiny proportion of the total revenue costs of the school. All this is soon to change.

The concept of head-as-manager is a relatively recent one and is largely the consequence of the economic pressures which have faced most LEAs since the 1970s. Their problem was how to use their scarce resources most effectively and the response by some of them was to experiment with schemes which involved changes in management practice, by devolving more financial decision-making upon those who are in the best position to make these decisions and who are most affected by them, namely the schools themselves. In this way a few authorities, notably Solihull and Cambridgeshire, anticipated some of the principles which the Education Reform Act (1988) will introduce from April 1990. The aims of the Act are far more wide-ranging than financial devolution alone, but the early experiments in delegation gave effect to the same supposition as in the Act – that schools will be enabled to make more efficient use of resources if they have control over them.

Cambridgeshire introduced its pilot scheme for Local Financial Management (LFM) in 1982. It was originally intended for secondary schools only but when the proposal came forward the head of

Buckden Primary School, a co-opted member of the Education Committee, was able to put the case for the inclusion of primary schools. The head felt the particular importance of primary participation; first, because if the principle of delegation was a good and sound one it should be capable of application across all sectors, and second, because there was almost no information at that time on the costs of individual primary schools. Until there was some real evidence to hand it seemed likely that the historical inequalities between the secondary and the primary allocations would continue unchallenged.

The benefits which the pilot schools (six secondary and one primary) derived from LFM encouraged elected members to extend delegation to all secondary schools and ten more primaries in 1986. Cambridgeshire is a county where individual initiative is encouraged and the scheme was the natural development of the pattern of management in schools promoted by the Chief Education Officer. The style of the LEA is characterised by its belief in directions rather than directives, a style which provides a good seedbed for the successful growth of local decision-making.

From 1986 the pace of innovation concerning management at school level has gathered momentum nationally, and at an astonishing rate, the culmination being the Education Reform Act. The Act itself does not employ the term Local Management of Schools (LMS) but it has become accepted practice to use it, following the recommendation in the Coopers and Lybrand Report (1988) to the government. The Act refers instead to a system of financial delegation and connects with the management of staff. Its conditions must apply to every primary school with 200 or more pupils, and smaller ones may be included if an LEA so chooses. Although it will take time in large local authorities to bring all primary schools into the scheme it would seem inevitable that they will all come in at some point. It makes no administrative sense to have the two systems running side-by-side in one LEA, as a permanent basis for organisation.

LMS is the most significant development for primary school management this century, not only because it will affect every one of them, but also because it goes so much further than its forerunner, LFM. The main differences between them are:

LFM	LMS
local	national
voluntary	statutory
few primary schools	all over 200
gradual implementation	prescribed time table
historic cost budgets	formula funded
inflation-proofed budgets	cash-limited

Most significantly under LMS, a governing body with a delegated budget will have greatly enhanced powers, especially in relation to the management of staff. The 1986 Education Act did increase the power of governors but it still left the processes of appointment and dismissal of staff within the overall control of the LEA. With LMS primary school governors will, for the first time, decide how many teachers and support staff a school will have. They will appoint and dismiss the staff without let or hindrance by the LEA, provided they meet legal requirements and act properly. They will also establish and operate their own disciplinary and grievance procedures for the staff employed at their school. It is expected that governors will want to consult with the head and the LEA, and they are required to do that in the case of most appointments, but in the case of suspension, for example, there is no such requirement. It is necessary only for the governing body to inform the head and the LEA that someone is suspended on full pay. Only the governors may end a suspension initiated by the head.

However, the LEA remains the employer of all staff and some tension may therefore arise because the relationship between employer and employee will be confused in a way it has not been before. There will be a marked change of role for local authorities in relation to primary schools with delegated budgets. On the whole LEAs have taken a more paternalistic stance towards the primary sector than to the secondary and therefore the adjustment in attitudes and relationships which will be needed may be the greater. Officers in all departments, not just Education, will have to become acclimatised to primary governors and heads taking decisions they have never before contemplated.

The clear implication of the Act is that LEAs will be less involved with the small detail of management and more concerned with a strategic role as providers and quality guarantors. That is, the balance of activities in their case will tilt more towards a supportive, advising and monitoring service and away from a directing and controlling one. The monitoring role is no new one for them but it may be a more complex one to fulfil in the future because of the extent of delegation required by the Act. Although LEAs are faced with a major reduction of central control over the deployment of resources (and therefore may be unable to promote educational initiatives to the same degree as before) they will still have a duty to ensure the quality of education for all children through the National Curriculum. Each child has an entitlement to an equal opportunity in education and it is the LEAs job to guarantee that s(he) gets it. A critical test of the new relationship which has to be forged will be how, and by what means, the inspectors/advisers set about doing this, when the management of staff and resources is in the hands of governors who may not share the same ideas on educational priorities.

As for the primary head, there is a phrase – 'the changing role of the head' – which gives rise to much debate, but it is one which makes an assumption that it *is* changing. In one sense that is true but in a more fundamental sense what is happening and will happen is an extension of the present role. Too much can be made of the changing role with the result that a whole mythology of 'the changed head' can be built upon it.

For instance, early criticism of LFM schemes usually came from members and union representatives who felt that the already too great (in their eyes) power of the heads would be further increased through financial control. They may or may not be correct in that judgement but alongside it were the dire prophecies of posts kept vacant, the appointment of cheap teachers, freezing classrooms and the like, all in the interests of saving money above all other considerations. As though, that is, when heads had a budget to manage they would promptly change role, foresake all professional standards and educational criteria and turn into accountants overnight. If it is any guide to the future, the experience of pilot schools indicates that both those heads who wanted financial management and those who had it thrust upon them differ not at all in seeing themselves first and foremost as headteachers and as budget managers very much second.

Nevertheless, there is no doubt that there are heads who fear a major change of role. They usually express this in terms of 'I didn't come into the profession to do X', X being the latest imposition upon them. Some primary heads truly dread the advent of LMS because the budgetary responsibilities seem daunting. They see a future for themselves being glued to the accounts all day or sitting before a computer screen making critical decisions about moving money around. In practice it is possible to run a budget satisfactorily without spending an undue amount of time, without accounting skills and without a computer. What is important to emphasise is that these same heads have managed their capitation budget without a qualm and that they are experienced already in management – in managing staff, in provision for the curriculum and in the organisation of the school. It should be a necessary part of any LEA training programme to reassure those heads who feel beset that guidance will be available, and to raise their consciousness that they are managers now, although they may not use the term.

That is not to deny that there are factors about which are shaping some change of role for the head. One of the factors is the pressure of time. Parents are more assertive and they are aware of their rights in selecting a school of their choice. There are far more visits for prospective parents now and they take up time. The governors too need more time from the head because many of them are unsure about their future role and some are frankly doubtful of their capacity to absorb all that is coming their way. Then the sheer volume of paper which is descending upon the head's desk is wellnigh overwhelming at present and everything is top priority. It will, presumably, ease off eventually but meanwhile the result is that a growing number of primary heads are no longer timetabling themselves for teaching and the change there is clearly less contact time with children. Conversely, another factor is the unavailability of teachers and supply teachers, which means the head is being moved more and more into the role of supernumerary class teacher.

Buckden is a village school which has been managing its financial affairs for seven years. It has a budget this year (1989/90) of £258,100, for 330 pupils aged four to eleven. There are twelve class teachers and a part-timer (0.4) – a cohesive and talented group who work extremely hard and have a strong commitment to the well-being of the school. The governors have deep roots in the community and take a pride in the school, which is the centre of many village activities. The interest of the school in having a del-egated budget came originally from a sense of frustration at being unable to direct funds to where they were seen to be most needed at the time. It was aggravating to watch money being spent on fixing draught excluders to doors which did not need them, when the really urgent requirement was for more furniture. It was hoped that local management would give the school the flexibility to respond to its own needs, and to respond quickly. That benefit has been realised time and again, and the ability to react promptly to a situation is an advantage the governors and head value highly, not least in the case of unexpected absence. There can be many circumstances when application of the local 'rule' that heads cover for the first three days of absence is inappropriate, and the decision whether or not to call in a supply teacher is best left to the head, who knows the priorities of the school at that time. If a supply teacher is unavailable and the head has to cancel other commit-ments to teach, there is under local management, an alleviation of necessity in the knowledge that the school, rather than the LEA has benefited financially by saving the cost of supply cover.

Another advantage has been the incentive to make sensible econ-omies, because any savings are retained by the school. An accumu-lation of small underspends, garnered through careful use of water, energy, telephone etc. can add up to a surprising total over a year. When the school is paying the bills and there is a tangible return in the form of the alternative use of 'profits', people are more of a mind to address themselves to the reduction of potential sources of waste. Primary schools have never been centres of prodigality but self-management does concentrate the attention on those areas of expenditure where a reasonable change in the spending pattern could result in another computer for a classroom. There is also an incentive to exploit the assets of the building, or the playing field through lettings, since the school sets the rate and keeps the income.

Local financial management seems to the governors and staff a practical matter of improving the quality of education by diverting savings made under non-educational headings to those areas which directly affect the classroom. Since the governors and head are responsible for the curriculum it makes good sense for them also to have financial control so that they can properly resource the curriculum plans they make. The advantage is that they know the cost of everything involved in a proposal – the cost of the teacher's time, the equipment, the INSET expenses, extra ancillary hours and so on – and they can decide upon options on the basis of accurate knowledge. The enablement to carry forward credits (debits carry over too) from one year to the next allows the school to build up over time a sizeable sum, which can be used for a project such as a small building alteration. It might be one which would never get into the LEAs minor works programme but one which could considerably improve the working conditions.

The real purpose of financial management is not about budgets, it is the making possible of local decisions which are to the benefit of the children. There must be pupil benefits if a scheme is to be worthwhile. Whether these are identifiable is another matter because the relationship between financial input and educational quality is exceptionally difficult to quantify and has defeated many an academic researcher. It is certainly not axiomatic that the ability to vire money from one heading to another will make for a better school. It is just as possible to make bad decisions about the alternative use of resources, as it is to make fruitful ones. The real imperative is to question the objectives closely and to evaluate the outcomes as best one can and be alert to the possibility that one can easily be seduced into thinking that there *have* to be educational benefits if extra money has been put in.

The system that has evolved at Buckden is not necessarily one that would suit every primary school, each LMS school will develop its own model of decision-making and accountability as it learns through experience. At Buckden it developed gradually but the aims upon which it is based have remained constant from the beginning. These were set down by the staff and governors in 1982 as follows:

– to create better learning opportunities

- to involve all the staff and governors in decision-making
- to make the scheme serve the curriculum
- to use any flexibility in the budget to make the most of the resources available
- to monitor progress regularly and to watch for adverse effects.

In the first two years a budget built up by the officers was used because the head had no knowledge of the costs of the school nor of the pattern of expenditure. Once they became clear then it was possible for the school to make its own budget. The LEA notifies the school of the gross sum in February and that is divided up according to local priorities under various headings – salaries, premises costs, capitation etc. and these are the figures used on the computer printouts which come each month from Shire Hall. (Figure 6.1).

Figure 6.1 – Buckden Primary School – 1989–90 Budget

Employees:	Teaching Staff	211100
	Supply Staff	1500
	Support Staff	11300
	Caretakers and Cleaning	10300
Premises:	Electricity	1000
	Gas	1400
	General Rates	11000
	Water	700
	Sewerage	500
	Window Cleaning	100
	Refuse Collection	200
	Cleaning Materials	400
Supplies:	Capitation	9000
Transport:	Car Allowance	400
Expenses:	Advertising	100
	Candidates' Expenses	100
	TOTAL	258100

There are differing levels of interest among the governors and staff – some are closely involved and others less so. The chairman of governors delegated all financial business to the vice-chairman, who works closely with the head. There has been no adverse reaction among staff and governors and the scheme, though not compelling everyone's ardent attention, is able to run in a collaborative climate. Commitment to the principles of local management has never been in doubt from anyone. Everybody wants to be involved in making financial decisions, but not in financial administration. That is done by the head. One of the initial concerns was how much time would be taken up – from the beginning the teachers said that the classroom was the first priority and that they did not want to spend time on administrative detail. Updates on the budget are regularly given in staff and governor meetings and there are certain times in the year when everyone meets together for making decisions about allocations.

The first year was hard work, mainly because of lack of knowledge about how budgets work, and anxiety on two counts – would the workload be too onerous and would the budget be adequate? There is no means of knowing until the first year has run its course, and one learns more in that year than in any other.

The amount of time spent on local management is one for personal decision by the head, but the workload need not be burdensome. It is important to distinguish between what contributes to the aims of the school and what does not, because it is possible to spend a great deal of time on detail. That is a natural tendency in the first year when it may seem essential to follow up every tiny discrepancy between the school accounts and the printouts, and when the urge to hunt out bargains is high. It is not the best use of the head's time to save two pence on a packet of gummed labels when the effort involved is to the detriment of other professional responsibilities. The need is to establish priorities early on and to use the scheme as a management tool. After the first year local management was found to *save* time at Buckden, and the average time spent on it is not more than four hours a month (excluding meetings and visitors!) The annual budget cycle is reproduced in Figure 6.2.

When all the bills have been paid it is hoped that there will be some money left over. That hope depends on many circumstances, especially the size of the base budget, but so far at Buckden there have been satisfactory results. The best year realised £9200, and last year a balance of £7800 remained. The allocation of the underspend is really a retro-virement, the school saves, then spends. In October all the governors, teaching and support staff together decide how they wish to allot the savings. This is a collegial exercise – everybody has contributed in their various ways to achieving the underspend and everyone has an equal voice in deciding how it will be distributed. Anyone can put in a bid for any sum of money but the proposal has to be backed by details of the educational

---

Figure 6.2 – Buckden Primary School – Budget Cycle

September	present financial statement to parents
	remind governors and staff re underspend
	total
October	allocation of underspend
November	check costs
December	complete underspend buying
	decide next year's curriculum priorities
January	do draft budget
February	LEA notifies funding
March*	finalise budget
	close accounts for current year
April*	notify LEA re budget figures
	open new accounts
May/June	receive *March 5* figures from LEA
	notify governors and staff re underspend
	total

* denotes meeting

---

intent behind it, and by accurate costing. That is because the pro-poser is likely to be questioned about whether the bid is based on current need, next year's possible priorities, or why such a large amount should go on just one curriculum area. The whole sum could be spent on one expensive item but in practice people take an across-the-board view of allocation and prefer to spread the benefits around. So they tend to trim some bids and they do not automatically agree to proposals made by the most persuasive or the most forceful advocates.

All bids are weighed against certain criteria:

– is there likely to be an educational gain?
– will it starve another curriculum area?
– are there more immediate pupil needs?
– does it benefit the environment?
– is it a repeat bid whose priority needs to be re-examined?

One recurrent bid is that made by the head for a contingency sum of £2000. That is always accepted because everyone wants the security of a reserve fund in case of unforeseen happenings. It takes time to build up a nest egg and the lack of one at the start contrib-utes to the anxieties of the first year. The contingency fund has never been completely used up and the balance rolls forward to start off the following year's reserves. The 1988–89 underspend was allocated thus:

		£
Extra ancillary hours		400
Under 5s		500
Library		1000
Colour printer		490
VTR		400
2 printers		330
Playground equipment		500
Extra teaching hours		1000
Extra cleaning hours		150
CDT resources		600
Special needs		430
Contingency		2000
	TOTAL	7800

This year's capitation and next year's underspend may need to be concentrated on the core subjects of the National Curriculum, simply because they are the most expensive.

From April 1989 Buckden moved to formula funding. At once the overriding importance of the number of pupils on roll was made uncomfortably apparent. The school suffered a loss of £7000 in the change from historical to formula funding, mainly because the roll had fallen by eleven children. The loss amounts to half a teacher but the pupil losses, as is usual, were scattered throughout the school, not conveniently concentrated in a single year group. It is pertinent at this point to re-state the main principles which underlie formula funding:

– that it should be related to the need to spend, while giving schools an incentive to make the most effective use of resources
– that it should develop an objective basis for allocation, rather than relying on historic costs
– that a school's budget should be determined in large measure by the ability to attract and retain pupils.

It is possible to support all of these principles but yet to see that the last of them will pose a problem for heads-as-managers. There is a finite number of children needing to be educated and they will largely be resident within the school's previously defined catchment zone. In rural areas many parents are quite unable to take advantage of open enrolment for reasons of distance, lack of transport or time. If there is no development and housing costs are prohibitive for young parents, the prospect for the school is a steadily declining roll and therefore a declining income.

There is much work still to be done on resource allocation formulae, and on the time-scale of the transitional arrangements which are intended to protect schools from too severe a change year-on-year. It is not easy to predict the effects on individual schools, when there are such variations among them. One variation is the cash-value per child. In the published schemes the value of one unit ranges from £600 to over £1000, before weightings are added. So two similarly sized schools, adjacent but situated in different LEAs, could find themselves with very different resources for educating the same number of children.

What changes may we see under LMS in the future? Where networking is not an early possibility there could be pressures from heads for cheque books and bank accounts so that ponderous administrative processes are speeded up. There may be moves for the extension of delegation – and there is no irrefutable reason why all the discretionary and most of the mandatory exceptions should not eventually be devolved. How governors and heads view that possibility will depend on their circumstances; those with an antique boiler or a flat roof will not be yearning to have structural maintenance delegated to them.

A lot more attention might, in the future, be turned towards exploitation of school premises, in attempts to generate income. We may see competitive ploys being used by governors who are anxious a) to recruit pupils – advertising? 'special attractions'? and b) to recruit teachers – spot salary + bonus? sponsorship? and, even, transfer fees? The early fears that governors would appoint cheap teachers seem a bit redundant now that the shortage of teachers in some areas is such that governors are relieved to be able to find any teacher at all.

There are interesting times ahead for primary schools. The principle of LMS is right, the processes and practice will need time to perfect.

Reference

Coopers and Lybrand (1988) *Local Management of Schools. A report to the Department of Education and Science.*

7 The deputy as trainee head

Derek Waters

It is frequently argued that the unsatisfactory and ill-defined nature of the primary school deputy head's job is the inevitable result of the failure of local authorities to provide an appropriate job description for the headteacher. The post of deputy is of fairly recent origin having been established in 1956. Although the position, by definition, was designed to be held by someone ready, willing and able to stand in for the head for short or long periods, there was little attempt in the early days on the part of the headteacher to ensure that the deputy was equipped to carry out that major responsibility. Too frequently it was the case that little training was provided to enable the deputy to develop any other kind of satisfactory role.

While some headteachers wished to preserve some of the mystique of their positions, in fairness it must be said that the heads themselves had had no training for their own role or introduction to such managerial skills as defining roles, delegating tasks, monitoring performance and so on. The net result of this situation has been over the years more a collection of *ad hoc* tasks than a properly defined role. In the Primary Survey (DES, 1978) HMI significantly failed to mention the deputy head but dealt at length with the work of the postholders; especially those with curriculum responsibility. They were concerned about the distribution of posts (eg the numbers of music and physical education posts being greater than those held for language work and mathematics) and the lack of influence of the holders on other teachers (ie only 25 per cent could be regarded as successful in this respect). Since that time the authority and expertise of postholders has increased to such an extent that in some schools they could be said to be affecting the work of colleagues to a greater extent than the deputy heads. In a recent report (DES, 1985) it was observed by the Welsh Office HMI that deputy heads were carrying out lower level tasks than the curriculum leaders. It is important therefore for every deputy to negotiate with the head in order to produce a job description which is appropriate to the position and status, and which articulates, in unequivocal terms, tasks and responsibilities which would make up a role satisfactory to all concerned.

Responsibility for leadership training

The job of the headteacher is such a complex, demanding and changing one that training to fit the incumbent for it must be regarded as essential. Over the last decade there has been a steady increase in the provision of training courses by some local authorities, polytechnics and such bodies as the College of Preceptors and the Educational Development Association. The programmes offered have varied in duration, content, rigour and quality. Some of the best include a high level of experimental activity and have taken account of the manner in which industry trains its managers. The Department of Education and Science have wished to encourage leadership training for many years and have mounted courses themselves on the subject. But with Circular 3/83 and later 4/84, the DES have provided finance for such training work in their One Term Training Opportunities (OTTO) programmes in various nominated regional centres. Usually experienced headteachers are selected for these courses with the twin aims of improving their leadership skills and to equip them with strategies to help train less experienced headteachers and deputies. Local authorities must then take up the responsibility for preparing and mounting 20 day courses. Deputies aspiring to headship should seek places on these programmes. Since these courses must have the approval of the National Development Centre for School Management Training based in Bristol, applicants can be assured that they will be well served when they attend.

In a recent report (ILEA, 1985) Norman Thomas (formerly Chief Primary HMI) said:

> We believe that nearly all deputy heads should be on the way towards becoming heads, and the heads should give them as much pre-training and experience as possible.

We are aware from Ann Mason's chapter on Staff Development of the role of the head in this respect. It would be expected that the deputy would be fully involved in the school programme – sometimes as a leader and at other times as a participant. But in addition there should be a planned programme to meet the specific needs of the deputy head. This assumes a willingness and a competence on the part of the headteacher to engage in this activity and similarly a cooperative attitude and an ability to benefit on the part of the deputy. Mutual respect and a sound working professional relationship between the two senior members of staff are prerequisites for the success of such a programme. The term 'programme' has been deliberately chosen since the activities and experiences would be planned to cover a period of two years. While much that will be proposed will need to be carried out while the school is in session, some items will have to be done outside those normal hours and both parties will need to commit themselves to this arrangement.

Where the head, because of pressure of work, is unable to give the same commitment to the task as the deputy is willing to offer, it will be important for the deputy to seek the opportunities which are suggested later in the chapter. It will be necessary for the deputy to indicate that the activities are suggested to enable the head's responsibilities to be carried out in the case of absence and to assist with personal career development. To enable some things to take place the cooperation of other teaching and support staff may be required and the deputy must be clear about what (s)he is requesting by way of assistance and why this is necessary. Some arrangements can be suggested which will be to the mutual benefit of all parties concerned.

Advisers and local inspectors who will be involved in preparation for headship courses and in appointments will wish to see evidence of training initiatives adopted in school, and will want to encourage the active interest of the headteacher in this process. In recent times some LEAs have designed courses which require the attendance of both heads and deputies, thus acknowledging the key leadership roles which each holds.

Gaining experience

In order to deputise properly, even for a very short time, the deputy head ought to know everything the head knows in relation to the school and what has to go on to make it function effectively and efficiently. So there is a need to systematically list all the tasks which the head engages in during a typical year. It could be useful to keep a professional diary to record experiences undergone with comments upon them. Alternatively a large notebook can be obtained, with different headings given to each page, an index to indicate cross references, and the facility to annotate the reports with personal comments. Ideally, if time can be found, the deputy and head should have regular discussions about the entries made in this training logbook to check accuracy, seek further clarification, indicate links and where further development or reinforcement is required. In the absence of such regular advice from the head, a critical friend eg another deputy or another head, can be asked to provide the counselling service. It is suggested that such discussions be confined to positive comments about the deputy's training progress.

Administration

Because of the demands of the Education Reform Act 1988 and other legislation there has been a great increase in the administrative work of the school. While a good secretary can relieve the headteacher of much of this, its sheer volume and complexity is turning the head into an administrator with less opportunity to be a professional leader in the school. The deputy could to the school's advantage take over more responsibility for the day to day running of the institution. But since the proposal is that the deputy should share the head's workload, administration must be included. Attendance at courses and conferences on such items as Local Management of Schools will mean that the demands of tasks will be shared, but also that on promotion to headship the deputy is already familiar with the theory and practice of financial management.

Headteachers will want the school to run efficiently in their absence and it makes good sense to show deputies both the standard forms and accompanying instructions for their use. The opportunity for training in a practical way will be to show with a real example how the details are filled in and procedures followed. On the next occasion when a return is required the deputy can carry out the prescribed procedure. In larger primary schools much of the administrative work is carried out by the secretary, and in some areas it is she who would be the obvious tutor to seek help from. Deputies should in the normal course of events assist the headteacher with administration but they should seek experience of all such work at different times. While they may not have to do all of it when they become headteachers, they need to know all about it, since they have to append signatures thus accepting responsibility.

The deputy should know about the filing system in operation and have access to it. Communications from the DES and LEA, including those marked confidential, should be available to the deputy. Letters will also arrive from other sources, including parents, and the head can be helpful to the deputy in discussing the appropriate form of reply to each since there will be no LEA guidance in this area. The deputy could be invited to suggest a suitable response, with the head commenting on this afterwards. It could well be that a mutual consideration of some correspondence could improve the quality of the reply. In most cases and certainly in those which are sensitive, a copy of the reply should be kept. The examination of a series of letters and replies could be useful to a deputy.

In the absence of the head or involvement somewhere else in the school, callers and those who telephone should be invited to speak to the deputy.

Experience of this kind should be seen as valuable training, as well as serving the needs of the school. Such interviews and even telephone calls can be stressful, and the deputy needs to be in possession of the facts, if the matter is going to be dealt with adequately. In cases of doubt, it is wise to listen carefully and sympathetically, promise to investigate promptly and to call back or arrange another meeting. A careful discussion with the head after investigation should be followed by a sincere request to be invited to continue to deal with the case or alternatively attend the promised interview.

At other meetings, for instance when children are transferring to their secondary schools, as well as being made familiar with procedures, the deputy should ask to sit in on the parental choice sessions.

Ritual practices

The deputy should be taking regular assemblies of the whole school. The head may be observed conducting such events but it is imperative that practice is gained. Some deputies feel a degree of reluctance to have other staff attend assemblies; it is better if they do, since it will be more normal for the children, and some early feedback can be requested from senior colleagues. Wise deputies always have an instant assembly ready in case the head is unavoidably detained and sends a note with the cryptic message 'Carry On'. Certain special assemblies, Harvest Festival, Christmas and Easter Celebrations, often require a different form of leadership. Once again, responsibility for this can be shared with the head. Some schools hold Prize Days or Leaver's Days and the form of these should be noted carefully. The deputy usually has a role to fulfil on these occasions and some enlargement of this can be suggested to gain further experience.

Visitors are a regular feature of some schools – HMI, LEA advisers, governors, students, other teachers and prospective parents. The deputy can volunteer to carry out this escorting duty following some careful planning and liaison with colleagues. A checklist can be prepared following such experiences and used subsequently as a guide.

Most schools make good practical arrangements to welcome the new intake of children and their parents in advance of the new term. As well as knowing the whole procedure, the deputy should ask to attend the welcoming session to see what goes on; how information is gathered from the adults; what the future pupils do at this time; how the new teachers are introduced and so on.

The deputy, especially if new to the school, should be observant of all the other ritual and practice which goes on, to assess its value to the social organisation of the institution. In one school the head might meet the staff informally before the children come in and to all intents and purposes conduct a staff meeting; in another the staff may have a social gathering once a term; in a third place the head may take all the children in the hall to allow staff to carry out classroom organisational tasks for the following week. The examples are legion, many of them idiosyncratic, yet most serve a useful purpose. Those that are might be noted for later use by a promoted deputy, suitably modified to suit the new context.

The Governing Body

By examining the Rules and Articles of Government issued by the LEA, as well as the plentiful literature on the subject (eg Wragg and Partington, 1980 and Sallis, 1980), the roles, rights and responsibilities of governors can be discovered. New legislation in parliament has increased the powers of the body, as well as clarifying their position vis-a-vis the LEA and the headteacher. (1986 and 1988 Education Acts).

If the deputy is the elected staff member then regular attendance and active involvement at the termly meetings will provide valuable experience. Where this is not the case, then the head should ask the chairperson if the deputy can observe on a regular basis. The latter would not be allowed to speak unless invited, and would have to leave during the discussion of any confidential matter (unlike the elected staff governor). It may be possible to attend staff interviews with the chairperson's agreement and to be allowed to ask questions, but (s)he would not be allowed to vote in the selection process.

It should be helpful to the head for the deputy to get to know the individuals on the governing body as well as possible, so that the responsibility of welcoming them to the school to special events or for routine visits can be shared.

The professional role

The deputy must always be seeking to improve personal classroom practice and provide a good example of professionalism to colleagues. Varied teaching experience should be sought. On a yearly basis, this should not be difficult to arrange but in addition, opportunities should be sought with colleagues to exchange classes for a period a week. This experience over an extended time should enable the newly appointed head to discuss primary practice, throughout the age range, with knowledge and confidence. Visits to other schools to observe good practice will be a regular feature of the training process. Often the chance to look around one's own school and discuss in open, frank and positive terms with colleagues what is going on in the teaching and learning process is often overlooked. The newest recruit to the profession has much to offer the experienced teacher and the deputy should be ready to receive new insights from those ready and able to offer them. Such professional discussions should boost the confidence of colleagues, especially those new to the profession. The deputy may be designated staffmember responsible for the professional and pastoral care of probationer teachers and students on teaching practice. Many LEAs have formulated programmes of induction which incorporates a school based element. There needs to be a degree of flexibility within the whole programme and this applies particularly within the school setting. This responsibility demands considerable skills in terms of providing assistance in various forms with such matters as classroom organisation, resource provision, motivation of children, and work planning. In addition, the need to build up and maintain a good relationship with a new colleague is paramount. This role of the deputy could expand to include staff development. The success of this enterprise will depend largely upon the attitudes and feelings of goodwill, cooperation, trust and mutual support fostered in the professional setting of the staffroom.

Where another member of staff has been appointed to take responsibility for staff training, the deputy head should offer the fullest cooperation as well as observing every detail of the programme.

Curriculum responsibility

It is important for every teacher to have the opportunity to exercise leadership in some aspect of the curriculum (Waters, 1983). The role in this respect for the deputy should offer opportunities both to help the school and the individual. In some schools either because there are too few members of staff, or there is a special expertise available, the deputy will assume a curriculum responsibility. With the advent of a national curriculum a wider role can be anticipated. To provide a broad and balanced curriculum a coordinator will be required and the deputy could be the most appropriate person for this task. In any case it will be important to be familiar with all the documentation which is being sent to the schools by the DES and LEAs. An active part will be expected from the Deputy in related schoolbased INSET, particularly on the organisation side but also in terms of providing active learning situations. Allocation of funding to curriculum areas will involve the deputy in decision-making activities with senior if not all colleagues.

Managing meetings

It will be unfortunate if the headteacher insists upon chairing every meeting in the school, and thus preventing other members of staff taking on this responsibility. The deputy should ask for opportunities to take on this role and then have the chance to discuss the process afterwards. As well as general business meetings, there will be gatherings of all or part of the staff to discuss curriculum matters, the organisation of special events, and emergency matters eg a discipline problem, a new directive from the education committee and so on. The size of the staff and the nature of the business will dictate the level of formality which is required. However many meetings are regarded as disappointing because no decisions are reached or action agreed upon. To aid in this process of managing meetings in a business-like manner, the chairperson must prepare adequately. This must include agreeing date, time, duration, place of meeting and its purpose. The form and amount of preparation that all, as well as particular members must undertake. The meeting itself should start on time and work steadily through the agenda, with the chairperson ensuring that different viewpoints are expressed and listened to attentively, summarising, seeking suggestions for action and so on. The keeping of records of the meeting is useful so that where agreements and action have been agreed, this is firmly stated with the people responsible for carrying out the decision by a definite date. It is a useful idea to adopt a flipchart for some, if not all, meetings so that everyone can see what is being recorded by way of suggestions and decisions. The formalities and courtesies must be observed by the chair who sets the tone of the meeting. Follow-up includes writing up the minutes, as well as prompting individuals to deal with issues they have taken on.

Parent organisations

Where there is a formal parent organisation, whether a PTA or not, the deputy should be actively involved both to support the head and to gain experience in dealing with parents as a body. Once again, opportunities for committee work and other forms of leadership can arise, as well as formally addressing the parents. The most successful groups are those which have developed a pattern of fundraising, social and educational activities and see themselves as being an active support of what the school is trying to achieve. The deputy is in a unique position to set a powerful example to the staff, be a source of practical and creative ideas and an energetic worker on behalf of the organisation.

Deputising

There will be occasional opportunities for the incumbent to carry out a deputising role. Sometimes this will be for a short period eg part of a day or the whole of one. There is unlikely to be supply cover for such occasions and so class responsibility will continue. Only emergencies are likely to arise, to be dealt with, if a competent secretary is on hand to deal with routine matters. However, problems can happen and the deputy should be ready and able to deal with a crisis. The head should alert the deputy when a difficulty can be anticipated and in any case should in a training setting have prepared the person concerned for most eventualities. The local office or a neighbouring head can be contacted in a case of real difficulties. Where there has been an incident the deputy should make a written record of it, and discuss it and the action taken as soon as the head returns. In the case of a longer absence by the head – from illness, course attendance, or during an interregnum period, then supply cover should be available and so the acting head can adopt the new role.

Familiarity with the day-to-day running of the school will be of great value. While the LEA can anticipate that no major changes will be made, it will expect more than a caretaking role to be carried out. Regular but not overfrequent discusions with the head would be a wise plan to adopt. In the case of a head-designate, arrangements should be made to communicate from time to time, so that the transfer of position can be made smoothly. Such behaviour should ensure a good working partnership later. While the new position for the deputy is different, good relationships even if slightly more formal, must be maintained if the school is to run satisfactorily, and a comfortable transfer back to former duties is possible. Occasionally the deputy can be invited to take on the acting headship in another school. This too provides some good opportunities for learning and a real knowledge of whether the position of headteacher is exactly what is desired. While there are some advantages in being in acting head in a different school, the development of new and possibly brief relationships with staff, pupils and parents makes particular demands upon the individual. To refuse such an opportunity may be unwise, however challenging or even uninviting the situation appears. Reflection on events and decisions will be useful to the deputy in deciding on further training needs.

Appraisal

A regular process of appraisal should involve all staff, including the deputy and the head as well as the school as a whole. Appraisal should be regarded as a two way exchange of views about the past and present with a view to creating an even more satisfactory and satisfying future. The deputy after a self evaluation should work with the head to build up a suitable agenda for discussion.

The final outcome should include the setting of realistic targets for development. These might include some change in the job definition as items like financial aspects, curriculum developments, working party membership are included. The removal of some responsibilities could mean further opportunities for other members of staff to enhance their roles. The latter proposals can provide an opportunity for the deputy to be actively involved in the development of other colleagues. In large schools or where the deputy becomes an acting headteacher, there could be appraisal interviews to conduct. To be able to carry out such activity, training opportunities should be sought.

Conclusion

These proposals are a far cry from the days when the deputy's responsibilities did not extend further than the preparation of the playground rota and collection of teamoney, and that person being 'dumped' in a head's chair totally unprepared to face the challenges of that post.

It is a demanding training programme which has been suggested in this chapter and should be seen as the practical element to complement the more theoretical input from one of the planned training courses mentioned at the beginning of the section. Much will depend upon the head, the relationship with the deputy, and the time available. Even without the headteacher's full participation there is much that can be done to prepare for headship. This book in its various ways will suggest further important areas for consideration to enable the deputy to engage in the process of self-skilling. As educational budgets are reduced more responsibility will be thrown back on staff to equip themselves for more senior positions. The art of management is concerned with successfully operating within the resource framework. Those who succeed best are those who are positive about the constraints and learn to manage themselves and their own development in a systematic way.

References

DES (1978), *Primary Education in England*, HMSO.
DES (1985), *Primary Education in Wales*, HMSO.
ILEA (1985), *Improving Primary Schools (The Thomas Report)*.
Sallis J (1980), *The Effective School Governor*, ACE.
Waters, D (1983), *Responsibility and Promotion in the Primary School*, Heinemann.
Wragg, E C and Partington, J A (1980), *A Handbook for School Governors*, Methuen.

Further Reading

Craig, I (1988) *Managing the Primary Classroom*, Longman.
Craig, I (1988) *Primary Headship in the 1990s*, Longman.
Day, C (1986) *Managing Primary Schools*, Harper and Row.
Everard, K B and Morris, G (1985) *Effective School Management*, Harper.
Glatter, R (1987) *Understanding School Management*, OU Press.
Paisey, A and A (1987) *Effective Management in the Primary School*, Blackwell.

8 The role of the subject coordinator

Charles Frisby

The title of this article may seem to be at odds with current Primary philosophy, fabled as it is in the commonplace expression 'We teach children not subjects'. That philosophy, if such it can be called, would see no role whatsoever for a subject coordinator, there being no subjects to coordinate, and any practising teacher reading this who holds to such a view would be well advised to lay the article aside. The catch phrase of course does not represent the actuality of teaching in schools, nor indeed the educational views (or philosophies) of most teachers. It does find favour with influential people who sit on committees and write articles and who, on the whole tend not to be practising teachers. Bennett (1976), Galton et al (1980) and HMI (DES, 1978) have all confirmed what any primary teacher knows to be the reality – that subjects are indeed taught to children in primary schools, and for most of the time too. The schools where mathematics, English, social studies (or 'topic work'), games and music do not appear as separate subjects on a timetable are few. This is not to suggest that any or all of these areas of study cannot be combined or entangled or interbred, but simply to acknowledge the fact that most children in most primary schools still receive each week hefty doses of these subjects. In any case the introduction of the National Curriculum with its firm subject base has effectively cut through the rhetoric to determine primary practice. The shibboleth 'We teach children not subjects' is semantic wish-wash. Nobody can simply teach children. We have to teach children something; how to tie their shoelaces; how to write their names; how to understand the Special Theory of Relativity, and it is this 'something' with which the subject coordinator is concerned.

But why a 'coordinator'? The primary school is the base for the autonomous teacher, the teacher whose dedicated skill, and whose cultivated relationship with all the children in his/her class somehow makes things happen, as if by magic, regardless of what can, and does happen next door. There are those who would point to teacher autonomy as one of the greatest strengths of the primary school. A strength it can be, but also a serious weakness, and the elevation of the pursuit of teacher autonomy to a position of priority in a school can lead to duplication and misdirection of effort, isolation, mediocrity and frustration. To illustrate a probable effect of this weakness upon pupil progress we might look at an admittedly simplistic description of two contrasting teacher styles.

Mrs B is a teacher of the old school. Kind but firm she is known to parents and children alike as a 'strict' teacher. She has been in the school for thirty years and some of the parents of her present class were taught by her. Indeed many of these parents have made representations to the headteacher, asking that their own children be placed in Mrs B's class. Mrs B relies a great deal on chalk and talk. It works for her. Her children do as they are told; they must put up their hands to ask a question or to request permission to leave their seats. The classroom is very quiet and there is an atmosphere of calm and hard work. The children's books are neatly presented and meticulously marked.

Mr C down the corridor doesn't believe much in chalk and talk, not because it is unfashionable but because after years of experience he has come to believe that it doesn't work very well for the kind of learning outcomes he has in mind. His children do group work, problem solving and 'projects' and Mr C acts mainly as a guide and counsellor. The children come and go as they please, about the classroom, to the library or the toilet. Mr C is too busy working with children to attend to trivial requests. The children work mostly in folders which are neatly and carefully presented and show much evidence of original research and interest. There is no disorder, just a sensible working atmosphere.

Both these stylised classrooms are effective mainly because the teachers know what they are doing and believe in what they are doing. Both styles of teaching can be effective, both have a place in any school. They can and often do coexist. But I would ask what it is that the children in these classes are learning as they progress through the school. Apart from the skills and concepts which each teacher plans for them, what else? Mrs B might say that her children are learning to do as they are told, while Mr C would perhaps suggest that his children are learning self reliance. I would say that at intervals of one school year they are learning both these admirable clusters. But there seems little doubt that children will need to unlearn many of the things they learn with Mr C in order to be successful with Mrs B. Mrs B spends a good deal of the first term cursing Mr C while retraining her new class. Mr C fumes with resentment and frustration because the skills he has fostered are now disregarded.

Now given a moderately wide spectrum of teaching styles even within a ten teacher primary school someone has to try to ensure that pupils get some kind of balanced treatment as they move from one autonomous teacher to another. Usually this is the job of a headteacher who will take such idiosyncracies into account at the annual reshuffle. But the point is that there is coordination. Somebody is taking on a responsibility for allocating children to classes in a rational way, because they know that some things will be learned more effectively when teachers adopt a style which is matched not just to the learner, but to the 'subject' to be learned. Moreover, really effective learning relies upon the application of teacher techniques which are consistent, persistent and continuous. If pupils learn to be self reliant one year and obedient the next, the chances are that they will soon forget to be self reliant while they are learning to be obedient. What we require are pupils who can be self reliant AND obedient, and can match their behaviour to the context. Some things, such as handwriting are more effectively (and efficiently) taught by chalk and talk with the class seated in rows. Other things, such as strategies for problem solving, cannot be taught or learned in that way. It makes sense therefore to try to ensure that every teacher uses a variety of techniques which are matched to the learning outcomes. *The task of ensuring that there is a fairly consistent approach to teaching strategies and learning outcomes (and that there is some attempt to match the two) falls to the subject coordinator, and the subject is to be more clearly perceived as the 'intended learning outcome'.*

Those who espouse the 'children not subjects' approach may care to reflect on the paradox that most coordinator posts seem to have been attached to the traditional subject areas: language; mathematics; reading; science; art and craft. Perhaps this means that primary curriculum design has not actually changed for a century. Perhaps all we do now is try to make the pint pot which in 1880 held a gill hold a litre. Perhaps we really ought to make a change after all this time. Maybe we could adopt an approach to curriculum design which looks at learning outcomes, at orders of priority, and at prescriptions for action. In some schools of course this might very well mean retaining and extending the traditional subject base, but in others it could result in new orders of learning outcomes altogether.

Setting priorities for the school

The first task is to select an order of priorities for development in the school as a whole. This must obviously be decided by the whole staff of the school with input from non-teaching staff, parents and pupils and must be led by the headteacher. The head will obviously suggest areas for priority consideration since he/she is the best person to take the necessary overview. It may be, for example that there is a general desire to raise the level of reading scores, or to provide a broader based scheme for mathematics. The school may wish to introduce team-teaching, or to base its social studies on the environment. It may be that the school has a problem with overnight and weekend vandalism, and that a high priority must therefore be given to establishing a more positive relationship with the surrounding community. This might well be more important initially than the decision simply to improve attainments in any one curriculum area, since it could well turn out that establishing good community relations will have the desired effect on pupil attainment anyway. Such things have happened.

Having ordered priorities, the coordinator, the teacher charged with the task of promoting and matching teaching strategies and learning outcomes, can be designated.

The introduction of Grade A posts, which can be allocated for a definite period, can provide a useful management tool. A post can be awarded for a specific brief over a limited time. This can focus the imagination wonderfully.

Defining learning outcomes

There is now a good deal of help available to schools in defining learning outcomes. The DES continues even now to shower upon schools papers and booklets listing learning objectives – pages and pages of them – and all very eloquently expressed. There really is little need to invent one's own. Whatever is to be thought about them they are, I think an advance on the evidence which Plowden (DES, 1967) noted, drawing attention to the fact that ' . . . some of the headteachers who were considered by HMI to be most successful in practice were least able to formulate their aims clearly and convincingly'. This may say something about HMI or it may imply that the less you know about what you are doing the more successful you may become, but it is not an argument calculated to convince the general public that primary teachers are any sort of experts. Partly as a result of this kind of misunderstanding we saw in the late 1960s and early 1970s some reported practices in primary

schools which, while assuredly aimed at creating 'happy atmos-
pheres', 'full and satisfying lives' and 'the development of whole
personalities' have nevertheless done enormous damage to primary
teachers by distorting the public perceptions of what primary
schools do. When we needed to be a little more hard-nosed about
telling the public that managing a successful primary classroom
required far more skill than mere brain surgery or University lectur-
ing, we went soft, spreading the glutinous flummery of post-
Plowden twaddle.

It must now be standard practice for a school to concoct a
statement of aims for submission to the apprehensive officers of
the LEA. In this respect the DES prescriptions are a godsend. But
they are useful only as starting points, neither full enough nor
detailed enough for classroom use. 'We aim to ensure that all pupils
can read fluently and accurately, with understanding, feeling and
discrimination' (Schools Council 1981) may look good on a Governor's Report, but a great deal more needs to be done before such
an aim can be carried through into practice. The coordinator's
contribution then is to lead the school staff in specifying required
learning outcomes, if possible as behavioural objectives. It will
simply not be enough to hope that because we specify a learning
outcome then that outcome will be achieved. We need to set down
the ways in which it can be *seen* to be achieved, not least by pupils
themselves. Much planning in schools proceeds on the basis not
of 'I think therefore I am' but of 'I say therefore I do'. Many teachers
are convinced that what they say is happening actually happens.
We need to cultivate a healthy scepticism. The perceptions of pupils
and parents about what is happening are often in conflict with
those of teachers. If at all possible, and few things are impossible,
it is a good idea to negotiate learning outcomes with pupils. It may
not be possible to negotiate learning outcomes with parents, but
at the very least parents need to be informed about what the
intended outcomes are, so that they can be brought into the process
of seeing that they are met. In any event pupils should be as much
in the know about learning objectives as teachers, not only because
this gives pupils a clear idea of what it is they have to learn but
also because, given a statement of objectives, many pupils will
teach themselves and each other as effectively as a teacher. Patricia
Broadfoot (1979) has pointed to the value of pupils' understanding
of learning objectives in enhancing motivation and hence
achievement.

Specifying learning outcomes – an example

The DES/HMI series *Mathematics 5–13* sets out a number of learning outcomes for most 11 year olds under five headings; facts, skills, conceptual structures, general strategies; personal qualities. Let's say we take one of these headings, conceptual structures, and specify a set of behavioural objectives leading to a definite aim – '. . . a thorough understanding of place value'. Now when we talk about a thorough understanding, how do we measure this? Is it to be hoped that if we provide enough graded workcards in place value exercises then the thoroughness of understanding can be measured by the pupil's position on the work card continuum? To some, notably the writers and publishers of graded work cards, the answer is clearly 'yes.' But practising teachers will say that they find countless examples of children who have worked through the graded schemes and are yet unable to operate in novel situations with the knowledge they are supposed to have gained! It might be better to measure understanding in ways which are traditional in primary classrooms, that is by applying the teacher's judgement. But the judgement needs to be informed in some detail and it needs consistent guidance throughout the school. It should be possible to develop a series of checklists which relate to the general aims of the 'subject' and which invite pupils and teachers to collaborate in a series of tasks designed to demonstrate understanding – a practical item bank. Compiling a draft checklist is an important responsibility of the coordinator, and it is necessary to realise that this is not an armchair exercise. There is a limit to what can be done away from the actual observation of children in the classroom. The coordinator needs to listen very carefully to the anecdotes of colleagues and to inform those anecdotes with his or her own knowledge and expertise in order to produce a credible format. The checklist needs to take into account the teachers' actual observations of how children perform in given situations. It should detail things which teachers have observed children actually doing and which are known to be crucial in the process of learning a defined outcome. In the example – an understanding of place value – children can be observed labelling sets of objects with numeral cards; they can be observed using Deines' blocks to play the 'exchange' game, thereby demonstrating an understanding of the process of exchanging 'units' for longs, flats and blocks, of whatever base; they can be observed representing a decimal number using counters on a card abacus. Mastery of these processes does lead to an understanding of place value and so the checklist will include them both as a pupil profile and as a teaching aid (or syllabus) for

Figure 8.1 – Sample checklist for place value

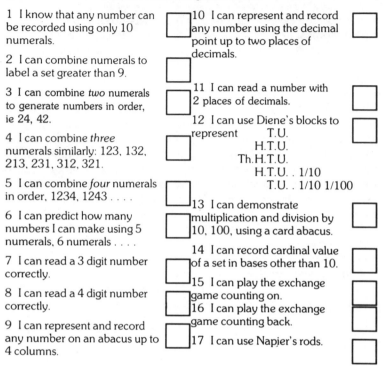

1   I know that any number can be recorded using only 10 numerals.

2   I can combine numerals to label a set greater than 9.

3   I can combine *two* numerals to generate numbers in order, ie 24, 42.

4   I can combine *three* numerals similarly: 123, 132, 213, 231, 312, 321.

5   I can combine *four* numerals in order, 1234, 1243 . . . .

6   I can predict how many numbers I can make using 5 numerals, 6 numerals . . . .

7   I can read a 3 digit number correctly.

8   I can read a 4 digit number correctly.

9   I can represent and record any number on an abacus up to 4 columns.

10 I can represent and record any number using the decimal point up to two places of decimals.

11 I can read a number with 2 places of decimals.

12 I can use Diene's blocks to represent   T.U.
                              H.T.U.
                           Th.H.T.U.
                              H.T.U. . 1/10
                                 T.U. . 1/10 1/100

13 I can demonstrate multiplication and division by 10, 100, using a card abacus.

14 I can record cardinal value of a set in bases other than 10.

15 I can play the exchange game counting on.

16 I can play the exchange game counting back.

17 I can use Napier's rods.

the teacher. A draft checklist then might look something like the list reproduced in Figure 8.1.

It is helpful if the checklist is presented in 'I can do' form. Children like to know when they can do something, and they can extend the list themselves if they can do things which are not on the list but which are connected with the area of study. The checklist can be revised periodically with input from pupils, teachers and parents. It is useful too if references to particular resources – text book pages, apparatus, number games, computer software – can be included. Children need to know where they can find practice items or exercises which can help them with particular parts of the syllabus, and many will enjoy working through the record themselves.

Having presented a checklist it will not be sufficient for the coordinator to suggest that the objectives, however clearly defined, should be met, and to persuade colleagues to this view. Teachers will need practical suggestions for strategies to help achieve them.

It will be obvious that a class teaching didactic approach will not be appropriate in managing pupils' progress through conceptual structures. The coordinator might therefore be called upon to demonstrate ways in which teachers can monitor progress through the programme, and this requires an examination of the teachers' methods, the pedagogy. But a pedagogy which puts 'individual instruction' at its centre is totally unrealistic. No teacher can possibly manage such a programme with 30 individuals. A strategy which does work is to group pupils by ability on the topic being presented. The class will need to be organised into five or six groups of sizes varying between three and seven. Any more than six groups means that the teacher cannot make regular contact with every group, and fewer than five will increase the size of the group. In practice a maximum group size might be six, a minimum three, with four or five pupils being the optimum. By grouping classes in this way it is quite possible for the teacher to spend at least ten minutes with a group at least twice a week, and to ensure that monitoring is done for every pupil – not just for the most attention seeking – while still giving time for class teaching summaries. 'Show and Tell' activities, and housekeeping and administration tasks. The use of systematic group work is appropriate not only in mathematics of course, nor does it promote the learning of mathematics alone. To be effective in such situations pupils need to practise a number of social and cognitive skills; listening and responding to another point of view; expanding an argument; drawing upon evidence; reasoning and questioning; exercising tolerance and restraint. These skills in themselves can form the basis for a checklist if the school felt it necessary to promote them. In that case the school might decide to use a traditional 'subject' like mathematics as a major instrument for learning group discussion skills.

Implementing change – management time

Defining aims, setting priorities, drafting behavioural objectives and suggesting strategies for managing their achievement are primary tasks of the subject coordinator. Ensuring that there is some consistency of approach throughout the school and that teachers get practical help *regularly*, requires that the coordinator be given the necessary time to work with colleagues in the classroom. Recent HMI studies of Middle Schools (DES, 1983 and 1985) suggest that coordinators rarely have sufficient time during the school day to carry out their duties properly. But Middle Schools, especially those 'deemed Secondary' are at least generally staffed with some flexibility available. The average primary school has next to none.

Unless a primary school receives special consideration it is likely that a ten class school will be established with ten teachers, a nursery assistant perhaps, and a headteacher. Given that the coordinator must have the time to work with colleagues, the headteacher must provide that time. It is curious that so few Primary teachers actually make any demands on the headteacher's time. Most headteachers of primary schools could find regular blocks of time to spend in classrooms enabling coordinators to be released to do their 'coordination' tasks. Besides, going into every classroom for an hour or so every week is an essential part of the headteachers' own monitoring function. If the headteacher has led the staff in the definition of priorities then the head must given support to the teachers who have been given the responsibility for ensuring their implementation. Such support is not just to be regarded as tacit. It must be active. It must be support which raises the status of the coordinator in the eyes of the rest of the staff, so that they see that there is an intention that the job is to be done. What greater demonstration of intent could a head give than to sacrifice his or her own time for the coordinator! Of course, priorities will change, and coordinators will require different allocations. It may be that the head will give three hours a week for one term to one coordinator, and two hours to another. The following term the priorities may change, and the allocation correspondingly reversed. But whatever the situation it can be taken care of by instituting on the timetable some 'management time'. In designing the timetable, the headteacher simply makes her/himself available for so many hours a week, during which time certain defined objectives are to be 'managed'. The coordinator then should be prepared to approach his/her headteacher with a definite plan for the use of management time. 'Mrs Jones, here is my detailed plan for implementing the changes we agreed. It will involve me initially in working with all the five 1st and 2nd year classes and their teachers, and I need one hour a day to do this. I would like you to take my class while I do it'. What headteacher could resist such an approach!

School record systems

A further way of implementing curriculum objectives is through the school record system. It might be assumed by now that all schools have such a system or systems, though it has not always been the case. The school record systems need to specify in some detail, the progress of pupils through the defined objectives of the curriculum. The coordinator needs to ensure that teachers understand the objectives and that they know how to translate objectives into practical schemes for delivery of the curriculum to pupils. A series of 'checklists' of the kind illustrated earlier in this chapter might form a school record system – defining skills and concepts in the various areas of experience, mathematical, scientific, physical, aesthetic and so on. Such a record system is extremely valuable not only to teachers in the school, but most importantly to pupils themselves and to their parents. An ongoing record system – operating day to day in the classroom and containing comments, notes, reminders, and assessment grades for example can act as a powerful medium for continuity, for motivation and for the involvement of pupils and parents in the detailed work of the curriculum. Periodically parents should have sight of the records and be encouraged to comment on their children's progress. Such a report is of far more interest and value to parents than the end of year comment such as 'English – a capable girl who works well' which says nothing about what a pupil is capable of – and the writing of which, all at one go, is a tedious business for most teachers (Frisby, 1982).

Specialist teaching

But it may well be that coordinator cannot persuade the headteacher to give up time to enable curriculum change to proceed, and record systems of the kind I have described do take some time to take effect in classrooms. How else then can a coordinator be effective? A headteacher might be persuaded to consider some form of specialist teaching.

Now specialist teaching in Primary Schools has not been too popular I know, particularly with those whose job it seems to be to define the primary teachers role from their positions in Training Institutes. However, it has always been carried out in schools, and the National Curriculum may help to bring it back into favour. When I started teaching in 1961 I taught music to other classes, and I assisted with 'boys' games'. The principle of using certain teachers with particular expertise is well established. It might now become more systematically applied in practice. For example, while Miss A is taking Mr B's class for music, perhaps Mr B could take Miss A's for, maybe, mathematics or science. Better still – given say four classes of 3rd/4th year juniors, there could be a rotating system of specialist teaching – music, maths, science, art/craft. This would enable a coordinator of maths, say, to work with pupils of all the other classes once a week. This experience is itself a very effective way of getting to know what other teachers are doing. Even now, too few teachers in primary schools have opportunities to take an overview of the work of the school. However, there is understandable reluctance to imitate secondary schools. In theory, the work in science for example should arise naturally from other work in progress, and the class teacher is therefore the person to decide on how and when the work should be planned. In practice the theory rarely leads to satisfactory outcomes. The dominance of the theoretical perspective may to some extent explain the relative failure of primary schools to introduce science in any coherent way. As in many other things – discovery favours the prepared mind, and the classteacher who has little confidence in science may very well as a consequence miss opportunities for scientific investigation which can, it is true, arise naturally. In any case – most children are more capable than we sometimes think and it really is too much to ask of any one teacher that (s)he prepares work matched to the wide range of abilities and interests of primary age children in several areas of experience. Knowledge is not a 'seamless robe'. The experience of literature is different from the experience of mathematics or science, and we are misleading children if we do not try to point out the ways in which these differences are mani-fested. Basil Bernstein (1970) has suggested that education is – 'the introduction of the child to the universalistic meanings of the *public forms of thought,*' and we do our pupils a disservice if we leave them with the impression that all knowledge is undifferentiated.

If a rotating system of specialist teaching is adopted, the coordi-nator (or coordinators since the system does allow more than one coordinator to pursue priorities at the same time) needs to establish an efficient communication procedure. If a coordinator works with another teacher's class for an hour a week, then the classteacher needs to have a clear and detailed idea of what is being done so that she can supervise the follow up work. The coordinator will need to provide detailed 'lesson notes' – with copies available at least to all those teachers whose classes are involved, and prefer-ably for reference by all other teachers in the school. It does no harm for the teachers of five year olds to know what is being done with ten and eleven year olds and vice versa, and other teachers in a school who may not be immediately involved will often add comments about the progress of pupil learning, or mis-learning, which can be very informative to a coordinator planning or modify-ing a scheme, a set of objectives or a record system.

Management of resources

The point about resources is that they must be *accessible*, and not just available. It has often been the case in my experience, to see a teacher using some piece of apparatus – perhaps sets of

Cuisenaire rods – and for another teacher to say 'Oh, I didn't know we had those – I could just have used them last term!' Books as a learning resource are always available in school – but to a pupil who cannot find them they are not *accessible*. Hence the coordinator's role must be to make learning resources, books, apparatus, audio/video tapes and slides, computer software, film strips, *accessible* to all pupils and teachers at all times. This means that all learning resources should be centrally catalogued, even if they are not centrally stored, and that pupils (and teachers) should be trained to use the catalogue system so that they can access the resources they need. It cannot be assumed that pupils know how to do this. Time and again I have seen children scrabbling about in a bookshelf for books about dinosaurs or policemen when they can have no certain knowledge that any such books exist in the school. Every school needs systems for cataloguing resources and programmes for teaching children how to use them.

Cataloguing resources takes time, but much of the essential clerical tasks can be done by groups of parents, who are very often glad to assist in work which they see is important to the school. The coordinator needs to arrange the time and opportunities for parents to take on this work.

The job description

The job description is all the rage now, but it is a pity that it seems to be regarded by some as a 'Management device' with which to pin teachers down. Management with a capital 'M' means 'them' – those in the education service whose job it is to manipulate 'us' and whose machinations must be resisted. In fact the job description *is* a management device which is of great assistance to teachers themselves in 'managing' (for that is what they do) learning in their own classrooms. A job description is not a contract, setting out conditions of service, but an instrument for assessing progress. A job description ought to set out some objectives which teachers think they can realistically attain. It is often said that a teacher's job is impossible really, that we can never attain our aims, that the job cannot be measured. This is partly true, of course because teaching has always been about 'ideals' which almost by definition are unattainable. But nothing is more likely to induce a failure of morale than the pursuit of vague and non-attainable aims. What we need to do is to set down a list of things which we think *can* be achieved. There is nothing novel about this. Teachers do it all the time. I might consider it realistic to teach a two-part carol by Christmas for example and usually I might succeed. Success in that endeavour leads to satisfaction and to greater motivation. Hence the job description ought to set out a list of objectives which the coordinator and the headteacher consider might be reasonably achieved in a certain period of time. Writing things down in this way also implies a sense of commitment. It is unlikely that a headteacher will agree on a job description which will prove impossible to carry out, and the head has a vested interest in seeing that the coordinator receives every assistance in carrying out the job which (s)he (the head) has sanctioned.

School based inservice training

I have up to now made no reference to the coordinator's role in developing school based inservice training. That is because I do not see this form of INSET as separate from the normal work in schools day to day. Some schools have adopted a model of INSET from the repertory theatre, where actors rehearsed one role while performing a different role and then on the following Monday night opened with their new role, having trained for it, while simultaneously dispensing with their old one. Such a model will not do in schools. Teachers cannot train for the new while practising the old and then hope to implement the new by a sudden transition. School based INSET is a drip-feed, we put in new things a bit at a time. In schools, thinking about things, talking about things and above all trying things out *is* inservice training. If the coordinator can persuade his colleagues in the school to adopt even one of the suggestions I have put forward, he will find that the consciousness of the teachers so engaged will be raised, however slightly. (S)he will be conducting school based inservice training whether anybody knows it or not.

References

Bennett, N (1976), *Teacher Style and Pupil Progress*, Open Books.
Bernstein, B (1970), 'A Critique of the Concept of Compensatory Education', in Rubenstein, D and Stoneman, C (Eds.) *Education for Democracy*, Penguin.
Bradfoot, P M (1979), 'Communication in the Classroom: A Study of the Role of Assessment in Motivation', in *Educational Review*, Vol 31 No 1.
DES (1976), *Children and Their Primary Schools (The Plowden Report)*; HMSO.
DES (1978), *Primary Education in England*, HMSO.
DES (1983), *9–13 Middle Schools – an illustrative survey*, HMSO.
DES (1985), *8–12 Middle Schools*, HMSO.

Frisby, C (1982), 'Records and Assessment', in *Forum*, Vol 24 No 2.

Galton, M, and Simon, B (1980), *Progress and Performance in the Primary Classroom*, RKP.

Galton, M, Simon, B and Croll P (1980), *Inside the Primary Classroom*, RKP.

Schools Council (1981), *The Practical Curriculum (Working Paper No. 70)*, Methuen.

Further Reading

Frisby, C (1984), 'Specialisms in Primary Schools, in *The Headteacher's Review*, Winter 1984.

9 The quest for a General Teaching Council

Robert Balchin

Not long after I had begun my first teaching post an elderly colleague was helping me to fill in a form for the Inland Revenue. 'What should I put for "job description"?' I remember asking. 'You don't have a job, you have a *profession*, put "Schoolmaster – *not* in Holy Orders"' was his firm reply!

Teachers have been referring to themselves as members of a 'profession' for hundreds of years but what exactly do we mean by 'a profession' and the epithet 'professional'? Have they something to do with a willingness on the part of a practitioner not to withdraw his labour? Do they denote some particular qualifications or skills? Do they imply values which mean that the teacher has more than a mere 'job'?

At first sight it seems easy to draw some clues from the Oxford English Dictionary's definitions of 'profession': 'originally, the public declaration, promise or vow made by one entering a religious order.' There is the implication here maybe that there are some special rules to be kept in a 'profession'. Also we read: 'a calling in which the knowledge of some department of learning is used in its application to the affairs of others', so 'knowledge and learning' appear to be involved and are to be applied perhaps to other people rather than to things.

If the criteria for the use of the word 'profession', however, were very tight in Chaucer's time, by 1600 a news sheet could contain the words: 'Their profession is to robbe and steale from their neighbours', and it was clear to the reader just what the author meant: that larceny was how they gained their livelihood: indeed there is the hint in the use of 'profession' that they were rather good at it!

Police today often refer to a particularly successful crime as a 'very professional job'; barristers and doctors are allowed to enter their 'professions' after a very rigorous training, and recruiting posters urge prospective soldiers to 'Join the Professionals'. Although the Victorians might have hesitated to use the word 'professional' of someone engaged in a manual craft, preferring to reserve the word for clergy, soldiers and the like, it makes perfectly good sense today to speak of someone as a 'professional builder' or 'builder by profession'. In fact, I suspect, if the word 'profession' does mean more than 'job' nowadays, it merely implies that there are some special skills to be acquired, perhaps over a period of time, but what those skills should be, or to what ends they should be used cannot be teased from the normal usage of the word, at least since the 17th century.

If the results of this admittedly skimpy analysis seem unsatisfactory, however, it is because there *do* seem to be occasions when the meanings of 'professional' or 'profession' seem very precise indeed. The doctor knows, for instance, the exact implications of the words 'professional misconduct'; 'unprofessional behaviour' covers a limited number of actions for a teacher and a 'professional cricketer' goes on to the pitch pledged to obey certain rules.

Certain groups of people, therefore, use the words 'profession' or 'professional' of themselves only when certain *extra* criteria, additional to those which specify the acquisition of some special skills, are in use. Briefly these are that the 'professional' should be elected or admitted to his 'profession' only by his fellow 'professionals'; that one of the conditions of admission is his agreement to a code of conduct (thus 'forcing back' into the meaning the original notion of religious vows); that only his fellow 'professionals' can expel him from his 'profession' and that only the 'professionals' are allowed (usually by statute) to perform the tasks of the 'profession'. Thus solicitors and actuaries, for example, have to pass certain examinations and to reach certain training standards established by a group of their older and more experienced colleagues before they are allowed to practise. They subscribe to a strict code of behaviour which has been devised by their colleagues; they can be expelled by them under certain circumstances and are not allowed by law to practise their skills, at least in this country, unless they are on a list kept by their colleagues. Finally the most important of these additional criteria is that the foregoing shall not just provide extra status for practitioners but shall also *afford special protection for the client*. To be more precise, solicitors manage their 'profession' by electing certain of their number to the Law Society, which regulates the training of law students by insisting that the institutions which offer law courses meet certain curricular criteria

(on pain of having its students excluded, of course), which establishes rules for professional conduct and which strikes those who
are guilty of breaking them from the Society's register of solicitors.
Only those on the register are allowed to practise in the United
Kingdom, thus ensuring that clients using a solicitor's services can
be sure that he is well trained and honest, and have a remedy if
he should prove not to be.

It was probably this restrictive use of the word 'profession' that
was intended in the founding Charter of the College of Preceptors
when it was issued in 1849, for the new institution was charged
'with the purpose of promoting sound learning and of advancing
the interests of education . . . ' by affording facilities for the teacher
for the acquiring of a 'sound knowledge of his *profession*'. The
college had at that time no firm home but was a group of schoolmasters convinced that it was necessary for them and their colleagues to become organised in a way that teachers had never
seen before.

Teachers hitherto, and indeed for a long time to come, were
mostly untrained in any formal sense and usually had a lowly status
in the community. Their calling had been damaged by the activities
of a minority of appalling incompetents who only a few years
before were castigated by Dickens in his resounding preface to
Nicholas Nickleby:

> Any man who has proved his unfitness for *any* other occupation in
> life was free, without examination or qualification, to open a school
> anywhere.

Only too aware of the Wackford Squeerses in their midst, many
teachers were determined to make their calling *exclusive*: they
would find a means of excluding the iniquitous and the inept from
their ranks.

At about that time medical men also wanted to dissociate themselves from the untrained quacks who harmed their standing, and
were feeling their way towards the General Medical Council which
was established in 1858. So successful were these early pioneers
in setting standards for their new 'profession' that in a few decades
their calling had become a prestigious one.

The reasons were not hard to see: underpinning 'professionalism'
is the clear presumption that if the members of a club or group
themselves are the sole arbiters of who shall be allowed to join
them as colleagues, then they will insist on high standards on entry
in order to preserve their own status and they will exclude all those
whose activities are likely to bring their fellows, by association, into
disrepute. This presumption has important consequences for the
client of the 'professional', of course, for he can expect a better

quality service. A correspondent to *The Educational Times* wrote in 1877:

> A clergyman can be suspended . . . a barrister may be debarred, a solicitor may be struck off the rolls, a doctor may be deprived of his degree and – paradox as it may appear – professional pride is fostered by these very penalties and dangers.

Satisfied that the experiences of doctors after the creation of the General Medical Council proved this presumption correct beyond doubt, teachers pressed Government throughout Victoria's reign for a 'professional' council of their own. Examinations of high quality could be set and a register kept of those who had qualified but unless no person could practise as a teacher if his name was not on the register, then 'professional' status would never emerge. This needed changes in the law analogous to those of the 1858 Medical Act to make registration compulsory.

Bills for the compulsory registration of teachers appeared two or three times during the last years of the 19th century; Sir Richard Temple's Bill (1891) would have confined registration to secondary teachers in England and Wales as a first step towards general registration. The examining bodies which provided secondary level teacher qualification were to be allowed eight representatives on the registering Council, the Crown was to have four, and four were to be elected from amongst the listed teachers.

By this time, however, a new phenomenon was on the scene. The growth of the trades union movement had encouraged teachers to gather themselves into associations and unions and these new bodies also wanted to be represented if a registering Council came into being.

Teachers, of course, had ceased during the two decades since the Foster Act to be mostly employed privately or to be self-employed or in the service of the churches and other education supplying institutions, and became the payees of the state through the Board Schools. Where there is one paymaster, collective bargaining is made easier and gradually the National Union of Teachers, the Teacher's Guild, the Irish National Teachers' Association and the Educational Institute of Scotland grew to be influential bodies. They sponsored, together with the Headmasters' Conference, Arthur Ackland's Bill for the registration of teachers. It was more comprehensive than the Temple Bill and extended the necessity for registration to elementary school teachers as well as those in Scotland and Ireland. It was considered by a Select Committee at the same time as the Temple Bill and evidence was heard for months. Everyone agreed that the principle of a 'professional' register for teachers was an excellent one, and that there should be an independent council to administer it. The questions which could not be answered were: which teachers should be listed and who should sit on the council? At length the arguments could not be resolved and neither Bill received a second reading, and there the matter rested for a further ten years.

The Board of Education Act of 1901, however, gave the new Board the duty of establishing a Teachers' Registration Council, and shortly after, a twelve person Council came into being: six teachers from the various unions and associations and six Government appointees. The new Council decided on a form of registration which was immediately boycotted by the National Union of Teachers, representing the elementary school masters and mistresses. These were all, of course, Government employees and certificated (and therefore listed) by the Education Department. The plan was that these teachers should be transferred en bloc compulsorily to the new register whereas the secondary and independent school teachers were to register individually and voluntarily. The NUT repudiated the whole concept as being unduly divisive and by the end of 1904 only 144 people had tendered their names and the whole scheme died of inanition.

The movement for teacher registration gained in strength again just before the First World War and a new Teachers' Registration Council was constituted by Order of the Privy Council in 1912. The Council this time was much larger, to take account of all the interests involved and eventually comprised 50 members: 11 drawn from the universities, eleven each from the elementary teachers and the secondary teachers, together with certain appointees of the Crown and other bodies.

The register had no divisions and all teachers registered voluntarily. The hope, of course, was that so many would do so that compulsion could be later introduced with few political difficulties.

At last things seemed to be going well and in 1929, when some 78,000 people were listed on the register, George V dignified them and the Council by allowing them to be called collectively 'The Royal Society of Teachers'. Members could place the letters MRST after their names and wear a distinctive academic dress if they so wished.

Alas, a further Act making it a matter of compulsion for *all* teachers to register never came and the Royal Society of Teachers, with only £100 in its funds, quietly folded during the War years and was wound up in 1949 by an Order in Council. Its proponents had signally failed to get Government to supply it with the necessary authority to make teaching a 'profession': all the time that teachers could practise without the necessity to register, it was powerless to improve standards.

The Royal Society of Teachers failed because it came too late: the state in the years before World War II was becoming looked upon as the 'natural' provider of schooling. Independent schools were thought by many observers to be on the decline, divisive leftovers from Victorian times. The principle of the state as the purveyor of education became enshrined in the 1944 (Butler) Education Act and by that time 95 per cent of teachers were on the state payroll. A hundred years before when the quest for an autonomous teaching 'profession' had begun, the employers of teachers were many and diverse and the teachers themselves without a voice to speak for them. Now nearly all teachers were local authority employees and had organised themselves in a growing number of unions and associations.

In the post-war era those teachers who still hoped to create a real 'profession' have had to face two problem areas: could the powers concerned with the admission, induction and possible exclusion of teachers, by now firmly vested in the Minister (later the Secretary of State) for Education, be prised away from the Government's grasp and passed to an independent body?

Would the teachers' unions see it as being in their best interests to promote such an independent body?

Both areas are fraught with difficulties. If a General Teaching Council were to come into being, using the general councils of the other 'professions' as models, it would have to be conceived along the following lines:

1 All teachers presently practising would have to elect some of their number to the new Council.

2 Teachers would have the majority of seats on such a Council, although there would also be representatives of say, the Department of Education and Science, the Local Authorities, the universities and other teacher training bodies, perhaps the churches and also some kind of 'client' interest (representing parents' associations). This predicates a large Council (fifty/sixty seats).

3 All currently practising teachers would have to register with the new Council and pay a fee (perhaps once and for all, perhaps annually). *No teacher would be allowed to teach, by law, unless registered.*

4 The new Council would devise a Code of Practice to which registering teachers would be obliged to subscribe.

5 The Government would hand over its lists of those currently barred from teaching (List 99) to the new Council and with it the right to exclude or suspend teachers who were found guilty of 'professional' misconduct from the register (and thus from teaching).

6 Government would pass the sole right to accredit courses of initial and inservice teacher training to the new Council.

7 Government would give the new Council control of the probationary

period for novice teachers and the power, of course, to decide whether admission to the register would follow at the end of it.
8 The new Council would advise Government on the question of teacher supply.

It is clear that immense political embarrassment could result if, during a period when a large number of teachers were required in schools, Government handed to a new autonomous body the power to constrict the supply of entrants to the 'profession'. If it is conceded that a General Teaching Council would set higher standards for would-be teachers (and this, of course, is the presumption which underpins the whole concept of 'professionalism') then either there would be fewer teachers, or higher salaries would have to be offered to attract better candidates. Neither choice has proved palatable to post-war Governments as the attempts to establish a General Teaching Council during the 1960s and 1970s demonstrate.

In 1966 a working party representing all the teachers' unions and associations then extant asked the Secretary of State to consider proposals to create a General Teaching Council for England and Wales. His reply was in no way encouraging.

The changes the associations are seeking would involve a transfer of control over the fundamental matter of teachers' recruitment from the Government to the proposed Council.

This he was not prepared to countenance at a time of teacher shortage.

In 1968 they tried again. This time, the Secretary of State, Edward Short (now Lord Glenamara) was more sympathetic for he had been a teacher himself. This initiative resulted in the Weaver Report (DES 1970) which was the product of a committee comprising representatives from the Department of Education and Science, the teachers' unions, the universities and teacher training interests and the Local Education Authorities. In the two years in which it struggled to find a solution acceptable to Government, the committee considered many patterns on which to construct the new Council. Its final proposals, however, kept the reins of teacher supply firmly in the hands of the Department. The authority to register teachers, to oversee probation and to discipline them (and if necessary strike them off) was to be available to a new teachers' Council but the management of teacher supply was to go to a different body and one which would have only five teacher members (out of twenty-nine seats) to represent their colleagues in the country's primary and secondary schools. The reason for two bodies was clear: the school population had expanded so much in the sixties that Local Authorities had difficulty in filling teaching posts and even had to advertise abroad. A General Teaching Council created on the lines discussed above would have made recruitment more difficult. The National Union of Teachers refused to back this hybrid solution saying quite rightly that a real 'profession' required that all aspects of admission and supply should be devolved to one body with a majority of teachers. The NUT was probably wrong to have refused a Council with even the limited powers on offer because a time would come in the 1980s when the birthrate would fall and thousands of teachers would be looking for jobs, which would not be available. Government nervousness about teacher supply would probably have diminished enough for the remaining powers to be handed over, and today perhaps teachers would be members of a 'profession'.

The dramatic increase in the number of teachers required to service the schools of the sixties and early seventies meant that the unions and associations recruited members as never before. These unions, especially the National Union of Teachers, the National Association of Schoolmasters (later to add the Union of Women Teachers) and the 'Joint Four' (see below) soon became accustomed to pronouncing on, and being consulted about, what were known as 'professional' matters and to 'speaking for teachers' in the newspapers and on radio and television. Clearly a new and independent General Teaching Council, especially if it became as prestigious in time as, say, the Law Society could be perceived as a threat to the status of the unions unless their own involvement in it could be guaranteed.

They conceived therefore a concept of a 'professional' Council in which, although all teachers would be obliged to register in order to practise, only those who were in membership of one or other of the unions would be able to take part in the government of the 'profession'. The teachers' seats on a General Teaching Council would be allocated only to those who were sent there by their unions; those teachers who did not choose to join a union were to have no mechanism by which they might be represented.

The formal reasons for this model were that it would be difficult for other constituencies to be arranged for teachers and, anyway, an election of some thirty or forty people by half a million practitioners would lead to practical difficulties of representation. Thus the Weaver Report recommended that the teachers (a majority) on its proposed semi-autonomous Council were to be appointed from the ranks of the unions as follows.

- National Union of Teachers: 10
- National Association of Schoolmasters (now NAS/UWT): 3
- Joint Four (now AMMA and SHA): 6

- National Association of Headteachers: 2
- Association of Teachers in Technical Institutions: 2
- Association of Teachers in Colleges and Departments of Education (now NATFHE): 2

The seats were to be allocated roughly according to the numerical strength of the organisations concerned, except in the case of the heads' unions. The NUT later repudiated this division as not reflecting accurately enough its number of members; this and its rejection of the other proposals concerning the powers of the proposed council caused the whole question of a General Teaching Council to be put back into that limbo in which it presently resides.

The concept of a General Teaching Council has always caused a *frisson* of difficulty for those teacher unionists who have conceived of teachers as an organised labour force marching solidly in step with their brothers and sisters in the other 'white collar' and 'blue collar' unions. They find it hard to accept the values of a 'profession' with its special overtones of exclusivity. I suspect that the NUT's opposition to the Weaver proposals was founded in part on a belief that if unity on 'professional' matters were to come, it ought to be through the aegis of the NUT. Some at least of its ruling members believed in those days (I am not sure whether they do now) that all the unions and associations ought to unite into one mega-union which would itself one day command the powers of a 'profession'. That this is muddled thinking, I shall show later.

The impetus for Weaver came partly from the success of Scottish teachers in achieving the establishment of a General Teaching Council for Scotland in 1965. The conditions for its creation were far more benign than in the South: teachers were not in such short supply and there was really only one union to speak of, the Educational Institute of Scotland. The council has the powers delineated earlier in this chapter. Teachers in Scotland elect members to represent them as follows:

- 11 are elected by primary teachers
- 11 by secondary teachers
- 3 by the further education sector plus 4 principals and 1 lecturer from colleges of education.

In addition there are a further 19 members representing the churches, the universities, the Local Authorities and the Secretary of State for Scotland, making 49 in all. Elections are held every four years and teachers are obliged to pay an annual subscription of £5.00 to remain on the register. This provides the finance for the Council which has a number of subcommittees to deal with aspects of its work. One is responsible for pre-service training (the Visitation Committee), one for probation, one for discipline, one for public relations, one for registration, etc. (It is an interesting aside to note that the register, of course, is held on a computer. One of the reasons advanced against the notion of an English Council used to be that it would be impossible to record nearly half a million teachers' names accurately. Now the National Trust holds details of its million members on a computer tape which would fit into a large briefcase!)

There are currently some 75,969 (GTCS, 1989) registered members of the General Teaching Council for Scotland, but alas only a minority of them seem to take an interest in its work, for at election time there is a disappointingly low poll – something of the order of 33 per cent. In its twenty-three years of existence the Council has worked hard to raise standards. Opinions are divided as to whether or not it has succeeded. To be fair, it is hard to find a standard with which to compare it. Conditions before its foundation by statute in 1965 were very different from those which obtain now; only now are those whom it admitted in its first five years coming towards positions of responsibility in schools. There is one other problem too, which may help to explain teachers' lack of interest in electing representatives to it: it is widely perceived as being union dominated. (It may be difficult, of course, for a teacher who is not backed by the Educational Institute of Scotland to obtain the kind of publicity which may win General Teaching Council votes.) This perception may be misplaced but still the biographies of many of the teacher members of the Scottish Council show active participation over the years in the organisation of the Educational Institute of Scotland.

In the early 1980s a group of teachers, of whom I was one, requested the Council of the College of Preceptors to espouse once again the cause of teacher professionalism and the GTC. Alas, the Council was dominated then, as now, by union interest groups, and it refused. Therefore I founded a pressure group of teachers who called themselves CATEC (Campaign for a General Teaching Council) to try to bring the idea of a 'professional' Council for teachers back once more into the arena of public debate. We were successful in persuading the then Secretary of State, Mark Carlisle, (now Lord Carlisle of Bucklow) to issue a statement. A lawyer himself, he was in favour of the principle of a teachers' Council and said as follows:

I will give all the help and encouragement I can to the establishment of such a Council, but I must emphasise that it would defeat the whole object of the exercise if Government itself were to set up such a Council. Such a Council, as with the Law Society, would be independent of Government – a separate self-regulating body for the teaching profession.

CATEC carried out both informal and official talks with unions and associations to see if there was any room for agreement amongst them.

It was clear from the start that the concept of a General Council was unwelcome to the National Association of Teachers in Further and Higher Education (NATFHE). Some of their members (especially those teaching certain technical or trade subjects) were not qualified in the sense of having undergone formal teacher training, and saw perhaps a future in which they would be excluded from registration. The other unions, especially the NAS/UWT, the Professional Association of Teachers (PAT) and the heads' associations, were broadly supportive of a new initiative, though it proved impossible to take up the challenge issued by Mark Carlisle before he was replaced as Secretary of State by Sir Keith (now Lord) Joseph, who publicly stated that he saw 'a great deal in the idea of a General Teaching Council for teachers, but little for their pupils.' He was said also to equate the notion of a General Council with that of a 'closed shop' and it is worthwhile spending some time in the examination of such a criticism.

The term 'a closed shop' is usually applied to an area of work in which an employer agrees that he will employ no one who does not belong to a certain union. Hence expulsion from the union, or failure to be admitted to it, means no work and no livelihood. Admission to the union depends on a promise to keep to its rules, and continued membership on actual obedience to them. So far there is no discernable difference between the notion of a 'profession' and that of a 'closed shop'. Both a 'closed shop' and a 'profession' demand the following of certain rules and in both cases the rules could be said to be promulgated to better the lot of the follower.

For instance both a medical doctor and a newspaper printer have to possess certain skills before they can work, both are assessed by tests and examinations. Without these skills, the doctor would not be able to save lives or the printer to keep his machine rolling. Both have to make certain promises before being allowed to work; however clever the surgeon, unless registered with the General Medical Council, he will not be permitted to practise; however dextrous the printer, if a 'closed shop' operates, unless he joins the appropriate union, there will be no employment for him.

We have to look more carefully at the relevant requirements for registration with a 'professional' body and for joining a union before the difference is apparent. The necessary and sufficient qualifications for, say, registration with the General Medical Council are all directly related to the skills required by a good physician or surgeon. The standards required on entry are clearly set down and both they and the code of conduct are a matter of public record. Anyone who reaches the required published standard and assents to the Code of Conduct will be admitted to the register and may practise. In a 'closed shop' however, admission is to a degree arbitrary and entry criteria bear no relationship to the skills needed for the job (as some employers have found to their cost) and are concerned only with a willingness to obey the rules of the union concerned. The arbitrariness arises because I could possess the necessary skills, I could offer to promise to obey union rules, there could be work available, but even though I have reached the required standard the union could still refuse to have me in membership because I was, for instance, unknown to the local committee. The nature of the rules reveal further differences. The rules of a union 'closed shop' are concerned *only* with the furtherance of the interests of its members especially with regard to pay and conditions of service. Those of a 'professional' body are concerned with standards of service and ultimately benefit the clients, although they may indirectly enhance the status – and possibly therefore the pay – of the practitioner.

Finally, the aims implicit in each term reveal clear differences also. A 'closed shop' restricts a client to the use of one group of employees, by threat of the withdrawal of labour, solely with the aim of gaining improved pay and conditions for its members. A 'profession' restricts a client, usually by statute, in order to protect the client from inferior service, and this has only an indirect bearing on pay and conditions.

If it is difficult to separate those criteria needed before a 'closed shop' operates and those which are the requisites of a 'profession', then it is no wonder that confusion exists when we look at the concept of a General Teaching Council as envisaged, for instance, by the Weaver Report. In the absence of a 'professional' Council, the teachers' unions and associations have adduced to themselves some of the roles of such a Council. They claim, with some justification, to represent the views of teachers on qualifications for entry, on inservice training, on disciplinary matters and indeed some of them have their own 'Codes of Conduct'. Some unions take their roles as quasi- 'professional' bodies very seriously, and genuinely try to look after client interests as well as those of their members. The Professional Association of Teachers members' Code of Conduct eschews strike action under any circumstances (although, as we have seen, there is nothing built into the concept of 'professionalism' which requires this, laudable though it may be. Indeed there could conceivably be times when a 'professional' *ought* to withdraw his labour for the better protection of his clients.) Here is a teacher writing in the journal of another union:

If the union were unguarded enough to take these recommendations further we might well be suspected of subordinating the real interests of children to the creating of employment for teachers.

Immediately the dichotomy is evident: is the union there to protect the teacher or the children?

If we assume that a teachers' union's duties are primarily concerned with improving the pay and conditions of service of its members (whatever else it may be free in a democratic society to do) then there are clearly disadvantages for the clients if a General Teaching Council becomes dominated by union interests. If a majority of teachers appointed to such a Council are there because of their commitment to the values of their unions then there is the danger that they could constrict the flow of practitioners into the 'profession', (by imposing arbitrary entry requirements), in order to coerce employers into better pay deals.

The quasi-judicial nature of a 'professional' council also makes it difficult to see how a union dominated body could deal reasonably and fairly with discipline cases. A teacher accused of gross misconduct could find himself being judged and struck off by members of the very union that is defending him. If they belong to other unions, the position could be worse given the perceived internecine instincts of the teachers' unions and associations nowadays!

1986 saw the creation of yet another initiative to keep the idea of a GTC alive. The Universities Council for the Education of Teachers (UCET) was upset by the creation by the Secretary of State of a new body of Government appointees (CATE) to oversee the quality of education courses for prospective teachers. The establishment of a General Teaching Council would, of course, provide the opportunity for the powers given to CATE to be wrested from government hands. Accordingly, representatives of the various teachers' unions and associations were invited by UCET to a series of discussions, and a sub-committee produced criteria for a GTC. Almost inevitably acrimony arose amongst the unionists about representation and even about the whole concept of a general council. The UCET effort died down, was prodded into life again in 1988 by a separate move, by the headteacher of an independent school to form an elected 'National Teaching Council', and died down again.

It is quite clear that only a General Teaching Council *which is quite separate from unions and associations* could concentrate on client interests, and, indeed, all the while that Governments remain the employers of teachers, it is the only model to which 'professional' powers are likely to be entrusted. If a future Council is to gain for teachers the respect which is the hallmark of a 'profession', it must not be concerned in any way with salaries or conditions of service and those who run it must be *elected* (whatever the practical difficulties) by the teaching body as a whole.

The intentions of those who, like myself, wish to see the establishment of a General Teaching Council must always be tested on one touchstone, and that is the question: 'Will your proposals, as well as enhancing the status of teachers protect and benefit children and their parents?' Only if the answer is 'yes' will a real teaching 'profession' come about.

References

DES (1970), *A Teaching Council for England and Wales (The Weaver Report)*, HMSO.
GTCS (1989), *GTC Link*, Journal of the General Teaching Council for Scotland.

PART II POLICY MAKING

10 Aims and objectives – are they useful tools in curriculum management

Calvin Pike

There are many and varied approaches to the job of curriculum management in the primary school. Differences are often characterised as much by the size of the school, levels of specialism amongst staff, or leadership style of the headteacher, as they are by the way in which teachers see themselves (as 'restricted' to the classroom or 'extended' to a concern with the whole school), attitudes to and perceptions of others' roles or the degree of support and consultation with Local Education Authority Inspectors/Advisors and Officers. All are important factors and much has already been written on each of them. In this chapter an initial focus will be made upon particular areas of more immediate concern so as to understand the question posed.

Firstly I shall attempt to clarify the background and development of the central concepts of 'aims and objectives'. I shall highlight some of the influences which have both shaped definitions of the term and led to curriculum models said to have been derived from them. Criticisms of the models will be reviewed. In so doing an interpretation will be suggested which lends itself to the current, post 1988 Education Reform Act, context of education. Implications for practice throughout this brief examination will be made evident.

Secondly, the sense in which the concepts themselves might be used as a 'tool' will be questioned. This, in turn, will lead to a review of changes in management strategies in the primary school with particular reference to more recent debate, advice and legislation.

Finally, and inextricably linked, will be questions relating to all important implications for Inservice Education of Teachers (INSET) with particular reference to the implementation of the National Curriculum.

Aims and objectives – background and development

The notion of 'aims and objectives' in the context of education is not new. The use of clear objectives in planning curriculum can be discerned as early as Cicero's taxonomy which later influenced Herbert and Spencer in the nineteenth century. In more modern day form, Bobbitt, in *The Curriculum* (1918) and *How to Make A Curriculum* (1924) clarifies his belief that 'Education that prepares for life is one which prepares definitely and adequately for these specific activities'. These activities were 'specified' through educational objectives described as being 'ultimate' or 'progress' for the whole school and particular age groups respectively. The concept has run through the literature since.

Following Charters' analysis of teaching in 1924, Tyler's work led towards what has come to be regarded as the classic definition of 'behavioural objectives'. As early as 1949 he considers the problem of 'stating objectives in a form to be helpful in selecting learning experiences and in guiding teaching'. Through questions of content, purpose, organisation and evaluation he suggests that 'one can define an objective with sufficient clarity if one can describe or illustrate the kind of behaviour the student is expected to acquire so that one could recognise such a behaviour if one saw it'. Bloom's *Taxonomy of Educational Objectives – Handbook I – Cognitive Domain*, (1956) sharpened the behavioural view. He divides objectives into three 'domains' – cognitive, affective and psychomotor – and offers a detailed classification of the first of the three. [A similar focus upon the affective domain came later in 1964.]

Four basic reasons for the use of such an objective model for curriculum planning may be identified. Kelly has clarified these as being the logical, scientific, politico-economic and educational respectively. The first, the logical, might be discerned from Hirst, Peters and others. They argue that if education is to be regarded as a rational activity then it must have a goal or purpose. Without being able to state our intentions our work is aimless. Mager (1962) has put it in another way, 'if you're not sure where you are going, you are liable to end up some place else – and not even know it'.

The scientific argument, underpinned by the predominant psychological theory of the 1920's and 30's, supposedly attempts to develop precision, accuracy and respectability in educational practice. The limitations of the behaviourist approach to objectives setting and measurement have already been alluded to and will be discussed further later.

The third reason for use, the politico-economic, is one which continues to grow in society today. Education, it is stated, is provided by the tax payer who is entitled to a clear statement of aims and objectives in order that s/he is aware how money is being used. Evaluation, in terms of such aims and objectives, monitors effective use of public money. The direction in which schools might be led – with overprescribed objectives – is an obvious danger in this otherwise very real argument.

Finally Taba claims that in order for education to develop, evaluation of effective teaching must take place. Feeling that 'those things that are most clearly evaluated are also most effectively taught' (1962), she makes the assumption that evaluation can only take place if educational objectives are prespecified. The only instruments of evaluation are, it is implied, related to characteristics which are predefined. Recent publications – for example by Hamilton (1976) or Manion (1984) have shown the limitations of such a perspective. Whilst these arguments for the use of an objective model are important, possible implicit assumptions must be considered before either the notion of 'aims and objectives' can be acceptable in managing the curriculum and/or both its weaknesses and strengths realised.

Throughout the description so far, though 'aims' have been 'broad' there seems little doubt that much of the writing on curriculum objectives contain the assumption that these objectives were behavioural – and behavioural only – in kind. This was certainly the case by the mid-60's. Hilda Taba's work in 1962 clarifies aims as statements of purpose and intention 'satisfied only if individuals acquire knowledge, skills, techniques and attitudes . . . usually referred to as educational objectives'; Popham (1969) informs us that 'satisfactory instructional objectives must describe as an observable behaviour or a product of learner behaviour': the Schools' Council's Aims of Primary Education (1964) look to 'what the child might do when the aim has been achieved'.

It is hardly surprising that this narrowed interpretation of 'objectives' should have developed. Not only did it grow out of Tyler's work, but draws upon early American experience of training personnel with objective testing of student attainment during the Second World War years – both of which relate closely to the field of behavioural psychology which was current in the United States at the time. In addition the view is associated with the work of the philosopher J S Mill. Being a neat and systematic form of scientific rationalisation, it leads to a separation of means and ends and a resulting statement of measurable objectives based on observable behaviour. These are significant factors in discussing the usefulness of 'aims and objectives' in managing curriculum today. Unless we make clear the type of 'objectives' in mind, through the use of aims that are educational in nature, criticisms of the behavioural must be addressed.

Macdonald Ross (1975) amongst others has given a number of very clear objections to the behavioural model. Some are:

(1) there is no consistent way of defining educational objectives using the behavioural model.
(2) such a definition inhibits the exploratory quality and character of the teaching/learning process.
(3) behavioural objectives become more easy to state as outcomes are trivialised.
(4) knowledge cannot be reduced to a list of desired behaviours.

These show the restrictive nature of such an interpretation. As has been shown by Holt (1983), it is no coincidence perhaps that Mill was a utilitarian philosopher!

Stenhouse (1975) has also provided a useful review of the criticisms of the model. He identifies it as, 'agree broad aims and analyse these into objectives: construct a curriculum to achieve objectives; communicate it to teachers through the conceptual framework of objectives'. Largely through a criticism of the work of Popham (1968) various objections are considered. The dangers of overstressing trivial learning behaviours are emphasised; the loss of use of unexpected and unspecified classroom opportunities are stressed; accuracy as well as the basis of measurement of behavioural objectives are questioned as being limited in educational value. Kelly and Blenkin (1981) further criticise the approach to curriculum management as it is said to 'reduce education to a scientific activity' with a 'passive model of man'.

The important question of interpretation and meaning was considered by many when the objectives model began to feel its influence in the United Kingdom. Innovation grew with the establishment of the School's Council from 1964. Clear statements of goals, aims, purposes and objectives were adopted and such a framework of curriculum planning soon spread to the classroom teacher. But concern to stress that educational objectives were not only 'behavioural' in nature became evident in the Council's projects; the Science 5–13 Project, entitled *With Objectives in Mind* in 1972 was a clear example of the change in definition and emphasis.

Paul Hirst in a paper in 1975 recognised the same problem. In this he rejects the idea that objectives are behavioural only with the suggestion that educational goals might be expressed in terms of forms of understanding and bodies of knowledge. This seems to point to an approach which is much more acceptable to those whose responsibility it is to manage curriculum in the school.

Through the work of Peters (1965) we are reminded of the distinction between the concept of education and other related concepts of training, instruction or indoctrination. The need to consider the individual's autonomy as learner and his engagement in activity which is of value for its own sake are seen to be essential criteria in defining educational practice. Kelly takes care to show that the adoption of an objectives model of curriculum planning not only fails to ensure that such educational criteria underpin practice, but, because of the nature of what is believed to be the prescriptive, prespecified elements of the model, actively operate against educational development. In other words a model which is likely to limit individual autonomy and curtail initiative within the classroom as a result of predetermined content, methods and evaluation, is said to act against what is regarded as being an 'ongoing, open ended process of education'. Pring's (1971) criticisms of the simplistic model of knowledge divided into domains and separated out into unrelated goals of curriculum support this view.

These are powerful arguments against a narrowed objectives model of curriculum planning and ones which must help in assessing the usefulness of 'aims and objectives' in curriculum management. If broad aims, defined with the criteria which have already been identified as implicitly educational, direct ways in which the process of education might be developed, then limited practice might be avoided. Schools might be more actively engaged in education. The potential of 'aims and objectives' for the curriculum manager might be realised. It is to these possibilities that I now turn.

Both the extent to which an 'objectives' approach to curriculum planning has developed from a behaviourist basis and the limitations of such a model have been noted by Eisner (1967). In a later paper particularly, *Educational Aims, Objectives and other Aspirations*, he paints a vivid background to the current picture, sounding appropriate caution for the curriculum manager today. After identifying the characteristic influences of American psychology as well as industrial models of management and military training programmes, he analyses the deceptive analogy between industrial and educational processes. He points to the complexity of the context of education and offers a useful alternative to what he regards to be 'an oversimplified view of the character of educational aims' in order ' to avoid reductionistic thinking which impoverishes our view of what is possible'. In spite of others' criticism of Eisner's previous work, this alternative directs us perhaps towards the ways in which 'aims and objectives' might be used for the curriculum manager. It offers clarify and support in implementing the curriculum elements of the Education Reform Act (ERA) of 1988.

Recognising that only a limited number of activities of the school can be reduced to prespecified behavioural objectives, Eisner considers two additional ways of conceptualising 'aims' the 'problem-solving objective' and 'expressive outcome'. In the former, students are given, or identify for themselves, problems to be solved. Instead of evaluating activities with objectives measured in terms of prescribed behavioural outcomes, judgements are made (rather than standards being applied) based upon criteria which relate to the process of learning which takes place, outcomes which pertain to the activity itself which has value in itself, and to the development of learning about decision making. The context of education is thus of prime importance; the process is seen as part of an on-going educational one and the product is identified only as an aid to reflecting on strategies used and sharing alternative solutions.

This latter type of educational aim is defined as an 'expressive outcome'. It is notable that Eisner has changed from a previous definition of expressive 'objective', the interpretation of which might have confused. Implications for preformulated goals as expressive outcomes are the result of 'curriculum activities that are intentionally planned to provide a fertile field for personal purposing and experience'. Unfortunately, Eisner does not clarify how the qualities of expressive outcomes might be appraised. In the same way that Hirst's 'Forms of Knowledge' might be said to be as yet still limited, Eisner's 'expressive outcomes' are also open to criticism. The complexities of such appraisals are, however, appreciated as being in need of our attention and inclusion in an educational context.

Though this concept is not necessarily limited to the Arts in the curriculum, Langer (1942) has gone some way towards identifying the nature of the relationship with a discipline which might lead to/bring about such 'expressive outcomes' in her analysis of 'artistic meaning'. Swanwick (1979) offers a similar objective in a hierarchy which looks towards 'aesthetic response' as an ultimate aim of music education. The contribution of both writers are of great value in developing a notion of objectives, which is not necessarily restrictive or reductionist, for the whole curriculum.

The interpretation of Eisner's work which has been given contains many of the features of the 'process' model of curriculum development. This too stresses the inadequacies of an instrumental, means ends approach to curriculum planning and management and must be appreciated in any consideration of the usefulness of 'aims and objectives'. Kelly (1981) has shown how the primary school tradition has been significantly influenced by the 'progressive' theories of education. Led by Rousseau and ultimately adopted by developmental psychologists of the present century, a 'process' view of education has grown which lends itself particularly to the work of the primary school. The view, identified by HM Inspectorate (DES 1979) points to an approach to planning which is broader and more comprehensive than the subject base of the secondary school. Rather than consider what and how to teach, there is an emphasis on what and how best children can learn. There is a concern for the creation of the appropriate context of learning and structuring such learning so that particular methods of enquiry, skills and concepts are developed. Activity of the pupil is stressed in an open atmosphere which is organised to encourage choice. Adequate time, it is suggested, needs to be spent in supporting each child so as to make appropriate assessments and to plan, observe and gain required knowledge of each child as an individual. The model is essential in identifying not only the philosophy which forms the foundation of the primary curriculum but also in considering its practical application.

Are they useful 'tools' of curriculum management?

The description above has been necessary in order to identify the various influences which have affected our understanding of the concepts of 'aims and objectives'. Clearly meanings which are attributed to the terms differ widely. The extent to which they might be regarded as 'useful' depends upon the interpretation held. It has been seen that their application might be extremely limited if viewed only in their original sense of prespecific goals which are measured in terms of anticipated outcomes and observable behavioural change. If defined more broadly, following the direction given by Eisner and others, educational objectives can be seen to be essential in planning, managing and evaluating the content, process and method of both teaching and learning involved in and leading from the educational experience developed within the school.

With this in mind the use of the concepts of 'aims and objectives' as a curriculum 'tool' should be clarified before considering further questions of curriculum management. If perceived in the sense in which we use a tool around the house or workshop so as to sharpen, fine-tune or repair, application of the concepts seem limited. As has been made clear, the notion of education objectives offers potential for curriculum development which is related to planning and evaluation of content, process and pupil-learning and teaching styles. Such objectives are developed and shaped from aims which are educational, being concerned for example:

> to enlarge a child's knowledge, experience and understanding, and thus his awareness of moral values and capacity for enjoyment: to enable him to enter the world after formal education is over as an active participant in society and a responsible contributor to it, capable of achieving as much independence as possible (The Warnock Report quoted in *The Practical Curriculum*, 1981).

Aims and objectives are thus not simply useful in adjusting and redirecting practice where appropriate. They are not brought to the curriculum whilst it is somehow in operation. Instead they must be realised to be at the centre of the curriculum itself, formulated in part before its practice and developing with its dynamic growth. The metaphor must therefore be extended. The concepts are more than curriculum 'tools'; they represent the curriculum machine itself. Implications for the management of this machine will now be addressed with the perspective of contemporary debate and development.

Until recently local education authorities and central government exercised little direct control over what was taught in primary schools. If we add to this picture the basic features of primary education with the autonomy of the classroom teacher it is not difficult to appreciate the assumption that curriculum development was restricted only by resources, talents, commitment, and energy. Kogan (1980) summarises the position thus:

> after 1956, the convention that schools create their own curriculum became part of the established wisdom of British Education.

Such autonomy is still reflected in the variety of institutions and organisations representing the primary sector; large and small scale; infant and JMI; horizontal and/or vertical grouping; open plan schools or more traditional classrooms.

In terms of curriculum management the English primary remained unique in that there were few policies which could be used to regulate or encourage curriculum change in classrooms. Whilst some saw this as positive (Fisher 1972), others regarded it as fragmented and negative (Rogers 1968). It is against this backcloth that the effect of direct intervention by the DES since the mid

1970s and implications for managing the curriculum through the model described should be understood.

Attempts to influence school curriculum with the national curricular framework over the last ten years and more have been clear. A series of reports and documents have led to the enormous changes inherent in the Educational Reform Act of 1988.

The basic structure required of primary schools had previously been built up in a report *Primary Education in England* (1978). Its main curriculum concerns were for standards, sequence and scope. Considering this and other documents of the period, six assumptions result, reflecting the need for a curriculum which:

– has common aims allowing for individual pupil differences;
– has a broad scope not restricted to basic skills;
– incorporates sequence of concepts and skills;
– caters for the needs of able children through more effective use of teacher expertise;
– reflects fundamental social values;
– provides for pupils' personal, moral and social development.

A centrally directed plan for curriculum change in the next ten years has thus become apparent. Priorities of this plan seem to include:

– the introduction of science and technology;
– a prediction of sequence of concepts/skills in all subjects;
– the incorporation of multicultural perspectives to all schools;
– meeting the needs of more able pupils;
– the development of applied learning and problem solving;
– a consideration of continuity, between and within schools.

The Organisation and Content of the 5–16 Curriculum (DES 1984) confirms both the priorities and the re-direction of the curriculum, especially in its focus upon planning which is 'whole school curriculum' and 'use of "subjects"' based. Such planning rests upon the strong case, made initially by HMI in the Primary School Survey, for scale post holders to act as curricular coordinators. The same document also makes clear the use of specialist expertise and teacher participation in decision making seems clear. Its publication, along with the introduction of subject specialist Educational Support Grants (ESG) and the new Local Education Authority Training Grant Scheme (LEATGS), heralded the changes currently being managed by each LEA, and more particularly institutions therein, as a result of the Education Reform Act (1988), including the National Curriculum.

This Act has been described as being 'the basis of a sequence of changes which will affect quite radically the public education service in England and Wales' (Leonard 1988). Quite how soon and in what way changes affect development will depend upon the clarity of the school's definitions of its intentions and planning for the future and the LEA's procedures for monitoring implementation of the National Curriculum in relation to the requirements of the Act. These requirements entitle all pupils in maintained schools to a curriculum which is broadly based and balanced which:

– promotes the spiritual, moral and cultural, mental and physical development of pupils at the school and of society
– prepares such pupils for the opportunities, responsibilities and experiences of adult life. (DES 1989, 5/89.)

A number of more general key points need to be highlighted in considering how the notion of aims and objectives might be interpreted and utilised by managers within the framework of the National Curriculum. They are as follows:

– The principle that each pupil should receive a broad and balanced curriculum relevant to his/her needs is now legally binding.
– The curriculum must be taken up by each individual child not simply 'on offer' at the school.
– Development within each of the curriculum areas must be promoted.
– Such development must serve the pupil as an individual, a member of society and a future adult.

More particularly the requirements of the National Curriculum within ERA, reflecting the framework for development offered by the Education (No. 2) Act 1986, are intended 'to take forward more quickly . . . across the country, the achievement of consistently high standards' (From *Policy to Practice*, DES, 1989). This curriculum for the nation comprises of:

– *foundations subjects* – 3 core and 7 other foundation subjects;
– *attainment targets* – up to 10 levels of attainment for ages 5–16, setting objectives for learning in terms of knowledge, skills and understanding that each pupil is expected to master;
– *programmes of study* – specifying essential 'matters' skills and processes that each pupil should cover at Key Stages of their education;
– *assessment arrangements* – related to the 10 levels of attainment.

Quite clearly the Act has, in many ways, been specific in its requirements for education in the present and the future. To what extent then, does it suffer the criticisms of the behavioural objectives model outlined earlier in this chapter? Close examination reveals that though the new law establishes a clear framework, its requirements may not be reduced to measurements of pupil performance which are exclusively in terms of behavioural changes, and its concerns are not simply with the acquisition of information. The pupil is required both to gain knowledge which is relevant and contextualised as well as a thorough understanding of processes. It will be necessary to develop appropriate skills so that individuals may become independent both as pupil/students and as mature adults in later life.

Moreover, the *way* in which teaching and learning is to take place has not been prescribed. The Act insists neither on particular teaching methodologies, for example within discrete subject boundaries, nor on special organisational arrangements. A 'reasonable time' to be spent upon each area of learning has not been defined as any more than that.

The Act quite distinctly adopts a model of curriculum management which highlights notions of aims and objectives. Whether this recent legislation's objectives may be optimistically interpreted as a balanced combination of curriculum models – as the description of Eisner's work earlier – continues to be debated. What is undisputed is that the 1988 Act places a firm responsibility for action and implementation on the decision-makers both at LEA and school levels. The latter being changed significantly as a result of the increased influence and powers of the lay governing bodies. Similarly the National Curriculum framework, its attainment targets and programmes of study, make *every* effort to support thinking and planning for all schools as,

- they provide clear objectives on which schemes of work can be based;
- they provide a framework for achieving continuity;
- they allow for and encourage progression whilst accommodating differentiation;
- they specify essential studies which each pupil must undertake;
- what is specified will allow teachers freedom in the way in which they teach, . . . etc;
- the requirements will be far from totally new.

The extent to which the aims and objectives in managing the curriculum will be useful has yet to be realised in practice. However pre-Education Reform Act reservations concerning the 'logic of the framework's assumptions' (Campbell, 1985) must be expressed still as concern is based upon the level of resources as well as appropriate characteristics of classroom teachers, headteachers and, more recently, school governors which have yet to be developed in many instances. It is to these considerations – for the development of individual staff, whole staff and governors – which I now refer.

Questions of inservice development and support

If a call for enriched management skills, subject specialism and collaboration and informed governor advice and leadership is to be answered then clear demands for Inservice Development in the primary sector must be addressed. Curriculum planning and innovation through shared decision making towards aims and objectives which may be evaluated and developed will require changes in many areas. The primary school which features the all powerful but isolated classroom teacher with a management which is represented in an autocratic head will need help and support in order to effect such change and seek the potential of National Curriculum aims and objectives in the school's development.

Research which preceded ERA has noted the extremely influential position of the headteacher in the primary school. The White Paper *Teaching Quality* pays attention to the crucial importance of the headteacher and other staff with management responsibility in schools. Circular 3/83, outlining the new initiative on headship training, clearly states:

> The Secretary of State sees a pressing need for headteachers and other senior teachers carrying out management functions to be better equipped for their increasing difficult and complicated tasks.

Part of the 'increasingly difficult and complicated tasks' in question will be to define the work of the school in order to maximise its resources and educational potential. In so doing, as Alexander (1984) has shown, the role of the headteacher and the postholders of responsibility will need to be made more clear, the curriculum will be planned through guidelines and meetings, and evaluation and self evaluation towards professional growth and public accountability will be major issues.

Each of these areas will be led, initially, at least, by the head. As a result, lessons to be learned of leadership style, characterised, for example by Nias (1980), will be significant not simply in identifying 'passive', 'bourbon' and 'positive' types but also in preparing for roles which combine firm leadership with staff involvement in decision-making. If aims and objectives are to be used to the full, INSET will be needed to assist heads to create appropriate balances between a 'concern for people' and 'concern for task' (Whitaker, 1983).

More participative forms of management will be required in order to deliver especially those elements of core curriculum which need not be associated with the 'specialist' as well as other cross-curriculum areas. Firm hierarchies will be less obvious. As a result of more teachers as consultants with curricular or organisational responsibilities heading working parties of colleagues, there will be more 'leaders' within the school. Heads will need assistance in managing through others in a way which is unfamiliar. At the same time curriculum managers must develop expertise in resolving inevitable conflicts which arise in promoting collaboration which does not always lead to concensus.

Inservice training will be required for the curriculum consultant too in handling group dynamics and developing interpersonal skills. In many cases the experience of leading and/or being led by colleagues of the same staff room is still foreign. Though the extent to which these changes will be possible must depend upon the way in which the role is perceived and enacted (Alexander, 1984), there will be a pressing need to become more able to use skills of negotiation and be aware of individual and group issues before objectives may be effectively developed which allow the flexibility and scope suggested.

Finally those responsible for INSET must also be concerned with the way in which individuals might influence whole staff groups during and post inservice development. Considering the changes which have been outlined, it might be wise to re-evaluate methods which remove heads from schools in order to retrain as is often the case at present. Greater collaboration might be promoted and a 'top-down' structure avoided if staff other than the head were to represent the school when 'external' course orientated inservice training is offered. Alternatively, the school as a whole might be the starting point for development with all staff involved in a review which fosters the growth of each individual's role as appropriate. These are questions not for the future but for the present.

It has been seen that school management and the management of the curriculum in the primary sector are closely connected; both are quickly changing. Current new directions might be regarded with suspicion as being restricting, over-prescriptive and in danger of heralding too much centralist control. On the other hand, they could be seen as presenting exciting opportunities for the growth of education through clear curriculum thinking, shared management and individual professional development. Which of the perspectives we share will depend not only upon our understanding of the key concepts of aims and objectives but the way in which they are developed within the school.

The chapter has gone to great lengths to show how this might be possible though warning of the need to consider management including inservice strategies throughout. The usefulness of the concepts must ultimately be realised in the extent to which they bring about the educational development of the pupils themselves. They after all, in the final analysis, are at the centre of and the reasons for our work. Schools Council (1983) has emphasised the point more clearly than most:

'. . . a precise statement of aims and objectives rooted firmly in what is known about children's growth and development. This must be our starting point.'

Summary

The chapter has attempted to investigate the place of aims and objectives in the management of the curriculum of the primary school. Initial descriptions of the background and development of the terms themselves have revealed clear differences in thinking associated with the concepts. Such differences have been seen to be significant as interpretations either restrict use to limited areas of curriculum or appear to hold much potential for the planning, development and extension of the curriculum as a whole.

It is in the second wider sense that aims and objectives are suggested to be at the centre of the curriculum machine rather than a tool which simply adjusts rigid sets of preconceived ideas during their implementation.

Changes in overall management of primary schools have been considered, especially within a comparatively recent context which more readily provides advice and direction to curriculum managers in preparation for the implementation of the Education Reform Act of 1988.

Finally, increased demands and an expansion of the roles of primary school governors, headteachers and teachers are outlined. Inservice development needs which might affect changes are briefly identified with implications for a more flexible interpretation of aims and objectives in a climate which not unjustly seeks to maintain high professional standards as well as effect increased public accountability.

References

Alexander, R J (1984) *Primary Teaching* Holt, Rinehart & Winston.
Bloom, B S (1956) *Taxonomy of educational Objectives I : Cognitive Domain* Longman
Bobbitt, F (1918) *The Curriculum* Houghton Mifflin
Bobbitt, F (1924) *How to make a Curriculum* Houghton Mifflin
Campbell, R J (1985) *Developing a Primary School Curriculum* Holt, Rinehart & Winston
DES (1978) *Primary Education in England: an HMI Survey* HMSO

DES (1981) *The School Curriculum* HMSO
DES (1983) *Teaching Quality* [White Paper] HMSO
DES (1984) *The Organisation & Content of the 5–16 Curriculum*, HMSO
DES (1989) *The Education Reform Act 1988; The School Curriculum and Assessment* (Circular No 5/89), HMSO
DES (1989) *National Curriculum: From Practice to Policy*, HMSO
Eisner, E W (1964) 'Educational Aims, Objectives & other Aspirations' in *Educational Imaginations* Collier McMillan
Fisher, (1972) *Learning how to learn: the English Primary School and American Education* Harcourt Brace Jovanovich
Hamilton, D (1976) *Curriculum Evaluation* Open Books
Hirst, P (1974) *Knowledge and the Curriculum* Routledge & Kegan Paul
Holt, M (1983) *Curriculum Workshop: an introduction to whole school curriculum planning* Routledge & Kegan Paul
Kelly, A V & Blenkin G M (1981) *The Primary Curriculum* Harper & Row
Kogan, (1980) 'Policies for the School Curriculum in their Political Context' in *Cambridge Journal of Education*.
Langer, S (1942) *Philosophy in a new Key* Mentor Books
Leonard, M (1988) *The 1988 Education Act: A Tactical Guide for Schools* Blackwell
Macdonald-Ross, M (1975) 'Behavioural Objectives: a critical view' in Golby, M *Curriculum Design* Croom-Helm
Maclure, S (1988) *Education Re-formed* Hodder and Stoughton
Manion, (1984) *Research Methods in Education* Croom-Helm
Mager, R G (1962) *Preparing Instructional Objectives* Fearon
Nias, J (1980) 'Leadership styles and job satisfaction in Primary Schools' in Bush, T *Approaches to School Management* Harper and Row
Popham, W J (1969) *Instructional Objectives*, Rand McNally
Pring, R H (1971) *Knowledge and Schooling* Open Books
Schools Council (1964) *Aims of Primary Education*, HMSO
Schools Council (1972) *Science 5–13 Project: With Objectives in Mind* Macdonald
Schools Council (1981) *The Practical Curriculum* (Working Paper 70) Methuen
Schools Council (1983) *Primary Practice* Methuen
Stenhouse, L (1975) *An Introduction to Curriculum Research & Development* Heinemann
Swanwick, K (1979) *A Basis for Music Education* NFER
Taba, H (1962) *Curriculum Development, Theory and Practice* Harcourt, Brace Jovanovich
Tyler, R W (1949) *Basic Principles of Curriculum and Instruction* University of Chicago Press
Whitaker, P (1988) *The Primary School Head* Heinemann.

11 A policy for combatting sex stereotyping in the primary school

Hazel Taylor

The need for a gender equality policy

Sex stereotyping is one of those phrases often bandied about, a piece of 1980s education jargon that can be easily uttered but little thought about. In fact, it is part of the cause of perhaps the greatest inequality yet to be seriously tackled in the education system. Stereotyping of children in school because of their sex or their race or their class leads to an immediate closing down of the opportunities available to them, because of the way in which teachers, pupils and other adults are influenced by the stereotype into behaviour which in fact reinforces it. The differentiation of treatment and expectations of girls and boys which is a function of sex stereotyping comes so automatically to all of us that we are largely unaware of it, and even less aware of its effects on the pupils in our care. Dealing with a largely unconscious process is difficult, because it requires consciousness to be established, then practices to be changed. Piecemeal attempts at change in individual classrooms have little effect when they are counteracted by a prevailing school ethos of sexism, and can simply lead to conflict.

It is very encouraging that the documents supporting the major curriculum developments of the late 80s – the National Curriculum, Records of Achievement, GCSE criteria, TVEI Extension – all have explicit sections on the need to provide equal access to the curriculum, and equal opportunity within it. There is still however relatively little dissemination of the ways in which this aim can be achieved.

To institutionalise change, an organised and consistent effort is required, and thus a whole school policy, led in its formulation, implementation and monitoring by the headteacher, is essential. Most public concern with equal opportunities has been expressed in relation to secondary school subject choice, and the clear sex differences in take up of modern languages, physical science, all the traditional vocational subjects – craft design technology, home economics, textiles, business studies – and the new vocational subjects, information technology and new technological courses. This will partly be redressed by the National Curriculum although sex differentiation in achievement still occurs in common core subjects like English and mathematics. A detailed study of these differences in choice, and how secondary schools can affect them, has been carried out by Pratt, Bloomfield & Seale for the EOC (1984). One of the effects of divisions in choice in secondary schools is that boys and girls are differently prepared for employment and at a time when traditional employment for both sexes is rapidly disappearing, boys, in their enthusiasm for physical sciences, CDT, and the new technologies, are preparing themselves for change much more appropriately than girls. Too many girls at option choice time are still caught in their belief in three myths: that office work is a nice job (one word processor operator does the work of six typists) (Huws 1982); that girls don't need careers (one in three marriages ends in divorce/women are 40 per cent of the labour force); and that science and technology are not feminine. For boys, the myths, while less work-related, are personally more damaging: that child care is women's work; a second European language is of little use; that personal relationships are less important than an interest in things. Changes in the balance of the population mean that there will be increased opportunities in the 90s for students to enter skilled technological work – for which girls must be as well prepared in the primary school. To survive in the world of the late twentieth, early twenty-first centuries, adults need a combination of the strengths of women and men and a sign of their maturity will be the extent to which they achieve this. An education which encourages the development of one set only of the sex stereotyped characteristics is failing them. The key place where the attributes, interests and beliefs about themselves which limit future options are being formed is not the secondary school, where the effects of those are made manifest, but the primary school.

It is important to examine in more detail how the stereotyping that inhibits equality is in fact fostered in the primary school, so that we can be clear about the measures needed to combat it. Gender differences, which are those differences which are culturally determined as manifestations of difference in the roles of women and men in a society, and which do not follow necessarily from sex differences, begin to develop in babies from birth, as adult perceptions of their sex shapes the treatment they receive. This has been well documented elsewhere (see for example, Oakley 1972). Children are aware of gender differences by three, and express them in doll play situations through making differences in dress and physical appearance (long hair for women, short for men) and through role play (caring roles for female dolls, work outside the home roles for male dolls). There is not space here to review the complex literature concerning the relationship between a child's ego development and sex role identity, but it is clear that by the time they enter school girls and boys already have notions of differences between the sexes which in no way relate to any innate differences in cognitive abilities, or achievement potential, but which do differentially affect cognitive skills. Within the school, experiences in the nursery and reception classes, and after, far from extending children's understanding of what is fitting for someone of a particular gender, actually reinforce a narrow view of sex appropriate behaviour and aspirations while at the same time apparently expecting equality in achievement and take up of opportunity.

We can examine common primary practices through questioning whether four basic needs to ensure equal access to the curriculum are met. Girls and boys need to feel equally free to make any choice, so they must not be constrained by sex stereotyping to reject certain choices as inappropriate: a boy should not, for example, feel he must reject pursuing an ambition to be a ballet dancer because it is stereotyped as a feminine activity. All children need to have a similar view of the importance of paid work and of fulfilling leisure, which means that girls and boys must not be constrained by beliefs that careers are more important for men, that caring for a home is essentially women's work, or that it is more degrading for men to be unemployed than women. They need to have the same feelings of self-worth and self-confidence if they are to feel able to aspire equally highly and equally widely, for feelings about oneself and one's capabilities are central to identity and ambition. They also need to have identical educational experiences so that they can make later choices from a common base of skills and knowledge.

However, role models in primary schools, methods of organisation, selection of activities made available, teacher-pupil interaction, and curriculum content, all need to be examined and probably changed if the prerequisites outlined above are to be met. Girls' and boys' absorption of sex stereotypes as ideal types to conform to is aided within schools first of all by the role models provided by the adults who work there. It is highly likely that the only men around a primary school are the caretaker, any craftspeople doing repairs and maintenance, and the headteacher or a senior teacher who probably teaches top juniors. Because of their scarcity value, male primary teachers tend to be rapidly promoted. The women in a school will be most of the teaching staff, the cooks, cleaners, secretary, nursery nurses, welfare assistant and school meals assistants. This presents a clear picture for children of 'normality': women in caring and servicing jobs, men in supervisory and technical jobs. It is immediately harder for a boy to wish to be a nursery nurse, because visibly no men do that job. At the same time, stereotyping is further encouraged within the nursery and the classrooms, through the way in which the philosophy of child centred education allows children to choose from a range of activities without questioning the processes through which a child comes to perceive her or his needs and interests. Girls who already are accustomed to playing out mothering roles at home, choose to play with dolls at school because they are familiar and because such play has been approved. Their need is partly for approval for what they do; their interest is secured by familiarity. They also have needs which they may well not meet because they do not know that they have them, to explore the physical world and to construct and observe how objects interact. Interests are essentially seeds which have been fostered into growth. Patterns of sex differentiated play have been well reported; we do not yet realise sufficiently how damaging they are for the development of the whole child. The five year old girl who says 'lego's for boys', or the boy who says 'boys don't play with dolls' and go unchallenged are being allowed to limit their horizons while their life has barely begun. In addition to the effect of reinforcing stereotypes about activities, different play patterns further develop sex differences in knowledge and skills, which then in turn have their effect in creating unequal access to later opportunities. Boys who spend hours in building activities are unconsciously learning and reinforcing their understanding of concepts about balance, properties of materials, area, symmetry, three dimensional objects, spatial relationships within a context which is enjoyable to them, and where their interest is developed through pleasure in the activity, the companionship of almost certainly same sex friends, and reinforcement from adults. All of this, added to the role of stereotyping, prepares boys well to 'choose' scientific, practical or technological activities again and again. Girls, while not eschewing such activities totally, will spend much less time on them, and gain far less from the effects of practice. The inevitability of sex difference in patterns of choice is further determined by the sort of feedback from adults that girls and boys receive in the activities they most commonly do. Social play receives different responses from object play, and that has different effects in the construction of ideas of capability and self-worth. Girls in general are reinforced in their pursuit of stereotyped feminity by teacher interaction which responds to their physical appearance and dress, their skills in social interaction and servicing other people ('Is this cake for me, Melanie? That is kind'), and fails their need for cognitive development. Julia Hodgeon's observation (1983) in nursery classes revealed a wealth of differences in teacher interaction with girls and boys, which had huge implications for learning. Boys in general are given positive feedback for physical and manipulative skills, and have their intellectual understanding extended.

At the same time as differences in skills and knowledge are extended, differences in perception of self worth are developed, not merely through differences in the type of feedback received from teachers, but in the amount, in its style of delivery, and in its frequency. Detailed analysis of gender differences as a determinant of teacher interaction with primary pupils by Delamont (1980) has shown that boys are accorded more attention in class, that the types of attention they receive are different and that consequently boys are more likely to develop cognitive skills. Boys are referred to more frequently by name, they are more frequently called to across the room, and they are responded to more quickly than girls. All of these things give boys and girls very different messages about their own worth and importance. Boys get the message that they can command attention, are important and that it is right for them to be prominent while girls get the message that they have to wait, that they are less important and it is not right for them to be prominent. As well as learning the message for their own sex, they learn the messages about the opposite sex, and play their own part in teaching them. This is the most central danger in perpetuating sex stereotyping: the perpetuation of the greater importance and power of boys and men compared with girls and women. Equality of opportunity and access to choice will never be achieved by common role experience, similar skills and knowledge levels, if the actual value placed on one sex is greater than that placed on the other. And for girls to value themselves equally with boys, teachers must change as well as the curriculum.

The curriculum is full of examples of stereotypes showing both difference and inequality. Reading schemes, information books, posters, packaging, the words of songs, all show women and girls in less exciting, less important, less active roles than men and boys. Women are not valued either for what they have done which men also do (such as run industry during the first and second world wars), or for what they do which men do not do. Lip service is paid to the importance of good mothering for instance, but it is not valued in the ways in which our society recognises value, by status, by financial return, by the recognition of high levels of expertise. The undervaluation of women's strengths leads both to an undervaluing of them by women themselves, and boys' rejection of them as strengths to foster.

This rapid survey of gender inequality in primary education, and its entrenchment in the system, shows how badly a concerted policy is needed in each school if equality is ever to become a reality.

The National Curriculum, in ensuring that much more science of a balanced kind determined by the programmes of study is experienced, will enable girls and boys to participate more in science and technological activity. Teachers must be aware though of the ways in which underlying expectations of sex differences in interest and performance can affect pupils' actual interests and development.

Content of a gender equality policy

A school policy on gender equality, to be effective, must be a substantial document, reflecting in its content a proper understanding of the causes of inequality and the harms of sex stereotyping. It must therefore cover all areas of school life, from outdoor play, to management, non-teaching staff, classroom organisation, curriculum content, interaction, and resources. It is helpful to formulate a policy under three main headings: the informal curriculum, school organisation and management, and curriculum areas.

The informal curriculum

The informal curriculum is responsible for transmitting many powerful values about gender and race equality, about class, about achievement and aspiration and commitment. Attitudes about sex differentiation, seldom made explicit, lie behind expectations of the behaviour, dress, interests and achievements of girls and boys, and however much teachers try to treat children as individuals, they cannot escape the overarching influence on them of gender as a means of differentiation between groups. A school policy therefore should require teachers to examine their own attitudes to gender equality and make explicit any different expectation they may have of girls and boys. Unquestioned assumptions that boys are more aggressive that they are stronger, that girls should be encouraged to keep clean and that it is unladylike to shout, need examining and testing against the four prerequisites outlined in the previous section. What are girls learning by being told not to shout when it is tolerated in boys? Are boys at eight *really* stronger than girls or is that a myth supported by differentiation in sex roles, lack of recognition of the strength actually used by women, and eventually created in adults by very different practice in using muscles and maintaining fitness? One teacher of ten year olds asked a girl to move a milk crate. A boy said the girl was not strong enough. The teacher then organised a milk crate lifting competition, and the girls' team managed more lifts than the boys' team, while individual scores within the teams varied greatly. It effectively demonstrated two central points: that there are great differences of strength within a sex, and that most girls' and boys' performances overlap. But the boys in the class were most reluctant to accept the very clear evidence, so deep was their engrained belief that boys are stronger. Here is crux of the problem of gender difference: the belief in male superiority.

To counteract such assumptions, a policy should recommend that all teachers explicitly discuss gender differences with their classes, to bring out the hidden beliefs and see if they hold true, and to counter the prejudices by example, discussion and experience.

A policy should also encourage the developing and sharing of common interests by girls and boys, because rivalry between the sexes leads to an intensification of identification within the same sex group and an increase in conformity to the stereotype. It should also encourage the open valuing of qualities in individuals which are not stereotyped – gentleness in boys and independence in girls – and it should require the same standards of behaviour from both sexes.

A policy should also recognise that sexist language is powerful in creating an ethos of gender inequality. The use of phrases like 'Don't be a girl' to an upset boy, or 'old woman' to describe someone who is fussing may go unnoticed, but they have a power-ful cumulative effect in forming attitudes. Similarly, any behaviour or language which encourages girls to think of themselves as poten-tial sex objects must be specifically identified in a policy and not used. This extends to removing the pages of newspapers with pinup pictures before they are used to cover tables for painting, and to praising girls for their appearance in ways that are not also applied to boys.

School organisation and management

A school's policy on combatting sex stereotyping must address itself to its own staffing if it is to be taken seriously. No posts should be sex-specific – such as responsibility for boys' PE – and positive efforts to deploy male teachers to teach infants should be made. Similarly, when appointing postholders for curriculum areas, the need for role models should be one of the selection criteria. A policy also needs to address itself to staff development, and present recommendations which take into account the need for all teachers to gain wide experience of school responsibilities, and equal access to management and other inservice training. This requires efforts by Local Education Authorities, too, to provide training at times when women teachers with home responsibilities can attend: while we may have a future where partners share equally in home and child care, it is not the universal case at present. A policy section on school organisation must also consider the roles of non-teaching staff in the school and the messages they convey to children through their attitudes and behaviour. A serious attempt to change pupils' attitudes in the classroom can be scuppered by the sexist comments of non-teaching staff, if they are not fully involved in the policy and do not understand its rationale.

The daily organisation of schools frequently involves unconscious practices which reinforce sex differences. These may seem trivial in themselves but they have powerful cumulative effects. Lists, playgrounds, lines, assembly seating, cloakrooms, registers, can all be found divided into separate parts for girls and boys, with boys almost always put first. All of these things imply that the sexes should be separate, that it would be abnormal for them to be together. Defenders of separate lines of lists cite convenience or habit in their defence without thinking of the message the children receive through the daily repetition of the practice. Separation is divisive, and school policy must cover all of these practices. There are many remedies, and the Brent Education Department guidelines (1985) cover them fully.

A policy must also address itself to the way the school presents itself to visitors: its brochure should explain its position on equal opportunities for girls and boys, its public performances should show its policy in action by avoiding stereotyping in refreshment provision and so on. The policy should also consider school dress: a uniform if there is one should give equal freedom of movement and flexibility to all pupils and if there is no uniform, pupils should be strongly encouraged to wear practical clothing and shoes. Girls are discouraged from many activities and games by wearing flimsy or insecure shoes, or dresses which may easily be torn, and fear of hurt or disapproval is a powerful inhibitor of freedom of movement. The effect of this in limiting potential development is so strong that the school has a clear duty to prevent it. As parents should have been involved during policy making this should be readily accepted.

The curriculum

A serious policy on sex stereotyping will review every area of the curriculum, and make recommendations in the light of knowledge and understanding of how gender inequality can be taught or changed. There is evidence available about sexism in all curriculum areas; much of it is reviewed by Judith Whyte (1983). Other work by Clarricoates (1978 and 1980) Steedman (1982) and Whyld (1983) can be referred to for detailed accounts. The APU surveys (1980, 81 and 82) have shown sex differences in performance and attitude in English and Mathematics in eleven year olds, and the GIST (Girls into Science and Technology) project survey (1984) of eleven year olds' science knowledge shows the sex differentiation in knowledge areas concealed beneath similar overall scores for girls and boys. Work by Harding (1981) traces differences in identity development and attachment to the world in girls and boys and links this to differences in approach and attitude to science and craft design technology. All of these findings need to be taken into account in constructing a curriculum which will genuinely foster gender equality. A curriculum policy on equal opportunities must ask for each subject area, five questions, and review its materials, content and delivery in the light of the answers. We can examine the possibility of sex bias in one curriculum area as an example. Science is a key area to consider, not only because of the very marked sex differentiation in science choices later on, but also because of the current emphasis on the development of primary science. If primary science practice is developed without an awareness of gender differences, then it will do very little to change the patterns of involvement in science after compulsory schooling.

The first question to ask when examining the curriculum for gender bias is this: Do girls and boys bring, from outside of school, substantially different attitudes to, and expectations of, that curriculum area? In the case of science they certainly do, because of the effects of sex stereotyping on the encouragement of scientific curiosity by parents and other adults, and because of differences in the encouragement of reading interests. There are class and cultural differences in the patterns of sex differentiation here, but broadly speaking boys very early on have a more positive attitude to what are later defined as physical sciences, and girls to biological sciences. How is that knowledge to be used in a science programme?

How can approaches be found which give girls a way of connecting with technology and boys of seeing the abstract science within biology? For while the divisions into types of science are not apparent to primary children, recognition that topics don't appeal to them in the same way certainly is.

The second question to ask follows on from the first: Do girls and boys come to the work of a given curriculum area with substantially different previous experience of it? While every child's previous experience of a subject will be different, broad sex differences are also likely. In our science example, if we include technology, then there will certainly be broad sex differences in tool use and materials handling from out of school experience. Immediately because of this there is not equal access to that part of the curriculum. So a school policy must consider remedies for this, perhaps by running familiarisation sessions for those pupils who need them (who may of course include some pupils of the other sex from the one broadly disadvantaged). Play experience will also have given girls and boys different amounts of previous contact with materials which develop scientific concepts, and a policy needs to include recommendations for monitoring early play, and developing children's experience in the areas they spend least time in.

A third question to ask is whether, once experiencing a subject in school, children develop different attitudes to it because of its content. In the case of science this will depend very much on the choice and presentation of topics. The study of flight which gives Amy Johnson as much prominence as Lindberg, and does not present her as eccentric or abnormal, and which looks at the human advantages of air travel as well as the mechanics of it, will interest girls and boys. It must be clear that there is a place for girls in the future study of a subject if they are to develop a real affinity for it, and therefore showing women's contribution to any science topic is very important. Books which show either only men and boys carrying out experiments, or show girls helping or looking on, or where there are about five pictures of boys and men engaged in serious activities for every one women, significantly depress girls' ability to relate to the content. Where resources can only be gradually changed, a school policy needs to consider ways of dealing with bias in materials, by making it part of the children's awareness for example.

Consideration of the effect of content on sex differentiation leads to the fourth question: do girls and boys also develop different attitudes to a curriculum area because of the teacher's behaviour, either through making assumptions about interest or competence based on stereotypes, or through using teaching methods which are biased? There is ample evidence from secondary schools that this is precisely what happens in many science lessons, where girls are helped in the use of apparatus while boys are questioned about the process and left to make changes for themselves. What happens when someone is reluctant to handle 'minibeasts', or when the bulb in the circuit won't light up? Girls and boys must be treated identically at this point. The phenomenon in girls and women known as 'learned helplessness' is easily developed. There is also ample evidence that boys and girls have different preferences for types of writing (APU), and that in later years, girls on average perform better in essay questions while boys do better in multiple choice (Harding). These findings have implications for task setting: science topics should be written about using the full range of registers, and incorporated in narrative and imaginative work, as has of course long been advocated by those concerned with language across the curriculum, but is still too seldom found. Boys can benefit from the opportunity to develop writing skills while girls can incorporate scientific concepts into their internal worlds through fiction writing.

The final question is the most important of all in coming back to the central problem of sex differentiation, that of unequal value. Do girls and boys develop a different perception of their own worth and competence through curriculum content or teaching methods? The monitoring of patterns of interaction is a first step towards answering this question. Where boys are allowed to interrupt girls, where boys are praised, or named, or chosen, more often than girls, unequal valuing is taking place. Where boys are told off for things girls would be allowed to do, because of fear of escalation in boys' behaviour, unequal treatment is being handed out. A group of articulate, well motivated girls in a class can together be a strong influence on interaction in a room and in every school such groups occur. But the prevailing pattern to be found is of boys dominating in classrooms, perhaps because the organisation has not sufficiently allowed for their needs. Whatever the cause, the message is clear: boys are more important than girls. While both sexes believe that, little else will change.

Making an effective policy

There are several important issues to be faced when making a policy to combat sex stereotyping in schools. The first is that there will not necessarily be initial staff support for such a policy, the second is that to be effective it will require a great deal of work, the third is that it will need considerable resources, and the fourth is that it will, because of the first three points, need to be put into effect over a fairly long period of time. Fifthly, like all school policies, it will require monitoring, evaluation and review, to see whether it is being fully implemented, and whether it meets its own aims.

A lot of ground work needs to be done by a headteacher or whichever member of staff wants a school to take gender equality seriously, and to propose a school policy is not the best place to start. Sexism is an area which attracts so many jokes, and such a bad press, that it can be dealt with trivially and meaninglessly if a school is asked, cold, to write a policy statement.

Gender, like race, is an area where people have deeply held personal views which colour their professional behaviour in a way that has considerable implications for the ways in which the topic is dealt with. Teachers can easily feel very vulnerable and threatened if they perceive criticism of their own life style, or of past practice which they have genuinely if mistakenly believed to be fair. To avoid a trivialising reaction, or a passing of responsibility very smartly on to everyone else – parents and the media being the main scapegoats – the head must show s/he takes the issue completely seriously, and that everyone will be involved in learning more about it in a systematic way until they know enough to have an informed opinion and can cooperatively make a policy. At least one member of staff, and preferably several, need to be very well informed about gender, and a first step should be to identify those most likely to develop such an interest, and encourage it. Local Authority and national inservice training should be demanded if not already available, basic reading identified and contacts made with other schools engaged on the same task.

Several casual references to findings about the effects of sex stereotyping, or discussions of items in the education press, or reports back from people who have been on courses, will make the issue familiar before it is formally introduced. Then a period of time will be needed for everyone to become better informed and more aware of the evidence of discrimination in their own school. It is a common reaction for teachers to acknowledge evidence from other schools but deny that it is relevant to their own. Rudduck and May's (1983) account of teacher investigations in Norfolk first and middle schools usefully indicates how evidence affects attitudes when the evidence is first hand. Teachers can be encouraged to carry out small scale investigations in their own classrooms and to share the findings. An outside consultant can be valuable in helping teachers to make links between evidence and theory, and between practice and effect. Some Local Education Authorities have effectively used small scale action research to promote equal opportunities in schools, providing adviser consultancy, and it is a model for school development clearly described in the GRIDS (Guidelines for Review and Internal Development in Schools) primary school handbook (McMahon et al, 1984).

All the evidence that is available suggests that parents of all ethnic groups and faith communities have similarly high expectations of the educational achievement of their children. It is also the case that there is within many families much greater acceptance of cross-gender role activities than is publicly acknowledged, or is reflected in the books read by children. The Newsons' (1968) study showed that Nottingham mothers taught their boys in particular to conform to 'masculine' norms in front of the neighbours. My own extensive experience of talking with groups of parents in an inner city area suggests that the great majority of parents want equal opportunities and support schools when the reasons for change are fully and properly explained. While teachers are becoming more aware, it is important to involve governors and parents in the equal opportunities debate. It is clear that the school must share with parents and its community a commitment to gender equality, and to changes that will bring it about, if it is not to be misunderstood or seen as undermining community values. It must be clear that educational achievement, not the imposition of specifically Western cultural values is the desired outcome. Many Western cultural practices in fact militate particularly strongly against girls' academic achievement.

When a suitable amount of preparation has been done, then a policy can be formulated, and targets set for its implementation. Many schools choose to set short term targets for organisational changes, such as alphabetical lists and registers, while also working towards medium and long term targets in resource development, analysis of book stock and curriculum review. It is important to add that pupils must be properly prepared for changes, or they may react with behaviour that seems to justify the original situation. Making all pupils in a class work in mixed pairs out of the blue will not increase co-operation between the sexes. One headteacher, new to a school – with separate playgrounds for girls and boys, first discussed the issue with teaching and non-teaching staff, allocated some thinking time, had further discussion, then fixed a date for the change. She used assemblies on play, safety and co-operation to prepare the children and arranged that each class should do some work with their teacher, for her, on co-operative play in the week the change took place, culminating in displays around the school. In that way, she ensured that her decision was not undermined within classrooms by those teachers who did not fully support it, as well as enabling the children to work through some of their ideas about coeducation and fairness.

Realistically, to review the entire curriculum in the light of gender equality objectives will take a very long time, and it is best done as part of a regular review of curriculum guidelines. It may be necessary to prioritise certain areas, or to delegate responsibility to examining each area to small groups of teachers, or to ask the postholders to report to a staff meeting about gender implications in each area. Development of all new work should of course take account of gender differences, as should the selection of all new materials. There needs to be a commitment of capitation over a period of years for the specific building up of a range of fiction that provides models of children and adults in non-stereotyped roles.

It is valuable as part of the policy making process to determine outcomes in terms of changes in children's behaviour, attitudes, skills and knowledge which can be monitored so that the policy can be evaluated. It is unrealistic to expect too much change too fast, because the side effects of gender role acquisition in terms of narrowing of individual development are so well embedded in all of us. However, increases in knowledge about what women can do, or have done, changes in expectation of girls' strength improved use of co-operative discussion techniques from boys, fewer interruptions, fairer use of questioning and allocation of praise, can all be measured. Teachers' record books should show how gender is being taken into account in daily work; interviews for new members of staff can ascertain attitudes to gender equality, and learning about the gender policy should be part of any new teacher's induction to the school. Regular reports to the governing body can be used as a public forum for information about progress. As a policy is formed and takes effect, so new issues will emerge which no one thought of before. The regular review of the policy will ensure that these are incorporated into revision and the development of everyone's practice.

A policy for combatting sex stereotyping is undoubtedly demanding to prepare and implement. It is, however, because of the enthusiasm generated among teachers who become involved in looking closely at sex differences in their classrooms, a potent motivator of the development of curriculum review and good practice. The more its need is accepted, the nearer our society will get to meaning what it says when claiming to believe in the equality of the sexes.

References

APU (1980), *First Primary Mathematics Survey*, HMSO
APU (1981a), *First Primary Language Survey*, HMSO
APU (1981b), *Second Primary Mathematics Survey*, HMSO

APU (1982), *Second Primary Language Survey*, HMSO

Brent Primary Gender Equality Working Party (1985), *Steps to Equality*, London Borough of Brent Education Department.

Clarricoates, K (1978), 'Dinosaurs in the Classroom', in *Women's Studies International Quarterly*, Vol 1, No 4.

Clarricoats, K (1980), 'The Importance of being Ernest . . . Emma . . . ', in Deem, R (Ed) *Schooling for Women's Work*, RKP

Delamont, S (1980), *Sex Roles and the School*, Methuen.

GIST (1984), *Girls into Science and Technology: Final Report*, Manchester Poly.

Harding, J (1981), 'Sex Differences in Science Examination', in Kelly, A (Ed) *The Missing Half*, Manchester University Press.

Hodgeon, J (1983), *Report of Nursery Observation Study*, Cleveland Education Department.

Huws, U (1982), *Your Job in the Eighties*, Pluto.

McMahon, A Bolam, R, Abbott, R and Holly, P (1984), *Guidelines for Review and Internal Development in Schools: Primary School Handbook*, Longman/Schools Council.

Newson, J and Newson, E (1968), *Four Years Old in an Urban Community*, Allen and Unwin.

Oakley, A (1972), *Sex, Gender and Society*, Temple Smith.

Pratt, Bloomfield and Searle (1984), *Option Choice: A Question of Equal Opportunity*, NFER/Nelson.

Rudduck, J and May, N (1983), *Sex Stereotyping in the Early Years of Schooling*, University of East Anglia.

Steedman, C (1982), *The Tidy House*, Virago.

Whyld, J (Ed) (1983), *Sexism in the Secondary Curriculum*, Harper and Row.

Whyte, J (1983),*Beyond the Wendy House*, Longman/Schools Council.

12 A multicultural policy for all primary schools

Rick Collet

The publication in 1985 of the Swann Committee Report (DES, 1985) turned out for many authorities and schools to be a significant milestone on the route to multicultural education. There are flaws and inconsistencies in its 800 pages, but, because of these imperfections (not in spite of them), it provides a useful state of the art description for many of us of a concept which is still emerging, surrounded, like most new educational concepts, by its share of controversy, apathy, and misunderstanding.

Perhaps the most striking feature of the progress being made is embodied in the Report's title *Education for All*: here was a Committee, established in 1979, to enquire into the education of children from ethnic minority groups, which after six years' deliberation and gestation, came out with an unambiguous statement of the central validity of preparing all children for life in a multicultural society. The key steps in Swann's argument are as follows:

1 The fundamental change that is necessary is the recognition that the problem facing the education system is not how to educate children of ethnic minorities, but how to educate *all* children.
2 Britain is a multiracial and multicultural society and all pupils must be enabled to understand what this means.
3 This challenge cannot be left to the separate and independent initiatives of LEAs and schools: only those with experience of substantial numbers of ethnic minority pupils have attempted to tackle it, though the issue affects all schools and all pupils.
4 Education has to be something more than the reinforcement of the beliefs, values and identity which each child brings to school.

5 It is necessary to combat racism, to attack inherited myths and stereotypes, and the ways in which they are embodied in institutional practices.
6 Multicultural understanding has also to permeate all aspects of a school's work. It is not a separate topic that can be welded on to existing practices.
7 Only in this way can schools begin to offer anything approaching the equality of opportunity for all pupils which it must be the aspiration of theeducation system to provide.

Here possibly is a ready-made agenda for an initial staffroom discussion. Firstly, do we agree? If not, can we spell out the alternative philosophy it is proposed to follow: eg, 'it is *not* necessary to combat racism . . . ' etc. Secondly, to what extent are we already implementing this agenda, and how can we go further? What might our school look like and feel like if we finally arrived?

We could turn for reference to see how some schools that have become multiracial in recent years have responded to a visible ethnic minority presence: how this has often forced the staff to re-think basic principles, about the nature of the school, its responsibilities as transmitter of culture(s), appropriate professional development, relationships with homes and parents and so on. Good practice is being documented (eg Twitchin and Demuth, 1985) from which all schools can draw some constructive lessons, and learning resources which have been devised for multiracial areas are of a quality to stand on their own merit in mainstream libraries (Klein, 1986). A computerised data base is now available which provides access to information on multicultural education materials produced by small-scale community publishers and local authority centres around the country (AIMER).

Still, the majority of schools are basically 'all white', and there is, as Swann documented, a disturbing tendency for those schools to cry 'we have no problems here' when asked about their attitudes to multicultural education. The first essential point to recognise about 'multicultural education' is that, in its fullest realisation, it is totally synonymous with good educational practice in general. So a multiracial school doing its best by its black pupils would equally be giving its white children the best possible education. Conversely, an all-white school, providing a sound education for all, will inevitably be 'doing' multicultural education, whether explicitly or not. For a sound education is one that is up to date and gives the pupils the knowledge and skills to function in contemporary society. Since that society is pluralist, a good education must, by definition, reflect and utilise cultural diversity. Failure to include a broad pluralist perspective constitutes, in Swann's terms, a 'fundamental miseducation'.

This is recognised and affirmed within the Education Reform Act

1988: paragraph 17 of DES Circular 5/89 on the School Curriculum and Assessment is unequivocal:

> 'It is intended that the curriculum should reflect the culturally diverse society to which pupils belong and of which they will become adult members. The requirements apply to *all* pupils – regardless of age – registered at *all* schools, including grant-maintained schools.'

Section 1 of the 1988 Act in fact extends the central purposes of the curriculum to emphasise the promotion of pupils 'cultural development and the development of society.' Such a perspective involves the sharing of cultures within a national identity, rather than 'teaching culture' or 'cultural preservation'. Details of content are less important than the reorientation of attitudes and objectives which determine curriculum selection and inform teaching processes and learning experiences.

'Sound educational principles' will include staff development policies, without which it is impossible to assimilate Swann's notion that 'multicultural understanding has to permeate all aspects of a school's work.' As Jon Nixon (1985) explains:

> Permeation becomes a cyclical process. Small-scale innovations create the need for a coordinated policy, the development of which requires consultation with a wide range of agencies and interested parties. This round of consultation and informal evaluation in turn creates the impetus for renewed innovations at the classroom level, thereby triggering the process once more. Conceived in these terms permeation as a whole school strategy takes a great deal of time and patience to develop. For it relies upon the willingness of teachers to modify, not only their practice, but also their attitudes and assumptions. The task of changing perceptions is central to the permeation process.

Where conditions for this process exist in a school, what might we observe as elements of good multicultural practice?

Let me take, as an example, what I shall call Cygnet Junior School. It is a decent 1950s building in a neat urban setting, sharing a site with the feeder Infants' School. About half of the school's 300 children come from Council housing, the remainder from private housing. Ethnically, the school is predominantly Southern British-English, with fifteen pupils of New Commonwealth origin, and eight of other European origin.

However, within this virtually monoracial school, there is a successful ethos of multicultural education, to the extent that, if through a trick of demography, the catchment area were to turn multiracial overnight, the systems and philosophy of the school would not need radical restructuring: it is already providing an appropriate education for all. And the school's experience in attending to the individual needs of all the children, would ensure that any special provision, such as English language tuition, was conducted on a sound educational base. As Swann points out, the best place for pupils to learn the language of study and academic opportunity is in the classroom, not withdrawn in the corridor, but this needs understanding by all teachers of the role of language in education. The starting point here for the teacher-pupil interaction is always an acknowledgement of what the child *can* do, rather than a checklist of failures and deficits. This educational ethos for all children ensures that a pupil for whom English is a second language will be received into the school initially with efforts made by the staff to ensure that the first language, the mother tongue, is recognised and celebrated and appreciated by peers and only then to move to an analysis of underachievement in a particular area and assistance.

This positive ethos has been endorsed by the Kingman Report on English Teaching (HMSO 1988): 'It should be the duty of all teachers to instil in their pupils a civilised respect for other languages and an understanding of the relations between other languages and English. It should be made clear to English-speaking pupils that classmates whose first language is Bengali or Cantonese or any other of the scores of languages spoken by the school population . . . have languages quite as systematic and rule-governed as their own.'

Such a school is an enabling rather than disabling environment. There is no way that pupils can be expected to acquire the necessary understanding and respect for each other's personalities and cultures without first having a base of individual self-awareness and self-respect, and having this reflected in the pupil-teacher relationship. Equally, unless we have an appreciation of our own and our peers' skills and talents, we lack the conditions for collaborative learning, for problem-solving activities and negotiation, for experiencing successful participation in a shared activity: another essential aspect of preparation for life in the wider society.

At Cygnet Junior, there is a coherence in the curriculum, evolving through collaboration with the Infants' School, to ensure continuity of approach. The head has taken care to appoint on to the staff a teacher with Infant experience and training as well as a teacher with a Secondary background, to ensure this continuity, and to maintain credible liaison systems. It is sad how much of the average pupil's school life is spent by teachers disparaging what has been done in the previous phase or even the previous class. It is encouraging, therefore, that the National Curriculum 'provides the basis for genuine continuity both within and between schools through a clearly defined common framework of attainment targets, levels of attainment and programmes of study' (NCC 1989). This should help to eliminate the demotivating effects of this part of the so-called 'hidden' curriculum, which is, of course not hidden from pupils at all. The integrity of the child's school career will suffer if there is no evident integration between the various components, and disillusionment and cynicism about the system soon result. Faced with incoherence, disjointedness and unfairness, Black pupils and some working class children often more readily express disaffection and resentment than some middle class children, acculturated not to make a fuss, but the latter feel the hurt no less. If we genuinely believe that education is a three-way partnership between pupils, teachers and parents, then we must work hard to ensure that the partnership systems within our part of the triad are setting a good example. At Cygnet, there are joint staff discussions with both the Infants and the Secondary schools. The school's aims and objectives are explicit, realistic, and dynamic, not immutable. Policies are evaluated with parents and governors, so that each partner knows what to expect and what is expected of them.

At Cygnet, the pupils are led to be responsible participants in their own education. With regard to 'basic skills', each child has a regularly updated graph of personal strengths and weaknesses, based on diagnostic assessments. A pupil can see that her reading skills are developing well, for example, but this term needs to concentrate on some element of mathematics, say, or graphic work. Peers, parents and the teachers can then be drawn upon for assistance in self-motivated, independent learning programmes, which, by encouraging experimentation in a range of techniques, let the pupils learn about their own learning. The knowledge and skills base thus acquired is important in itself, but more significant is the awareness of one's capabilities, a gift that develops the potential to continue learning in adult life.

Recently, Cygnet pupils worked on a language project, an integrated whole-school activity, with appropriate tasks and goals for each year group. Examples of languages were collected and analysed, ordinary homes, as usual, providing quite extraordinary resources. As usual, too, a cluster of parents and grandparents became fascinated as well and brought in, with the same degree of involvement as the children, stamps and coins and other regalia. An English boy proudly found a Punjabi newspaper in the local shop, but needed his Asian classmate to get some value from it. Swahili and Chinese appeared, and stimulated exploratory groups, while another group patiently transliterated the names in the register into the Cyrillic alphabet. Folk tale and song blossomed beside computer languages, and the Domesday Project incorporated a survey of all the language competence locally, including those learned at school and for casual interest. An assembly on the Wordhouse (Fisher and Hicks, 1985) vividly illustrated the give and take of English and other world languages, and this underlying concept of inter-relationship and inter-dependence was not lost on the pupils. They had had another opportunity to see the world from someone else's point of view, surely a key component of a sound education. They had experienced again the concept that difference is not to be equated with deficit: that other systems have validity besides our own, and that our familiar language, culture and lifestyle should not be perceived as norms from which all others are inferior deviations.

There had been extended opportunity for practice in basic skills, for information and study skills, for disciplines such as geography, history and (with all the imported foodstuff packaging) home economics. Underpinning this – or perhaps 'permeating' it – is the school's philosophy on multicultural education being put into practice. It is modest, but clear and uncluttered.

To develop in every child a critical understanding and respect, both of their own cultural background and the cultural background of their neighbours, so that:

- children may be helped to make sense of themselves with particular reference to the culture of which they are part;
- children may be helped to decide what kind of person they wish to grow into;
- children are better equipped to become responsible members of their community, respectful of the views and cultural backgrounds of their neighbours.

This statement, which needs to be read alongside allied statements on moral education, religious education, and other areas of experience, has been formulated and negotiated by the staff together. It is accessible to parents, governors, to the pupils themselves, and the schools connected with Cygnet. The process of permeation, described by Nixon, is constantly in train.

The activities described above in the thumb-nail sketch of the languages project are, of course, replicated each term in countless primary schools up and down the country. What perhaps makes schools like Cygnet rather special is the 'accountability' element, the fact that each staff member can articulate what they are doing – and why. The philosophical and policy base set the context for the practical activities and their conduct and evaluation feed insights back into the policy, cyclically.

No one plods on till the holidays with an exhausted topic, nobody begins the task of finding a theme for next term by dusting down the resources cupboard, noone advances that frequently heard, but least educational, argument: 'we've always done it this way'. Some school activities, methods, assemblies, systems were designed for other times and other people, possibly with a desire to turn out white, male, middle-class, Christian replicas of ourselves and our cultural totems. Perpetuating this immediately disadvantages a large proportion of all our pupils, and obsolete systems, no longer appropriate or necessary, can be racist in outcome if they disadvantage and humiliate ethnic minority pupils, for example, in matters such as dress and diet, totally monocultural learning materials, arrangements for parents' evenings, and so on.

Our world, our society and our culture are changing fast, and teachers, if they are adequately providing for their pupils, must at least reflect this change, if not promote it. A fresh look at our practices and procedures may result in abandoning some irrelevant rituals, but not with the result that our pupils will be victims of turmoil and insecurity, because proper policies will be there to maintain stability, coherence and a steady goal.

The pupils at Cygnet Junior are being equipped to cope with change and its implications, through a key component of their curriculum – 'Education for a Developing World'. The starting point of the policy statement is the overall aim:

> to encourage and develop social awareness and responsibility so that children are led to an understanding that we live in a complex and interdependent world.

There follows a list of objectives in terms of attitudes:

1 The development of an interest in events and situations which will lead to questions about causes – not only HOW? and WHY? but WHAT?, WHERE? and WHEN?
2 The development of a sense of empathy, that is, a capacity to imagine what it is like to be in someone else's position.
3 A growing respect for the ideas, opinions and rights of other people.
4 A concern and respect for the evidence of others and for the experience which others have had.
5 An understanding of roles and responsibilities.

Then comes a set of objectives in terms of skills, including information-gathering, testing evidence, organising material with appropriate oral and written activities, exploring attitudes, values and opinions, working in groups, and so on.

The realisation of these objectives should lead the pupils to:

– a better understanding of themselves;
– a better understanding of and response to other people;
– a clearer understanding of their immediate community and the wider society of which they form part;
– an understanding of their ability to influence the direction of their personal development.

Five key questions are then posed for consideration:

Issues   What are the issues which affect people's lives?

Values   What sort of world do people want to live in?

Problems   What are the problems in the world today which prevent people living as they would like?

Background   What is the background to these issues and problems?

Action   What can be done and what is being done about them?

Through this consideration, three key concepts should emerge, those of interdependence, responsibility and change. Only when we have reminded ourselves of some of the pitfalls and prejudices (of both teacher and pupil) that may initially cloud discussion, do we start to examine some possible topics that will incorporate these concepts, skills and attitudes:

- My family – a starting point for consideration of how a society works;
- Local community – including 'My school as a Society';
- Waste; Celebrations; Work and Responsibilities: 'Who does what for whom?', etc.

After working through the project, the staff became concerned that this theme of Education for a Developing World might be becoming isolated from the curriculum and be too distant and issue-based, 'bringing the world into the classroom', rather than starting from the needs of the child. They are now working, through a 'whole-school' inservice activity, to re-cast the guideline document to ensure a projection outward from the individual and the immediate environment of child, home, school and community. A valuable contribution to the discussion is the teachers' handbook (Button 1989) which includes a section on how the national curriculum can be given a global dimension.

Placing the pupils as the central focus assists both their independence and interdependence which is exemplified in all sorts of ways within the school. Pupils know how to respect each other as human resources and that it is worth working together. Other adults, besides the classteacher, are regularly in the classroom and are drawn into the learning process. Assemblies, always open to parents, make little attempt to ape adult worship, but seek to celebrate the worth of some shared experience, some particular achievement within the school or community. A school council, of staff and pupils, and a school meeting, organised by the pupils themselves, debate and negotiate aspects of administration or facilities and maintain the school ethos. An understanding of the unacceptability of racial abuse, name-calling or graffiti starts here, not with an edict from above. The head 'makes' the school policy, not by promulgation, but by providing the conditions in which the policy will emerge from among the participants themselves. This corporate, participative, model of school policy is endorsed by the Elton Committee (DES 1989) when it recommends, for example, that:

'Headteachers and teachers should encourage the active participation of pupils in shaping and reviewing the school's behaviour policy in order to foster a sense of collective commitment to it' (R76). Additionally: 'Headteachers and staff should work to create a school climate which values all cultures, in particular those represented in it, through its academic and affective curricula' (R90).

But, of themselves, central government or local authority edicts can do little to change things for the better in a school. In a fascinating recent study, Troyna and Ball (1985) survey the attitudes to the issues in multicultural education among heads and teachers in an authority with a very positive and well-established policy document. The limited and partial impact of the policy in schools is due, they argue, to a failure by the Authority to consider the complex processes of curriculum innovation, and too great a reliance on the policy initiative alone to function as a change-agent.

Genuine progress only occurs when 'top-down' directives are matched by 'bottom-up' initiatives. Schools in one large shire county, for example, do appear to have moved ahead from the ostrich-like 'We have no problems here' cliché which the Swann Committee found so depressingly widespread in 1985. Kent carried out an extensive consultation exercise (KCC 1988) on its Curriculum Statement 5–16, a document which included sections on Equal Opportunities and Multicultural Education. There was a substantial response regarding multicultural issues from a wide variety of schools, including those with little cultural diversity. They recognised and underlined the importance of addressing multicultural issues in all schools, supported by INSET initiatives and resources. In this case, policy formulation seems to be proceeding step by step with the perceptions and ambitions of the grassroots professionals, a characteristic essential for genuine policy implementation (eg. NAHT 1987).

A useful analysis of the features affecting the failure and success of innovation within the school is provided by Robin Richardson (1985). Though written with reference to the implementation of the Swann Report in schools, his article repays close study, as the

conclusions are generalisable to all aspects of educational innovation and change.

Among the factors which indicate that a project is likely to fail
are: a lukewarm or negative attitude from the head; lack of understanding and discussion among the staff; a sense that the project
has been foisted on them from outside; lack of adequate knowledge
and skills base among the staff; a sense of threat, suspicion or
frustration; meagre material resources; a sense of low prestige for
the project among pupils and teachers and so on. On the credit
side, however, a project is likely to succeed if for example:

1 The head and senior staff are clearly seen to be committed both
formally, eg, in meetings and statements, and also informally, in everyday conversations.
2 The staff most involved in the project:

– feel that the project belongs to themselves, that it is home-grown;
– were involved from the start in diagnosing the problems to be solved,
and in pondering and deciding what should be done;
– have an excellent graps of aims and principles;
– clarify doubts, uncertainties and disagreements in discussion with each
other;
– agree on the meanings of basic key terms.

Richardson goes on to examine the factors outside the school
which affect failure and success of an initiative, including the LEA
stance, inservice support, parental and community interest,
additional resources, and so on.

There is an added complicating factor to innovation in multicultural education, subject as it is to tensions and pressures from within
itself and from outside, in that it is perceived as a controversial
issue. Thus, schools have a good excuse for inaction, for keeping
a low profile, for not getting involved. It is time that more all-
white schools began to address the issues with the same degree of
courage that many multiracial schools have shown in facing up to
their responsibilities. (Mulvaney, 1984).

If pupils raise concerns of injustice and inequality that they perceive, it must be educationally valid to follow them through, despite
possible grousing from the armchair critics about 'political' education. The head of Cygnet was approached by a group of pupils
who were disturbed that the local council appeared to have broken
its promises with regard to a development on a neighbouring site
that they had come to know and care about. The (perhaps conventional?) response of ordering them back to the classroom to get on
with their work would not have been counted as 'political': it might
be authoritarian, arbitrary, colluding with injustice, but not political!

In fact, the head sat down with them, and channelled their anxiety

into the task of researching and documenting the evidence, identifying the appropriate officer, and preparing and arranging a depu-
tation to present their point of view. This 'political' project turned
out, in fact, to be a memorable and beneficial learning experience,
probably because it was so fuelled by the interests of the children
themselves. They also, incidentally, made a successful case.

The ability to accept and foster this independence of mind, this
articulation of concern for justice and responsibility (whether the
subsequent Secondary schools like it or not) is important in current
debates within multicultural education. It is relatively easy for a
school, whether all-white or multiracial, to bring in some colourful
aspect of other cultures or countries: an assembly on a festival like
Chinese New Year, a wall-display, an international evening, the
type of activities sometimes known as the three 'S's' – samosas,
saris and steelbands. Because it is easy, it can be merely exotic and
superficial, 'tokenist'. The story is told of a multiracial school where
a group of white parents came to complain about their children's
involvement in Diwali celebrations; sensing prejudice, the teachers
remonstrated with them. 'Nothing wrong with Diwali' replied the
parents, 'only why have you used the same theme and the same
materials for the last five years? Is there nothing else from India
our kids could do?'

Tinkering with pretty aspects of other cultures and countries
does not constitute adequate preparation for children for multiracial
Britain, although it may be the first, necessary, stage of opening up
the issues (Grinter, 1985). There must be facilities for moving on
to, or incorporating, what has become known as an anti-racist
approach, one that helps pupils identify and challenge the structural
and institutional injustices and inequalities in the community, the
society, the world economy, and so on. This would develop a
critical awareness, not just in issues of race, but of gender and class,
accent and dialect, difference and prejudice in general.

Clearly, the school itself must provide a foundation of genuine
equality of opportunity: at Cygnet every effort is made to avoid
reinforcing unhelpful stereotyping, such as in differential opportunities between the sexes in games, crafts, dance, and in roles
within the classroom. Textbook and library materials are scrutinised,
not by one decision-maker doing good, but by the collective efforts
of staff, parents and pupils, with the opinions and sensitivities of
black parents particularly sought. A group reading project is organised around a theme, using a variety of sources; differing opinions,
conflicting facts emerge: which is right, which is valid, which is
obviously biased? Practice in the ability to appraise and evaluate
sources of information, images, the media, hidden messages, is an

essential contribution to the young person's intellectual equipment and can be developed in any school in the land.

I began with the question of how we might recognise multicultural education in an all-white school and have taken examples from a school where I have often had the opportunity to observe what I take to be multicultural education in action. This, of course, is a particular example of a marriage of theory and practice, and is not being proposed as a normative model to be replicated. It happens to work, within its own 'ecology' of staff, pupils and the community, with their particular qualities and relationships.

What I have tried to demonstrate is that our newly-articulated statutory commitment to multicultural education has nothing to do with abandoning the core of good practice for the sake of some exotic marginalia. Cygnet's curriculum has all the necessary features of breadth and balance, differentiation and relevance. It starts where the pupils are, but sets clear goals, and seeks to assist all to achieve their potential. Without compromising this, it also manages actively to promote the skills, attitudes and concepts related to responsibility, interdependence and change.

The school prepares its pupils appropriately for society, because it is in some respects a scaled-down model of that society.

The curriculum of the school maintains the integrity of subject areas within an integrated project framework; the ethos of the school fosters the worth and self-awareness of each child within a corporate community. This reflects the view of society that acknowledges the access of ethnic minorities to social integration within an expanding common core of values, rights and duties, while preserving their integrity in terms of cultural, background and lifestyles.

A sense that the school is designed for the pupils, not for the convenience of the administration, encourages a view of a society that is for its people, whatever their similarities or differences, where good relations are built not merely upon the concessions of tolerance and goodwill but on articulated standards of justice and equality.

A school community where accountability and involvement are paramount posits a world which is explicable and negotiable, not governed by dogma and prejudice.

Idealistic, possibly; but education without ideals reduces to the level of the conveyor-belt. As Robin Richardson further observes in his article: 'a map without utopia on it, it has been said, is not worth consulting. Admittedly, there are disadvantages, in dreams and ideals, the disadvantages of unreality and abstractions. But frequently, also it clears and strengthens your mind if you venture to dream for a while, as concretely and practically as possible, about the ideal situation to which all your current efforts are, you hope, directed. It may be very valuable, for example, in the present context of a school's planned response to the Swann Report, if head teachers and teachers write brief descriptions of what they hope their school will ideally be like in about ten years' time, and if they then compare and contrast these ideals in discussion with each other.'

Discussion, the interplay of ideas, is paramount. Given a pyramid diagram of power relationships, one would expect to place policy-making at the top, and the implementation of practice at the base. A genuinely effective policy in multicultural education or education in general, does not remain 'on high', but has to be absorbed by the intended beneficiaries of the policy, in this case, the very pupils themselves. Reciprocally, good practice – features like collaborative learning, empathy, ability to handle evidence and controversy and so on – has to permeate back to the top, to the policy-makers. As Chris Mullard (1984) succinctly observes, theory without action is sterile, and action without theory is futile. The success of a policy for multicultural education will be judged neither on the elegance of its phraseology or its exhaustiveness, nor on the colourfulness of the classroom displays, but on its outcomes in terms of equipping each and every future citizen appropriately and adequately for life together in a pluralist society in an interdependent world.

References

AIMER (Access to Information on Multicultural Education Resources). Details from: AIMER, University of Reading, Bulmershe Court, Earley, Reading RG6 1HY.

Button, J (1989), *The Primary School in a Changing World*, Centre for World Development Education.

DES (1985), *Education for All (The Swann Report)*, HMSO.

DES (1989), *Discipline in Schools (The Elton Report)*, HMSO.

Fisher, S and Hicks, D (1985), *World Studies 8–13: A Teacher's Handbook* Oliver and Boyd.

Grinter, R (1985), 'Bridging the Gulf: The Need for Anti-Racist Multicultural Education', in *Multicultural Teaching*, Vol 3, No 2.

HMSO (1988), *Report of the Committee of Inquiry into the Teaching of English Language (The Kingman Report)*

KCC (1988) *An Education for Life: Curriculum Statement 5–16*, Kent County Council.

Klein, G (1986), 'The Best of British', in *Multicultural Teaching*, Vol 4, No 2.

Mullard, C (1984), *The Three O's*, National Association for Multiracial Education.

Mulvaney, M (1984), 'Multicultural Education in the Primary School', in

Straker-Welds (Ed) *Education for a Multicultural Society: Case Studies in ILEA Schools*, Bell and Hyman.

NAHT (1987), *A Model School Based Anti-Racist Policy* National Association of Head Teachers.

NCC (1989), *Circular Number 3: Implementing the National Curriculum in Primary Schools*, National Curriculum Council.

Nixon, J (1985), *A Teacher's Guide to Multicultural Education*, Blackwell.

Richardson, R (1985), 'Each and Every School: Responding, Reviewing, Planning and Doing', in *Multicultural Teaching*, Vol 3, No 2.

Troyna, B and Ball, W (1985), *Views from the Chalkface: School Responses to an LEAs Policy on Multicultural Education*, Centre for Research in Ethnic Relations, University of Warwick.

Twitchin, J and Demuth, C (1985), *Multicultural Education: Views from the Classroom*, BBC.

13 Discipline: ideas from Britain and abroad

John Pease

At present, in the vast majority of State schools there are good to acceptable levels of discipline. It is the exception that makes the news which is then stretched for the maximum advantage of journalists with a pecuniary interest in the headline and of politicians in search of a public image.

Pupils and teachers also need each other since both are forced by circumstances to be members of the same communities – pupils by law and teachers to earn a living. For many teachers their own training leaves them with qualifications of little value elsewhere; and so their bonds are just as binding.

At the lowest level, both pupils and teachers have a vested interest in making life as interesting and bearable as possible – and to this end there must be the give and take without which no society can survive.

With the passing of authoritarianism the alternative has been to aim for an atmosphere relaxed and devoid of tension; and it is the degree to which this is attained that establishes the 'tone' of a school.

However, the achieving of good standards is by no means entirely in the hands of the teachers.

Schools are shaped by the societies they serve – but everywhere is uncertainty and turmoil. Traditional ways – including those of maintaining order and respect are undergoing drastic change. Chesterton said that tradition was the democracy of the dead; and this applies to much of the traditional ways of maintaining discipline: simple, easy to understand and cheap, with children obeying or children being punished. This includes physical punishment. In my LEA, until September 1985, headteachers were advised that 'Reasonable corporal punishment may be administered by the headteacher or another teacher authorised by him.' In a survey of the County schools it was most interesting that the vast majority of the governing bodies wanted this right kept. This was put down by one elected member on the Education Committee as indicating that governors were simply following the dictates of headteachers. It never seemed to occur to him that many governors were present or past parents. Short of canvassing direct they were the nearest thing to a parent poll.

A change in County policy banning corporal punishment from September 1985 was mainly hypothetical. The vast majority of schools never knew the use of the cane. Some of the longest serving headteachers had never owned such a weapon. They were lucky to have had a choice. Times had changed since Frederick Stone said in 1931 – just before he died at the age of 83 – that the job he hated most as Officer of the Watch in The Royal Navy, was having to flog the midshipmen for inattention.

In Britain the State Educational system survived for many years having corporal punishment; but with inbuilt safeguards against the wilful abuse of children: this being the approval or disapproval of governors; the support or alienation of the staff and above all the reaction of parents and pupils. Possibly the greatest safeguard was the fact that headteachers were promoted from the ranks. They were not outside administrators having little in common with the teaching staff and limited knowledge and experience of discipline within the classroom. Headteachers had to establish their attitudes towards discipline while class teachers and deputies – and these attitudes were well known before their appointments. All in all, we still have a system which works well and is possibly unique.

During the thirty odd years I have been in teaching – to me the major change has been the attitude of teachers towards children. In my first post a Senior Master summoned me to his classroom for a lesson in 'how to maintain discipline.' There were over fifty 15-year olds seated in rows from wall to wall. He called out names rapidly and threw books across the room. Two boys were summoned and the first duly caned. The Senior Master stood in front of the second – a large, black-haired youth in shabby hand-me-downs. 'You . . . are . . . filthy.' He spoke slowly and for the benefit of the class. 'Look at you!' he sneered. 'You're dirty . . . you didn't wash this morning, did you? Your neck is black . . . Do you ever clean your teeth? . . . They're yellow!' 'The secret is to get them off balance,' he confided.

It was the generation of teachers returning from the 1939–1945 war who changed all that; and pioneered a relaxation of atmosphere where respect, liking and humour could replace sarcasm. It meant that pupil and teacher would get to know each other as individuals.

The second major change stemmed mainly out of the Primary sector where teachers removed competition as expressed in class positions and tried to make it a personal affair much like a runner measures the effect of his own training programme. It was to the teachers' eternal credit since it involved much thought and preparation to teach narrower ranges of ability than classes as a whole. The third major move by the teachers was to create parent interviews and seek shared solutions to educational and behavioural problems.

It was Mr Justice Coburn who ruled in 1865 that a parent, by placing a child into the custody of a teacher, delegated to that teacher all of the parent's authority as far as it was necessary for the welfare of the child. This seems to have no counterpart elsewhere.

In France there is an entirely different concept: teachers are not even expected to remain on school premises when they are not teaching. They are there to impart knowledge and then go home. Teachers, by tradition, are not responsible for discipline and this is delegated first to *surveillants* (often students earning money to support themselves through university) and second to an official disciplinary committee. This is served with outside help and run by the school administrator.

As far as the French are concerned present problems with school indiscipline are largely of their own making. About 1968 France underwent a revolution against the old imposed methods of keeping law and order within schools. There was an awakening, liberalised society which resented external authority and demanded 'self-discipline' as a proper right. In some areas this has been a disaster with widespread breakdown in discipline: mugging, destruction, graffiti and extortion becoming common. Absenteeism developed on a massive scale. The general atmosphere even in primary schools became one of inattention and continual noise.

In the USA, as in France, headteachers are unknown and administrators have the day to day running of the schools. The disciplining of the children is largely in the hands of the 'Developmental Counsellors'. These are ancillary workers following the theories of well known child psychologists: the 'Logical Consequence Theory' where long periods are spent trying to get a disruptive child to see that by being naughty the class as a whole is prevented from operating: and trying to get the offender either to conform or go into 'time out' voluntarily ie self-exclude. Another fashion is the 'Reality Theory': What were you doing? (not anyone else involved)

Were your actions good or bad? What are you – the child – going to do to put it right? It all takes time and staffing resources – especially as these helpers are within each school.

Yet again we see a society struggling to solve the problems of indiscipline – where, at its worst, *surveillants* have become patrolmen carrying guns.

With the abolition of corporal punishment as a sanction against indiscipline the all important question is whether ways that are left can cope into the future. There are still many parents who doubt that they will. One example was a caring father who gave his small son a smack since it was the only way to stop him running into danger near a main road. He wonders how an infant teacher deals with a naughty child who is defiant, causes disruption and won't listen to reason. He views with concern that in 1989 there should be a campaign by those who would make it illegal in all circumstances for him to exercise judgement and to physically chastise.

Eternal vigilance to good practice is the price that has to be paid even to stand a chance: providing a relevant curriculum to minimise boredom; carefully matching the work to the pupil's ability either to prevent under achievement or unreasonable pressures which might lead to stress; marking carefully and being interested in the work produced; keeping adverse criticism to a minimum and being as encouraging as possible.

You don't talk about good behaviour – be an example. In Springfield Virginia, part of the assessment for all teachers is: showing respect to the pupils; considering what others are saying to be important by not interrupting; not sounding intolerant; taking an obvious interest in the welfare and safety of the pupils; taking responsibility for general behaviour round the school; handling sensitive matters in a caring and sensitive way and being positive in communicating.

What they are saying is that the teacher, being the adult, should make the positive moves.

If it is at all possible then turn a negative into a plus: one school had a litter problem despite long exhortations and clean-up parties as a punishment. Eventually a bright member of staff came up with the idea of buying pick-up tongs like they use in parks. Each class now takes responsibility for a week's clean-up and the children are chosen as a reward for effort. Litter is now largely a thing of the past.

You have to look for ways of giving children responsibilities and beware 'favourites'.

You must always think before you judge – listen to the other side and make every effort to be fair; and don't be afraid to apologise if you get it wrong.

If you are going to reprimand then wherever possible, do this in private – with the statement that you do not want to make it public to other teachers, pupils or if necessary parents. The reasons for privacy are not only to preserve the pupil's self-esteem but to avoid confrontation which might lead to defiance where the pupil feels it necessary to maintain a 'macho' image and perhaps cause amusement at your expense. I well remember the joy it caused me at school to watch a teacher chasing one of my friends in and out of the rows of desks while vainly thrashing the air with her cane. I know who had my admiration and respect. So keep your cool.

One of the commonest forms of sanction is to make children stay in. You must be sure of supervision – never leave a pupil in the class for a punishment while you go off for a coffee break.

Give detention to complete work by all means; but do beware of destroying work ethics and the interest in any subject by using it as a punishment: it would be extremely doubtful practice to make anyone write out the ten commandments fifty times.

If you are going to threaten a sanction – make sure first that you can deliver – and make sure that you always keep your word.

As long as you are being fair, just and reasonable – then you are in the right and deserve the support of the parents; senior staff within the school and above all your education officers representing the local authority.

Punishment can no longer be simplistic, punitive and just a deterrent. Where a pupil regularly misbehaves the aim should clearly be to try and discover the causes and not just be content with suppressing the symptoms. To this end all schools need a good pastoral system – the main aim of which should be preventative.

It is at this point that schools come under strain. Politicians are long on moralizing but short on providing either the staffing ratios allowing time for counselling or even sufficient facilities away from the mainstream schools so that disruptive pupils can be withdrawn for tuition and guidance. In many authorities sufficient money is not even made available to provide materials needed in order to resource more practical approaches for the less academically minded.

Looking into the psychological, social and emotional problems of a difficult pupil sounds such an obvious thing to do until you examine the logistics. A recent case conference in Slough involved the time and expertise of:

- 2 Welfare Officers.
- 1 Social worker
- 1 Educational Psychologist
- 1 Schools' Counsellor
- 1 Social Services Officer

- 1 Chairman of Governors
- 1 Headteacher
- 1 Deputy Headteacher
- 1 Youth Group Organiser.

There were also numerous visits to the parents. To find a day when all these busy people were available was an enormous task. The headteacher concerned remarked that organising D-day must have been less of a strain.

Teachers in the classroom carry the main strain of keeping discipline. It has never been the tradition to pass on problems readily for, in a way, they feel that they have lost face both with the children and senior staff.

From now on there will be an added incentive to conceal problems. However desirable it is for teachers to have the confidence to approach their heads for backing they know that real power is being invested more and more with the Governors. By April 1993 at the latest in Dyfed, for example, the Governors will control the budget in all schools with over 176 on roll – this being the smallest size school with a non-teaching head. Those who control the purse strings will also control the teachers they employ.

The Elton Report states quite clearly that:

'if there is no prospect of the teacher involved achieving an acceptable standard of competence in classroom management, we believe that governors should not hesitate to recommend dismissal'.

For sure there are recommendations of professional support and supplementary training for a teacher experiencing difficulty in maintaining discipline, and also that there should be consideration of transfer to another school. However teachers are well aware that professional support and training needs competent helpers and costs money, and there can exist no transfer as of right to another school.

People lose their jobs in many walks of life and many can take up similar employment elsewhere. For teachers dismissal will likely be final.

It is of utmost importance, therefore, to recruit in the first place those who are likely to stay the course.

Personality and character probably count more than just academic ability especially as the degree to which discipline can be imposed is limited. It depends more and more on consent and the degree of respect forthcoming from the pupil. Discipline in our schools depends on the quality of the teachers. Lord Elton's Committee recommends that a student spends some time 'observing' the work of a school before the start of initial training as a test of their interest in and capacity to enjoy teaching.

Surely 'observing' is not enough. Students need an opportunity to find out if they can cope with children. It is not enough to be concerned with the standard of entrants to teaching – there must also be concern for the demoralizing impact on any young 'learner-teacher' committed to college or university only to be rejected as a result of failing the classroom test.

The Elton Committee obviously realised that it made sense in money and human terms to discover unsuitability for teaching as soon as possible.

A solution could be sought: it would be logical if students delayed entry to colleges in order to have work experience in schools. The aim would be to find out if they were unsuitable at an age early enough for them to take up higher education in another direction without prejudice. Such experience might also make up the minds of many 'waiverers' to enter the profession.

Discipline also depends on the quality of the support given to teachers and they are entitled to know that support is readily available and exists in real terms. Schools must have arrangements for removing difficult pupils from lessons: keeping them away from their friends during lesson breaks; taking them, if necessary, out of certain lessons where their lack of control might cause danger eg swimming; removing them for long periods to a withdrawal room and even escorting them to the washroom. 'Time out' as it is known in the States, still needs staff to supervise – although it is unlikely that we would go to the lengths of one school in Seminole County where a child is placed in a room, given boring and uninteresting work, then watched through a one way mirror by one of the school secretaries.

At the end of the day you are moving towards exclusion from school by a series of steps: getting together with the parents for a mutually agreed period out of school to allow for a 'cooling-off' – but with suitable work provided; formal suspension for a short period with return subject to guarantees of good behaviour both from parent and pupil; transfer to another school – perhaps for an exploratory period; permanent transfer to another school; sending to a 'sin bin' away from the school site or providing 'home tuition' until there is rehabilitation. There must be in-built safeguards so that the right to expel is not abused. On the other hand, if a school needs to protect the interests of the vast majority of children, then it needs to be able to take positive and swift action.

It is not only the politicians who need to be convinced of this. The State system in England and Wales is such that administrators at Authority headquarters have only needed a minimum of two years experience teaching before becoming eligible for entering local government. It was not even necessary for them to have reached managerial rank within the schools. It then takes them some time to reach senior positions in a completely different profession. With the best will in the world their recollections are rusty and they might not understand changing problems at grassroot. Take, for instance, the problems of lunch-time supervision. During these break periods children are released from the close control of trained teachers in order to become highly mobile under the supervision of untrained dinner controllers – invariably ladies from the local communities. This is the time when children are least organised; likely to be bored; come to harm and when fights and bullying take place.

It is obvious that the persistent offender needs to be debarred from the school at lunch time – first for a short time as a warning period. It is obvious that the parents will have to be informed and if possible, their co-operation obtained. Yet in one authority in England it took three years for the officers to agree that headteachers could do this. One of those who opposed it most wrote that he could not see that there was any difference between debarrment during the lunch hour or during normal school sessions. In the meantime the headteachers could not wait on semantics. Their local association decided to turn this attitude of mind to its own advantage and advised its members as follows:

Dear Colleagues: As you know the Education Department takes the view that there is no difference between a child being disobedient in the classroom or a child being disobedient at lunch times; and therefore disagrees with debarrment – insisting that the children should be suspended.

Until this view becomes more realistic we suggest you use the following procedures in dealing with bad indiscipline during the lunch-time breaks:

First letter to parents   Your child's behaviour at the mid-day break is a source of annoyance to other children and to the controllers supervising the play period. If it does not improve I shall have to take more serious action. I am seeking your co-operation in warning your child that this behaviour has to improve.

Second letter to parents   Your child's behaviour has become intolerable during the mid-day break for the following reason(s). (Here note possible reasons for this action – eg Is a perpetual nuisance to controllers; has been guilty of bullying other children; has been guilty of downright disobedience to staff; has acted in an irresponsible way endangering him/herself and/or others).

It would be helpful if you could make alternative arrangements for lunch at home, or with a neighbour during (say – one week) as a cooling-off period. I suggest that this commences on (date) leaving school at (end of morning session) and returning at (start of afternoon session).

Third stage The third stage is to suspend.

The headteachers reckoned that the three stage procedure involving parents in the debarrment exercise provided an opportunity for parents to discipline their children. They considered the effect of this agreed procedure could bypass LEA objections. At the end of the day the Authority agreed what the heads were already doing. They monitored it for two years but there was no evidence that it was being abused by debarrment-happy heads. They really should have learned to trust their *teachers*. Co-operation with parents should always be sought and from the very first meeting headteachers and members of staff should make it clear that home was expected to work with school in overcoming not only academic, but any behavioural problems that might arise. It might even be necessary, from a punishment point of view, for the parents to be asked to act as an extension of the school.

Unfortunately co-operation will not always be there. There has been a noticeable increase in tension brought into schools by pupils from families suffering increasing financial pressures perhaps from redundancies and associated stresses causing insecurity. Often a child's life style is affected and marital problems abound. These tensions produce anti-social behaviour demanding more and more pastoral care and contact with parents. More and more children are being physical in their reactions to other children – and one headteacher reported an 11 year old boy who had reached the stage of 'mother beating' now that his father – a 'wife beater' had left home. A new generation of parents is emerging – they either cannot, or do not wish to control their children.

A recent survey of schools drew the following conclusions: some parents do not support traditional sanctions – many of them encouraged by what they have been told about 'parent rights'. One headteacher was told that he had no authority to take away a child's privilege of a play time. Another school reported that many sanctions were now ineffective: lines; copying; detention and extra work – even with home liaison and a positive programme. Yet another school reported occasions when parents entered the premises and dragged their children from the detention room. Teachers were told 'Punish . . . in your own bloody time and not his.' One boy actually had a stroke with the cane for spitting in the face of a lady meals controller. The next morning the headteacher was accused of being a sadist and then physically threatened. Those parents were not even slightly bothered by the anti-social behaviour of their son.

In Florida a Principal can expel and the child does not return until the parents have attended a case conference. In practice alternative schools are provided where classes are small and curriculum is interesting and well resourced. It costs a great deal and to some extent might encourage a child to be disruptive. Since 1976 in France, Disciplinary Boards are called upon to decide upon exclusion of pupils. Boards are typically composed of: Principal; a member of the administration designated by the Principal, two representatives of the parents; two of the teaching staff; two of the pupils and two from the local community. Parents are forced to pay attention and can be hit in the pocket by losing various child allowances.

In the USSR teenage problems are not the same. Teachers and pupils have been secure within a completely controlled curriculum since the beginning of Primary education. The system is centred on developing technical competence and not individualism and is very strong psychologically. The basis of the philosophy is that 'all will succeed'. They do not accept that anyone is not capable – people just develop at their own pace. This – with the notable exception of Jews and Catholics – extends to ethnic minorities who are given two extra years to get to the standards of the Soviets. They are allowed their cultural differences and given extra lessons to learn Russian, being taught by their own ethnic teachers. Discipline problems are not really known. First day of term is a 'welcome day' when the pupils bring the teachers flowers. It is rare for the student not to feel part of the set-up: mainly due to the long period of socialisation which goes on. Pupils are grouped into fours and this is known as the 'Link System'. If any one pupil performs badly then the others are accountable. Each group is then responsible to the whole class. You can either regard this as encouraging people to be responsible for each other or take the view that it encourages reporting on each other to the authorities. Be that as it may, parents are very much held to be responsible for their children. If there are problems at home then the parents are helped – much like welfare. Since everyone knows that the first approach will be one of support – then why should anyone oppose the system? Parents who do not conform risk being castigated publicly at work by a Union representative.

In the USSR education is all important since it determines the future of the country – it gives the skills which help determine the efficiency of the economy. This means that education becomes something to be valued and with an end – it is not just something to be endured with no rewards. The whole national concensus is to support education and those with professional qualifications expect a higher standard of living than the average. Education is not looked at as being something to broaden the mind and which ends up by restricting the receiver within the narrow confines of poverty.

In West Germany academic excellence is recognised as a virtue. A German friend told me that, in his opinion, the English suffered from inverted snobbery in this respect. Although a lot of the young doubt parent values – and although there is rising unemployment – they still have a belief in the value of learning. As in the USSR there is a national perception that education underpins the system and is vital to the nation. Ever since the unification of Gemany in 1870 it set out to be an industrial nation. From being a non-country Germany overtook Britain despite two World Wars and complete devastation and foreign occupations.

The system is much less regimented than in the USSR. There are no uniforms and pupils are treated as adults.

Parents know that the pupil will suffer consequences if not up to scratch. The burden is on the pupil to learn and the parent to give every support.

Homework is set – though the teachers are under no obligation to mark. After all, homework is something which cannot be guaranteed as being entirely a student's own effort.

Teachers must set formal tests in all subjects ever few weeks and it is not considered to be the teachers' fault if the pupil does not work.

The pupil has to learn and the effective motivator is the monitoring of performance. This is a great help to the teachers since they have high expectation that the work will be done and can spend their time on following-up and not chasing-up.

The system has one major advantage for the pupil. Since tests are frequent it does away with the stress of 'mugging' up a whole year's work.

Subjects are graded one to five and the test results are averaged out to give the final year mark. The average of a bottom five in any subject means the risk of a repeated year in all subjects. Results are measured – not just effort – and failure for more than two years means transfer to a remedial sector.

Students have to make an effort in all subjects – they can't opt out just because they may not like a teacher – and they can't afford to regard any subject with contempt.

Suspension means that the pupil misses work and risks being held back for a year suffering public shame and not going on with their peer groups.

Repeated years are also part of the system in France where it is known as 'redoublement'. Up to a third of Primary children are late in getting to Secondary school; and some are held back for two years.

Yet again teachers are employed to teach – the onus is on the student to learn. With curriculum nationally defined teachers are secure in knowing what to teach yet have some flexibility as regards methodology via council decisions in individual schools.

In the Federal Republic of Austria parent involvement is mandatory. Every term there are parent-teacher meetings and these are during two days when teaching does not take place. In Britain teachers are expected to give of their own time for evening consultations – when the teachers are tired from a day in front of the children. Here it is thought to be more important not to inconvenience the parents and put them to the bother and expense of taking time off from work to discuss their children's education. Both parents in Austria must be available when needed. It is the duty of the parents to support the work of the schools and also to provide the means for study. The laws and the courts can be used to make the parents face up to their responsibilities. In Austria and Germany teachers are much respected.

In France they are recognised as professionals with clearly defined hours. They are Civil Servants with security and pay and status much greater than here. They do not come cheap and are not, therefore, regarded as of little value.

In the USSR teachers are amongst the most respected professionals in society.

In all these countries education has purpose – therefore it has value – therefore its practitioners gain respect.

We also live in a society where many parents are career conscious for their children even before they enter mandatory education at the age of five; and there are many groups devoted to providing formal training for pre-school children.

Sooner or later children themselves realise that they have to earn a living. You would think that this realisation would engender support for the teachers. It might – if it were not for massive unemployment. That makes the pupils challenge the relevance of what they are being taught. The quieter element will continue to work and pray that what they are learning has some job implication – but trouble invariably happens when students see little point in what they are doing. In 1987 six out of ten students leaving school took no further part in formal education.

It is exceedingly difficult for the teachers to extol the virtues of a system which so obviously has not brought them financial success – not even job satisfaction judging by the number escaping to other jobs or taking early retirement. It is ironic since the teachers must have been in the top group of those who succeeded within the system in the first place.

Since 1865 and Mr Justice Coburn teachers have been considered to be 'in loco parentis'. The idea clearly stemmed from a private school system and a tradition where the rich first handed over their children to 'nannies' and then packed them off to boarding school where they could be neither seen nor heard.

In other countries parents remain in loco parentis even when their children are at school and so retain responsibility for their good behaviour.

There is no doubt that making parents responsible for their children's actions is fraught with difficulties; but the Elton Committee has moved in that direction with a recommendation that

'the Government should explore the possibilities for imposing on parents civil liability for their children's acts in school . . . we would encourage the Government to consider how, in suitable cases, the courts could provide for family counselling as an alternative to damages, fines or other punitive measures.'

In this country the only duty mandatory upon the parent is to send the child to school – though, in practice, enforcement is slow and by no means certain. A school, in its prospectus, can make it absolutely clear which sanctions it adopts; and can indicate that, by accepting a place at the school, the parents thereby have agreed to support those sanctions – but, this does not impose a duty on the parents other than a moral one.

On the other hand parents can demand every right to challenge the school for special consideration both for their individual children and of their own personal opinions on how things should be done. This is very time consuming and can lead to a school defending and justifying every action when there ought to be no need to do this. Teachers and headteachers are well used to the threat of going to higher authority – be it Chairman of Governors or Director of Education.

There are no reciprocal stresses put on even the most unreasonable of parents. They are only able to get away with non co-operation where they feel that LEAs and Governors are afraid to stand up and support their teachers.

An obvious need for support is where a teacher has been assaulted; yet experience has taught teachers over many years that when this happens the first reaction of the authorities has been to sweep it under the carpet.

With attacks on teachers becoming more and more commonplace some authorities have taken some steps in the right direction. Four years ago in Berkshire, the Unions had little difficulty in prompting the authority to make a general statement of intended support: that an assault on a teacher would be its concern whether it occured on or away from school premises provided that it arose in the course of or out of the performance of a teacher's work. The authority also agreed that any pupil concerned be suspended as soon as practical having regard to the headteachers' legal obligation to ensure the safety of the pupil eg where it proved impossible to get in touch with the parents.

The only costs that the authority was willing to incur was to grant leave of absence with pay if the teacher were required to give evidence in court. In the case of disablement, the authority should consider the possibility of paying compensation in accordance with the Conditions of Service for Teachers. All other expenses were to be met by the Teachers' Unions – ie the teachers themselves since the Unions operated with the money that they received in members' subscriptions.

To reiterate the self evident: discipline in our schools depends on the quality of the teachers and the degree of support given to them.

All experience and common sense indicate that if sanctions are non-existent or non-effective then you encourage an insulting 'I know best' or 'What can you do to me now?' attitude from those who contribute nothing but stress and unreasonable demands on finite resources.

The maintenance of discipline should be a contract between school and parent. If a parent will not accept reasonable rules of behaviour in a school then the school should be under no obligation to accept the child. Refusal by a parent to support the rules which then resulted in non-attendance would be a deliberate choice of the parent and there are legal means of dealing with this.

Parents only have the right to expect their children to be in an atmosphere conducive to learning – and where there is good discipline as understood by tradition – if they come to the support of a teaching profession under pressure.

Someone has to teach the children.

Reference

DES (1989) *Discipline in Schools (Report of the Committee of Enquiry chaired by Lord Elton)*, HMSO.

14 Internal Review and Development

Brenda Ebbs

The plethora of change now being experienced by schools is both daunting and fundamental. Viewed from a positive attitude it could also prove exciting and challenging. The Education legislation of the 1980's will have a dramatic impact not only on the curriculum but on how schools are managed.

> 'The new requirements represent a considerable challenge for all concerned, but . . . they offer the basis for exciting developments. Teachers will want to grasp the opportunity afforded by the introduction of the National Curriculum to further their professional development by building on existing skills and learning new ones.'
> (*National Curriculum – From Policy to Practice* D.E.S. 1989)

The National Curriculum will begin to be implemented in schools from September 1989. ERA established the principle that ' . . . entitles every pupil to a curriculum which is balanced and broadly based.' In essence it reflects what many good Primary Schools are already undertaking in practice. However any period of change can bring uncertainty, stress and feelings of alienation.

How can the Headteacher work to secure the entitlement of the National Curriculum for the pupils in the school?

How can the Headteacher work effectively with staff, with Governors and with Parents in order to ensure that these changes are implemented in a positive way?

How do you examine old practice and relate it to new requirements?

No school can undertake a review of the whole curriculum at any one time. If sanity is to remain intact then planning priorities is a necessary step. Using the 'Elephant' technique might be useful! You can eat an elephant if you take one bite at a time.

There may be a new National Curriculum but we need to examine our current practice to see how it relates to new policy. We will still need to work out the details of our own curriculum policies.

'There will be a great deal of scope for teachers in schools to carry out curriculum development . . . indeed, the introduction of the National Curriculum seems likely to stimulate a lot of work at local level on aspects of the content of the curriculum and its organisation and to help focus this on the essentials of what teachers and pupils need'.
(*National Curriculum Policy to Practice*, D.E.S. 1989)

For a number of years there has been pressure on headteachers and schools to undertake a systematic evaluation of the work of their schools. Many local authorities produced guidelines to assist the school in self-evaluation. Some imposed procedures where the purpose of review was for accountability purposes. Many schools have developed systems of Internal Review where the headteacher and staff look at the work of their own school. It is the purpose of this chapter to share with you the developments within the school of my first headship as we attempted to undertake internal review and development.

This method of internal review and development worked well in the first school where I was headteacher, but it has continued to be a valuable tool for managing change and curriculum development in my second and very different school.

At this time of unprecedented change it is proving a worthwhile method to help us identify our priorities for reviewing and developing the curriculum and aspects of school organisation to match the requirements of the National Curriculum.

We were greatly helped in our work by using guidelines produced under a Schools Council Programme, *Guidelines for Review and Internal Development in Schools*, known as GRIDS. It was produced by a team based at the University of Bristol School of Education.

Why the need to produce yet another set of guidelines? One reason was because so many of the books on evaluation and review are just a checklist. They ask you to look at *every* area of your school and then stop at the review stage. There were no adequate guidelines on how to go on and develop the area under review. It reminds me of an incident with my youngest son. He came in from the garden one day, happily dirty, after having helped his father to dig out the compost heap. I took one glance and said, 'Just look at your hands'. A little while later when sitting down for a meal I noticed that his hands were still dirty, when remarking on this he replied, 'Well you told me to look at my hands, but you did not tell me to do anything about them'.

Many of us are feeling overwhelmed with the amount and the depth of change that we are being asked to undertake. We need help and support to sort out our priorities and undertake the changes in a systematic way. We need support to examine what is happening in our school, to discover areas that need attention, but we also need help and guidance to show us how to go on and develop the area that we know needs change.

As a headteacher I found a group of good professional teachers prepared to work very hard. However each teacher was working independently in their own classroom box. Many had stayed with the same age group for many years. There was no written down policy for curriculum. Of greater significance there was little discussion on a professional level between teachers over curriculum content. I found no sense of teachers feeling part of a team working towards common goals. There was certainly a closed climate. My immediate predecessor had done a great deal in a short time but most of the staff were still used to a style which had long dominated the school where the headteacher was concerned with being head and making decisions. The teachers saw their job or role as being a teacher of a class. They expected decisions to be made by the headteacher. There were no job descriptions and no curriculum responsibilities. My early attempts at staff participation were not very welcome, it was seen as my job to make the decisions and I should get on and do it. My efforts to involve staff in discussion and include them in decision-making were very clumsy, there is nothing, I have discovered, like learning by experience.

Words such as evaluation or appraisal of work individually or collectively were almost unheard of at our school, but this probably reflected the national picture at that time. It became obvious to me as a new headteacher taking stock of the school, that some coordination of the curriculum was necessary. As I began to look at the work of individual classes I found that some areas of the curriculum were not adequately covered, whereas other areas were painful in their repetition.

So we began the work of curriculum review. Our first attempts were not very good and did not have a lot of depth to them, but we had made a start, and were learning together. This came about not because of any external pressure but as a result of internal need. It came because of a concern to offer to the children a curriculum that had relevance to their needs, that gave continuity to the pupils work and guidelines, support and resources to the teaching staff. We began to have regular staff meetings for the purpose of looking at the curriculum of the school. The value came in the level of discussion and the subsequent changes that were made had their source with the teachers. The curriculum guidelines that we started to produce were not imposed by me, the head-teacher. I believe that imposed change would have resulted in alienation by the teaching staff, and I wanted agreement to change because it had been internalised by the staff.

At first I found it difficult to get staff working together. We moved very slowly and certainly we would have benefited from the use of guidelines on how to go about the review of the work of our school and how to move on to development of the area under review. Some of the difficulty that we encountered was because of my lack of experience at leading a team of staff in review. I had not been given such experience as a teacher or in my post of deputy headteacher.

The areas of the curriculum that we first looked at were those where it was obvious that something had to be done, and where staff were willing to admit that they needed some help and support. Over the next five years we used regular staff meetings and inservice days to look systematically at various curriculum areas. We produced aims and objectives for our school. The staff began to get used to a collaborative style of work, and we built up a consistent pattern. I discussed the new area to be looked at with my deputy first. The staff then held an initial discussion about the new area to be reviewed. Teachers would then be given a period of time to work individually on their own particular aspect of the work. Eventually I would collate the individual work, which was then produced in draft form.

After further discussion and any necessary changes, the final draft policy document would then be put into use. It was revised again in the light of problems encountered as we began to put it into use.

This method of working became the normal pattern, as we built up guidelines on each area of the curriculum. It was not that I had a mania for getting everything down on paper, there would have been little value in simply producing words on paper. The value came in changes that were slowly taking place in the classroom. For me it is what is happening at the level of the children's learning that is important. As a headteacher I could have tried to impose upon the teaching staff content of curriculum or certain styles of teaching, but had I chosen to try this I doubt whether they would have had any effect upon the interactions in the classroom.

It was in this climate that our school was asked to become a pilot school to try out new materials being produced, now known as the GRIDS project. It was explained to us that guidelines were being developed to help the individual school to review the work of their own institution. By undertaking a review of the school, choosing a particular area to review in depth and then to go on to develop the work in that area, improvement could be made to the teaching learning process within the school. We were already committed to the idea of evaluating our work and to spending time looking at one area in depth. For this reason I felt that we should go ahead and accept becoming a pilot school for this GRIDS project. The method of working seemed compatible with our existing working style.

What is GRIDS?

GRIDS stands for 'Guidelines for Review and Internal Development in Schools'. So much easier to just say GRIDS. The book published, deals in depth with the background for the production of these materials, its rationale. Anyone considering using this method of approach will need to use that book. I can only deal with how we used it in our school and to look in a simple way at how this method worked for us.

I feel that I must emphasise that the Guidelines produced in the GRIDS project are to:

- help a school look at itself;
- help it with a review of the school;
- help it develop the work of the school.

A school is made up of people and it is the people of the school, that are collectively involved in the review of the school.

We are now learning how to involve our school governors and parents in curriculum review. Governors now have greatly increased responsibilities and many need support and guidance from the professional, if they are to have any chance of fulfilling the responsibilities placed on them.

The guidelines are only guidelines, it is not necessary to follow exactly every detail for it to be effective, they can be used to suit your situation. It is also important to remember that review of any area of the school normally leads to development in that area, and that this review and development is for internal use.

It is also vital to state that we are looking at a view of the whole school and not at the work of individual teachers. I believe that there is a useful place for the regular review that a headteacher can undertake with members of staff on an individual basis. There are many benefits from an effective performance appraisal process. However this chapter is to deal with the collective process of a staff working as a team and does not focus on the performance of the individual teacher, it carries no threatening overtones.

So we began to use the guidelines produced by the GRIDS

project team. Since we were trying out the materials as a pilot school the programme was to last for one year. We have since used the materials at our own pace.

The guidelines are in various phases:

Getting started To decide whether the GRIDS method is right for your school, consult with staff and decide how to manage the review and development.

To carry out an initial review of the school This involves all the teaching staff in collectively identifying a priority area, and reviewing the needs of the whole school.

To take one or more priority areas and carry out a specific view This involves looking in depth at one area of the school and identifying the needs and concerns of all the staff.

To take the action To take action on the recommendations that are identified in the specific review.

Evaluation and feedback To assess the effectiveness of the action taken.

If this is not very clear to you, try to keep reading, as it might be clarified as I link the theory of the stages of the GRIDS process to what has happened at our school.

Getting started

The first time that we used these materials I met each teacher individually to explain what the GRIDS method of review would involve, and then held a full staff meeting to give the opportunity for joint discussion. This is because you do need a staff to be reasonably committed to it. In our schools some staff were more committed than others, but none were actively opposed. I made an early mistake. Due to day to day pressure I saw some staff members over a period of several days. By the time I reached the last member of staff they were already feeling left out! If a headteacher decides to see staff individually it is important to do this quickly. As we continued to use this approach it has been important to fully explain to any new teachers what is involved.

Initial review

The first task is to carry out an Initial Review of the school, and the purpose of this review is to identify an area or areas that can be looked at in depth. The Initial Review enables you to sort out the priorities for Review and Development. In order to carry out this Initial Review the GRIDS project book has a survey sheet which covers most areas of concern to a school. Staff are asked to indicate on the survey sheet which areas they feel would benefit from a more detailed or specific review. Which areas they see as a strength or as a weakness of the school.

The survey of staff opinion asks staff to consider:

The curriculum   This is broken down into a number of areas eg communication skills:

- Speaking
- Listening
- Reading
- Writing

and so covers the curriculum areas of the school.

Pupils   This is also divided into a number of areas eg methods of grouping pupils, pupils records etc.

Staff and organisation   Once again this is divided to cover a whole range of areas eg staff development, and also includes all the boundary areas like parental involvement.

Internal review and development

There is also space on the survey sheet for the individual school to add their own topics not included in the survey.

We give out the survey at a staff meeting and then use the meeting to clarify what the survey means. It is as well to check if there is any misunderstanding of terminology. We also discuss if any extra information is needed before staff fill in the survey sheets. In our case members of staff have a staff handbook which includes schemes of work as well as basic information. It may be that staff need specific information on particular areas in order to give an informed decision. We then find it useful to allow staff to fill in the sheets on their own rather than sitting together at a staff meeting. Teachers need time to reflect quietly on their own.

Teachers do not have to put their names on the sheets, but we found that no one seemed to feel the need for secrecy, and teachers completed the survey sheets independently without discussion with colleagues.

When undertaking this work for the first time as a pilot school we appointed a member of staff to be a coordinator. I saw the chance to appoint a member of staff as a coordinator as an opportunity for staff development. The results of our surveys show staff feeling about all the areas of the school. The survey includes curriculum areas but also includes areas like staff and organisation. In fact it includes all the areas for which the headteacher is responsible. This exercise alone has been of benefit to me as a manager of the school. In order to plan development I should know how staff feel about all these areas. My own attitude has been that I am willing to accept the staff decision upon looking in depth at any area that shows up as in need of specific review. I have also felt that staff have a clear idea of the needs of the school. In our previous work I had decided the area for review so this was a great change for me. Headteachers considering using the GRIDS method for Review and Development should consider seriously the management implications of this approach. There are some headteachers whose management style is such that they might not be happy with this approach.

The surveys undertaken at our school have shown up a number of areas as in need of a specific review, they have also shown up several small points that we have been able to deal with quickly and do not need a long specific review.

Our first survey showed three main areas as in need of a specific review:

Mathematics,
Children with special needs,
Physical education.

We used a staff meeting to give teachers the results of the survey and to discuss the major areas that needed a specific review. We all agreed that we could only tackle one area at a time but found it difficult to reach agreement on which area we should look at first. Eventually we decided to postpone our decision for a week to give ourselves time to reflect and talk informally about these areas. At the next staff meeting it was decided by a narrow majority that physical education should become our first priority area. I was pleased at this decision since this was the one area that we had not worked on as a staff. We lacked staff expertise in this area, had constraints in our building and needed help.

So we have covered the first stage of review, to identify an area that the staff will collectively focus on, thus initial review is completed. As we move to the next stage, that of the specific review, I recall that the first time we undertook this I began to have doubts about this method of working. The specific review is very detailed and asks you to make a thorough examination of present practice. The first time we used the materials we only decided to stick to the guidelines because we were a pilot school and had to report on the materials. In fact this turned out to be the stage where we learned the most, and the guidelines have proved most valuable. Before, when undertaking curriculum work we have always rushed into the action stage with a feeling of 'Let's get on with it and decide what needs doing'. The guidelines made us spend a long time looking at the present situation in our school.

How necessary it will be to take time to examine current practice and how it relates to the requirements of the National Curriculum before we rush headlong into action.

Our first specific review was on physical education and we had little documentation on this. All teachers wrote down what they had been aiming to achieve, what they actually did. The coordinator collated this and gave a copy to each member of staff. This exercise took place over the period of one term and gave us some surprises. We began to realise that any child who had attended our school must by the time they left be an expert on curling and stretching! We had managed to include it in our curriculum for just about every age pupil in the school. Next time that you visit Weston-super-Mare, look out for those who can give a superb performance at curling and stretching and you will know that they attended our school. Specific reviews that we have undertaken since that first one, have been on areas that we have previously worked on together, and have involved looking at previous curriculum guidelines.

This sharing of experience has enabled teachers to learn from one another. We used an inservice day and further staff meetings to discuss our current practice and the basis for these discussions came from the material that each teacher has written down. By talking together and by all teachers having the chance to examine what others felt they were doing we realised the gaps that we had in our work with the children, and the repetition of certain areas. The written down version of our present curriculum was also useful as a start when we later came to re-write our own curriculum guidelines in the action development stage.

The importance of looking in depth at the current practice cannot be over-emphasised. We have been willing to be open and share because the whole exercise was for our own use. The spirit in which this is done is very important. It is useful to be self-critical and even to be able to laugh at yourself. During the specific review we have always struggled to come up with our criteria for assessing the effectiveness of our present practice. The struggle has always been worthwhile because by looking at the criteria that we have drawn up we are able to decide why and how we are dissatisfied with present practice, and then to go on and to list our particular difficulties. The best thing about this whole exercise is that it is related to our school, our staff and our resources.

By the end of the specific Review we have achieved the following:

1 Written down or looked at our present aims and objectives for the particular area under review.
2 Recorded our criteria for judging the effectiveness of our practice.
3 Written down, or looked at our present curriculum.
4 Recorded our list of difficulties.
5 Written down our recommendations for the action that is needed.

Action development

As we move into the next stage we now have a clear idea of what action needs to be taken. This is why the specific review is so valuable. It is not a hit or miss affair. Our next job is to take action on our own recommendations.

So what type of action have we taken. First of all, over a period of time we are involved in a lot of thinking, reading and talking. While physical education was under review I have never read so many PE books in my life. Later when we went on to review mathematics we took nearly two terms to look at numerous maths books and schemes. A very useful action, is to involve the outside consultant. We involved our first outside consultant in the form of our LEA PE advisor. She came into an inservice day and discussed with us what we were doing and gave some valuable advice. We have also involved a local lecturer from a College of Education. He came into our school to work with our teachers and children. In many ways this proved more useful than teachers going out on courses. This was working and thinking about our reality, working with our children and our resources. Staff also tend to apply for courses for the area under review and this is also useful.

We undertake the re-writing of our own curriculum guidelines. We also purchase resources. This has to be within our normal budget, but I have always tried to link the spending of our capitation with the area that is under review. The implementation of LMS will still mean we have to work within budget restraints but it may well give us greater flexibility. There are usually other more simple forms of action, like the reorganising of apparatus. At the end of the action stage we have dealt with all the difficulties that were on our list of recommendations for action.

As we have completed the action stage we find that evaluation needs to come after a space of time. We need a chance to see how effective our action has been. Also before one action stage is finished teachers are usually anxious for needs in another area to be dealt with. So the cycle begins again, we do not need to immediately repeat the staff survey but go on and deal with the other areas that the original survey show as needing review. The time that it takes to complete a cycle on the whole Review and Development process will obviously vary from school to school. It will depend on the staff of the school, the area chosen for review and many other constraints. In some larger schools staff may be able to tackle more than one area at a time in a specific review. We found that for us the whole process can expect to last over one academic year. It takes us this time to look in depth at one area and to undertake the action and development needed. We do of course still expect to deal with other issues that arise and looking in depth at one area of the school does not mean that you give no attention at all to other areas that the school has to deal with.

We continued to use the GRIDS approach to Review and Development. There was no pressure on us to do this, but this method worked for us. After we had dealt with the areas on the first staff survey sheet we went on to complete a new staff survey. After a period of time our needs change, new members of staff come into the school and so the whole process begins again.

I have looked back in a very positive way at the use of these guidelines, but each school has its own set of circumstances and must decide for themselves if this approach could work for them. It is also important to reflect on some of the problems that can be linked with Review and development strategies.

Some of the possible problems could be linked to an imposed system. Either imposed from outside or imposed by a headteacher on their staff. To be effective Review and Development needs to take place in an open climate. The headteacher and the individual teachers need to consult together within a trusting relationship, and to build together towards a mutually acceptable set of criteria. This is of vital importance at a time when so many changes have been imposed on us. When staff are involved in the process of decision-making there is less resistance to change than if the change had been imposed. There is a need for this to take place in a non-threatening context. No group of teachers are going to admit to deficiencies in the same way if the exercise is for accountability purposes only. Unless difficulties and problems are openly admitted there will be no commitment to dealing with them.

Relationships will also affect the whole Review and Development strategy, while it needs the open climate to flourish individual members of staff can sabotage the collective work of the team. It is also vital to question the criteria used by staff in judging the effectiveness of their own work. Judgements will be made against the views of their own educational philosphy and individual experience. It is difficult to be objective and for this reason external consultants can have a useful and valuable contribution to make.

A realistic look at the problems involved need not deter us from undertaking Review and Development work in our school because there are many benefits to be gained.

The whole purpose of our schools is that the teaching/leaning process can be effective for the individual child. It therefore makes sense for the teaching staff to work together to consider what is really happening in the school. It is useful to share experience and expertise and not to be afraid to be held accountable for the schools performance. Its activities should have a relevance to the lives of the children and the staff need to make a collaborative effort to consider the work of their school.

The advantages for the school are:

Improved internal communications This will happen when a group of teachers sit down together to consider the work of their school and how development can take place. Day to day activities do not give time for communication at this level so time for this had to be planned.

Improved overall performance The headteacher and staff have a joint opportunity to say what they are thinking and feeling. Difficulties and problems can be explored and this should lead to the finding of solutions.

More effective and efficient use of personnel As individual teachers gain particular strengths through experience and inservice training the school can gain by making use of those strengths. Expertise can be shared by all the staff. Postholders for a particular curriculum area have the opportunity to share their expertise and also listen to the problems and difficulties faced by other teachers in a particular area.

Motivated teachers The headteacher can become aware of the thoughts and feelings that individual teachers have and being aware of problems can try to deal with them. As all teachers and sometimes non-teaching staff and Governors are involved in the collective process of review all have the opportunity to influence changes in the school. Teachers are usually more motivated to implement changes that they have helped to formulate.

Future planning It is useful for the headteacher as manager of the school to know how staff feel about every area of the school. To understand and explore the problems that face teachers in their classrooms and which it is so easy to forget in the headteachers office. By understanding the priorities for development there is the chance to plan systematically to deal with problems, and imposed changes of the National Curriculum.

The advantages for the individual teacher are:

Clear understanding of the needs of the whole school Each teacher may be aware of their own needs and the needs of the children in their age group, but they also need to be aware of the collective needs of the teaching staff. To be aware of the development needs of the children of other age groups. There is a need to be part of a continuous process of education in the school and a need to discuss their own problems and seek their own solutions.

Opportunity to increase capability through an agreed development plan Discussions on problems or weakness can be linked to professional development or training. As teachers collectively discuss the needs of a particular area it will possibly throw up individual needs for teachers to seek:

- further education: to give increased knowledge in a subject;
- individual training: to give improved performance in a pedagogic skill;
- relevant experience: to have help for a particular task or a change of responsibility.

For the headteachers who have considered the problems and benefits from undertaking a collective style of Review and Development with their staff there are some final, obvious and important consideration to take into account before embarking on a Review and Development process in their school.

The attitude of both the headteacher and the staff is more important that anything else. If the headteacher and staff really want to start upon such a process it is more likely to be successful. In my own school the teachers who put the most in to the process got the most out of this method of working. There is no doubt that this process takes extra time, and the headteacher has to be realistic about the time staff are able to give to Review and Development. There is a fine line between extra commitment of time and energy that will eventually be rewarded by helping staff to carry out their teaching commitments and too much work resulting in an unfair burden on teachers already overloaded with work.

If a school has never participated in review and development work then the GRIDS materials should be very supportive in making a start in this area. My advice to schools undertaking this would be to follow the procedure as it stands even if at first you cannot see the value of all the stages. We did not see the value of the specific review until we had completed it. However use your own commonsense if some of the stages do not apply to your situation.

The management implications for the headteacher need very careful thought. It is vital that the headteacher is supportive. Does the headteacher wish for staff involvement in some areas of the school? It is putting the development of the school into the hands of all the teaching staff. The initial review cannot be predicted. The headteacher must first ask themselves if they are willing to accept any area that the staff choose to review.

One should also consider resource costs. It is useful to link spending of school capitation to the area under review. Usually review of any area throws up a need for some resources to help development work. The staff need to be realistic and work within the existing resource possibilities. There is also the resource cost in terms of personnel. Individual teachers in my school gave more time outside of school hours, but there was also extra work placed on the school secretary to type reports etc.

Conditions that will help are co-operation between staff and a willingness to share together. Working in this way will enhance this co-operation. If I need a criteria for judging the effectiveness of our Review and Development it is this. We enjoyed this way of working. We learned a great deal about the curriculum area under review, we chose to continue with this method of working. Most important is that practice has changed. We will approach this period of educational change with greater confidence knowing that we have developed the means to review and develop the work of our school. The benefit will be for our children.

References

GRIDS (1988), *Primary School Handbook (Second Edition)*, Longman for SCDC.
DES (1989), *National Curriculum - From Policy to Practice*, HMSO.

PART III RELATIONSHIPS OUTSIDE THE SCHOOL

15 Involving parents in the life of the school

Elsa Davies

One of the nicest things about parental involvement is that it can be such fun. All too often, in concentrating on the more serious aspects of this complex subject, one can forget the warmth of feeling, the confidence of support and the laughter-sharing times which happen when the relationships between people are founded on sufficient trust and respect to become relaxed, understanding and caring. The pleasure and joy in sharing a child's education with parents needs stating, for it is all too easy to become enmeshed in the problems and difficulties which appear to beset the pathway to warm and sincere home school contact.

Having said that and having acknowledged the complex nature of the subject, it seems both sensible and economical to begin by attempting a definition of terms. This is not easy for parental involvement in school life occurs at every school organisation level and it is subject to widely differing perceptions and interpretations. In this chapter, the term 'parent' is used in the main to refer to the people responsible for a child's welfare, upbringing and education. At times, too, it embraces other members of the family, close family friends, neighbours and members of the community who care about the school. Where the term 'family' is used, children themselves are included, as they are also in the school community which is sometimes referred to as the school family.

In the main, the interpretation of the term 'involvement' follows the standard dictionary definitions based on a significant association with, in this case, an enterprise. In its breadth, it covers practical participation in the school and the classroom during the school day. It also covers the more representative level of participation on home school associations and governing bodies. Both these forms of parental involvement are taken as given, in that they are currently accepted practice in the majority of primary schools. A more personal and idiosyncratic interpretation of involvement allows for the 'significant association' to include less tangible elements of felt support and goodwill to be placed on an equal level of importance as practical participation. In that parents and teachers are involved in a shared responsibility for children's education through schooling, there is assumed in this interpretation, an implied mutual obligation on both parties to work together for the best educational experience for children. It is this 'working together' principle, in its broadest sense, that this chapter on parental involvement addresses.

Perhaps the most pressing argument for headteachers approaching parental involvement in this broader sense is the vital nature of the effect of reciprocal support on children, their parents and their teachers. Parental involvement is so complex, diverse and all embracing a concept that it pervades the whole ethos of a school. It calls into question the philosophical beliefs underpinning a school's broad aims and for this reason, deserves the most serious and considered study by headteachers, staff and governors. Alongside these deeper concerns, recent legislation (Education [No. 2] Act, 1986 and the Education Reform Act, 1988) make it imperative for heads to draw parents more closely into the life of the school. Historically, statements to the effect that schools:

> are more likely to discharge their responsibilities wisely when they ensure that parents and others understand their intentions and the reasons for them (*Curriculum 5–16* DES 1985)

have now been translated into the statutory Governors Annual Meeting with parents and the National Curriculum profile components. Added to this, there is an intuitive understanding in many teachers that involving parents in school life carries with it many advantages ranging from the various talents and opportunities parents bring to school life to the important chance it provides for reducing and eliminating areas where children can manipulate conflict between parents and teachers. Other advantages include the opportunity of proceeding more effectively in a child's learning by involving their most natural teachers (parents) and certainly, not the least advantage to a caring professional, is the awareness it raises of not having to undertake the whole weight of responsibility for a child's development when there are others to share it. Finally, there are lessons to be learnt from management research (Peters and Waterman, 1982) which strongly proclaims the importance of an organisation staying close to the client and of listening intently and regularly to them. In order to respond sensitively and to give the best possible service, teachers need to generate a dialogue with families and to listen carefully to them. Teachers also have a responsibility to offer the benefit of their professional expertise as they look together with parents, governors and others for the best way forward for the children in their school.

The essential purpose of good school management is to enable the easier translation of school aims into practice. In relation to parental involvement, this means the creation and maintenance of warm, working and interdependent parent teacher relationships. Therefore, as a framework, the chapter takes broad areas of managerial concern such as communication and decision-making and looks at how they inform and extend the concept of parental involvement and in particular, at how the development of active parental support can help teachers proceed more quickly and lastingly in children's learning.

Communication

One of the major managerial functions of the headteacher's role is the development and maintenance of communications in a school. It forms one third of a manager's executive activity (Mintzberg, 1973) and aspects of it pervade almost every area of a manager's work. Interestingly, Mintzberg labels the relevant role category as 'Informational', which serves to emphasise the importance of communications as a means of sharing information. Although the sharing of information may be regarded as an end in itself, it is but the first step in a process which leads towards supportive parental involvement. Through sharing information with school families, a realignment of lay/professional boundaries occurs, which results in an increased commitment of all parties to the primary aim of securing a child's well-being and progress. This common ground is where the mutual respect and trust essential to warm and sincere relationships in a school are nurtured.

Non-verbal communications

Beginning, however, on a contradictory note, there are times when communication is not a matter of sharing factual information in words. Sometimes the items are more tangible. Mentioning a cup of coffee as an important aspect of parental involvement may appear trivial on the surface. Yet, the underlying messages behind the provision of coffee making facilities for parents at school is very powerful. It is strong and tangible evidence that they are welcomed and it helps people to feel part of the school family. In the same way, similar messages are conveyed by the schools who choose to share space with parents in the form of a parents, family or community room or area. Equally, schools who share their buildings with parents by allowing access to classrooms and corridors are encouraging easement in some parents' initial feelings of apprehension about the school.

Spoken communication

In returning to the theme of sharing information, it is clear from many years of experience that this happens at its most informal and individual level when parents and class teachers meet at each end of the school day. Often such contact is brief and specific but it is a significant and essential feature of parent-teacher communication. It gives both teachers and parents the chance for example, to mention something praiseworthy, to express anxieties and to acknowledge tacitly their mutual support.

Much less satisfying and far less important in relation to encouraging parental involvement are the occasions which arise for formal talking at school functions, education evenings and parent association gatherings. Amongst these events, the Governors Annual Meeting with parents is a significant innovation. At such events there is plenty of opportunity for dissemination of information by professionals but less chance for constructive feedback from families. However, despite their limitations, these events are useful for the other functions they perform in relation to school life (Coulson, 1984) and for the starting point in parent contact they provide for some schools.

Equally important but on a different and rather more individual level are the opportunities parents have for discussion about their child's development with the head and the teachers. Formal consultations involving individual families and classteachers need still to be a part of our provision as professionals but additionally, there are times when a parent or the head may wish to raise a matter of specific concern, for example, over the provision for a pupil with special educational needs. Access for discussion is important at these times.

It is also useful to offer an invitation for discussion at various times when children have completed particular stages of their learning (Davies, 1980a). The National Curriculum designates 7, 11, 14 and 16 years of age as statutory reporting stages but concerned parents and teachers would probably regard this provision as a minimum level of involvement in a child's learning program. More positively, schools could use the National Curriculum levels of attainment in particular subject areas as bases for offering regular parent/teacher/pupil discussion opportunities.

At these times, the child's school record (which can be initiated in the parents' presence when their child begins school) can enhance discussion with children and parents. Parents appreciate knowing that whenever they need they may have access to any notes which school staff make on their child. There are also times when parents are glad of the chance to add information to this working document. Encouragingly, Macbeth (1984) regards this open access to personal educational data as measure of the degree of success which the parent teacher partnership has achieved.

Written information

Apart from the unofficial 'grapevine', the first contact most families have with schools is their initial visit to enquire about enrolling their child. On this occasion, it can be helpful to give the school's introductory booklet. Such introductory publications not only need to provide enough information for parents to make a considered judgement about their child's early schooling but they should also project the feelings of warmth and purposefulness which characterise a caring, educative community.

The importance of the style, content and presentation of the introductory booklet is also applicable to all forms of written communication with parents. Yet, while clarity of content is highly desirable, it is the welcoming tone and sharing nature of the notes which encourage parental support. Many schools produce regular information circulars which are much appreciated by parents (Davies, 1980b). Some newsletters appear two or three times a term and carry information ranging from curricular items and organisational matters to special events and general news. Some also offer opportunities for parents to make contributions to the content as well as summarising meetings where parents have been involved in decision making. A casual and informal style of writing can encourage parents to suggest the inclusion of information items which might be relevant to other families.

It is also worth noting that regular newsletters can be effective in developing the spirit of partnership in recent legislation. They can, for example, enable governor concerns to be shared with parents in a natural way which integrates governor activity into the working life of the school.

Even though newsletters serve families in many ways, there is still a need to provide opportunities for parents to make direct contact with other parents as a group. Some schools provide 'family noticeboards' for this purpose and such ideas, along with the brief but friendly notes of home-school associations to families, are initial steps in encouraging parent to parent contact. However, in order to make progress in this area, some activity by individual parents is to be desired. More advanced stages of parent to parent contact are in evidence when individual or small groups of parents can produce information leaflets or organise educational or social events for children and/or parents. This activity involves parents communicating orally and on paper with each other and is indicative of the extent to which a really trusting bond exists between teachers and parents. Extending opportunities in this particular aspect of communication is one of the future development areas in the progress of parental involvement and an important step towards realising the concept of 'equal partnership' with parents.

Teaching/learning involvement

In recent years, the most significant advances in home school relationships have centred on maintaining active parental involvement in their child's education once school has begun. The logic behind such moves is the commonsense, economical approach of harnessing the natural talents of the parent-as-teacher in supporting the expertise of the professional teacher. In terms of a child's enhanced progress and motivation for learning the dividends are great and research in the Inner London Education Authority (Griffiths and Hamilton 1984) and Sandwell (Stevens, 1984) support personal experience. They are equally noteworthy in relation to the development of purposeful parental involvement through providing parents with a deeper understanding of the joys and the difficulties arising in more formalised teaching. They also serve to emphasise the unity of purpose in the aims of parents and teachers.

The Inner London Education Authority PACT (parents children and teachers) scheme is a particularly notable, documented example of continuing parental involvement in a child's learing. In this scheme, children are encouraged to take books home to read with a family member who is then asked to make a brief note of the experience on a progress card. With the addition of the teacher's response, these progress sheets gradually become a form of conversation between parents and teachers which focuses specifically on a child's learning. This strategy can be adapted to suit the learning programmes of particular schools, for example, where skill mastery is the style of learning, then books accompanied by brief suggestions on specific supportive activities can be made available for parents.

Another method of supporting home learning is for teachers to produce information leaflets on specific educational topics, particularly those concerned with the content, organisation and delivery of the National Curriculum. The possibilities for themes are endless but examples might include leaflets on the contribution of children's play activity to design and technological capability , the value of sand and water play, teaching alphabetical order, activities for developing visual and aural memory and so on. Even further along the path of providing opportunity for the expression of parental desire to help their child's learning is the channelling of a particular and regular professional activity to these ends. In schools where teachers prepare forecasts of work, a brief summary shared with parents can bring rewards, particularly in relation to thematic work. In this way a child's activities within the family can be complementary to the school based work and parents can also share expertise or knowledge with the class. Brief though such contact must inevitably be, it can give parents an indication of the knowledge and experiences their child may be exposed to as the term proceeds.

In the area of teaching/learning involvement, a considerable onus lies upon the professional to produce tangible output to support active and continuing parental involvement. However, even though the reciprocal input by parents is less visible or concrete, it deserves, nevertheless, to be highly valued. Parental teaching involvement gives impetus and motivation to a child's learning. It also allows teachers time to concentrate on learning areas needing professional expertise. Not least of its advantages is that the dialogue it engenders carries latent messages of trust and understanding between parents and teachers.

Other developments

As technology becomes ever more sophisticated and the constitution of school groups change, schools will need to consider alternative means of communicating with families. Some schools produce video cassettes to tell parents and prospective parents about their aims and activities. Similarly, audio cassette tapes can substitute in many cases for written information. Such provision can be particularly helpful to handicapped parents. If the cassettes are available in different languages, families from different ethnic groups or from abroad can be made more warmly welcome. On the multicultural theme, where possible, it is both courteous and respectful for the school to try to have all their publications, particularly their news bulletins, translated into the various languages used by parents.

As time proceeds, forward thinking schools will be producing lending libraries of their own computer software packages, specially designed to support their learning programmes. They may also become involved in projecting their school activities through interactive video techniques. In these and all the aforementioned ways, schools can be engaging in that vital dialogue with parents which supports a child's learning.

As education business partnerships develop, schools will see ways forward in sharing the teaching/learning elements of their activity with those parents who might find closer involvement difficult. Bulletins outlining new educational developments or school organisation patterns, for example, might be circulated to local companies which employ significant numbers of parents. Similarly, articles in local trade magazines, union bulletins or newspapers can also help share good news about how schools are helping children learn.

Decision-making

Opportunities exist in all aspects of parental involvement for lay professional tensions to emerge and this is especially so in decision areas which are intimately bound with policy making. Although teachers have long felt this policy making function to be a professional preserve, the reality is that schools exist to serve children, and through them, their families and ultimately, society. To achieve the most effective match between parental expectations and professional expertise, teachers need to talk purposefully with parents about ways in which the school can best serve its families. Sometimes the Governors Annual Meeting is the proper arena for such discussion but most likely, a slightly less formal setting achieves better results. Whatever the setting, it is important to note that the dialogue can only be successful if it is founded on the principle of equality in the home school partnership. Only then can sincere consultation and genuine involvement over school improvement lead to stronger family commitment to the school in general and more specifically, to the development of the individual pupil.

At present, most schools have two long established decision making bodies, namely the staff group and the governing body. Schools may also have a relatively newer group in the form of a parents association which, in relation to the other groups, has the disadvantages of seeking to represent a non-cohesive group of people and of having, for various reasons, a very weak influence base within the structure of school life (Merson and Campbell, 1974). In the past, none of these groups fully served the headteacher in discovering the best response the school can make to family needs. Although the new governing bodies could be deemed to provide some answer to this problem, their residual formality and restricted membership constrains their effectiveness in some respects. Consequently, there is still a need for heads and governing bodies to search for innovative ways of discovering and channelling a wealth of talent and goodwill to the betterment of educational practice. An historical example of one creative response was the setting up of school policy advisory body (Davies, 1985) which drew all the parties together to look critically and constructively at the school practices and procedures. Discussion areas ranged from the highly practical provision of directional signs in the school building to more complex areas such as transition between school and supplementary provision in curricular subject areas. The important thing was that, whatever the topic or level of discussion, the school and its families were both the focus and the beneficiaries of the outcome.

Similarly another different but currently valid way of involving parents more fully in school decision-making is to open out areas more closely regarded as professional issues. An example of this kind could be the annual decision necessary on alternative school structure patterns. Parents are often anxious over decisions to undertake such options as 'vertical grouping' of pupils in classes. It can help greatly if they along with the staff, have looked seriously and together for the best option for their school.

Such arrangements not only serve to vitalise parental involvement in school life but they also help to bridge areas between the three distinct decision making bodies previously mentioned. In an ideal world, with everyone working for the best for the child, it would seem sensible for these groups to strengthen and focus their effort through coming together (Davies, 1986). Until then, concerned heads and governors will find the ways they can to bring together all who care about the school in the search for continuing school improvement.

Managing conflict

When parents are involved in the various aspects of school life, and in particular, their child's learning, many of the traditional conflict areas disappear. For example, school files on children which once were secret generated far more interest and anxiety in parents than when access to them was available. This was because the teacher trust in according access is matched by parent trust that school documents contained professional statements related to a child's education. In any good working relationship, there are times when differences of opinion may occur. It is then that the role of the headteacher is critical in identifying dysfunctional conflict and channelling all efforts to creative and constructive discussion. If, for example, suggestions offered by parents are unrealistic, impracticable to undertake or at their worst, involve serious compromise of professional knowledge, headteachers and their staffs need to be explicit in defence and justification of recognised principles of educational practice. Likewise, a responsibility rests upon parents to add considered comments to the debate.

In supporting and encouraging both professional and lay contribution to group discussion, the headteacher can lay the foundation for the innovative style of decision reaching which offers the optimum for school improvement. More appropriate for the 'equal partnership' concept is the adoption of a 'worrying at' style of decision making which puts the onus on all parties to contribute. Such a style eschews consensus in that it leaves some contributors with little or no commitment to the new proposal. Neither is it based on compromise, with its implication of the outcome being less than the best that can be achieved. When sufficient 'worrying at' the problem to reach an outcome occurs, everyone can take some form of commitment forward into the new scheme, if only that accrued from sharing in the decision making process.

Implementing change

Once decisions involving action have been taken, the work of the headteacher in providing the right sort of organisational environment for these initiatives to flourish is vital. Charged with managing the change process, heads can encourage parents and teachers to be venturesome in making suggestions or trying out new ideas, by arranging flexibility within the school system (Davies, 1984). The National Curriculum framework is designed to enable this to happen. Heads can also offer evidence of their trust in parents by delegating authority for undertaking proposed schemes. Such proposals might include the organisation of a group to take responsibility for a school nature area, a 'teach-in' on computer programming, a pre-school family club or a visit to the seaside or the ballet – the list could be endless. If a decision is made to arrange for example, school assemblies involving increased parental and community input, then the head might have to exercise considerable supportive activity with staff and parents as problems are revealed. As well as alerting people to the usual stages of difficulty in the change process, heads are called upon to show tenacity in ensuring the new scheme has a fair chance and fearlessness in deciding to shelve the idea if it proves impractical (Nisbet, 1975). Yet, even in these onerous areas, sharing the decision making responsibilty with parents, teachers and governing bodies can alleviate some of the weight of responsibility headteachers often feel (Gray and Coulson, 1982). There are times when both groups, either separately or jointly, can be drawn into the necessary formative appraisal which should accompany a new scheme. If, for example, in the early operation of a new style of school assembly, it receives a mixed reception from parents and teachers (despite their initial desire for it), then regular review discussions within the staff group and governing body or policy advisory group can help the headteacher support those people implementing the change.

Conclusion

The benefits of encouraging mutual support between parents and teachers are found at all points within the school system. On an individual pupil level, parental support has its outcome in the extension of natural (and more lasting) learning which enables the professional to proceed more speedily and specifically in a child's learning.

At system level, schools founded on a person centred organisational and educational philosophy, encourage a dialogue with parents which enables them to respond more pertinently and accurately to needs of families. Through sharing information, policy making and even through sharing expertise with parents, such dynamic schools reap the precious reward of active and felt client support and goodwill.

Although this chapter has attempted to look at parental involvement in school life through some areas of managerial concern, it is important to note that effective school management is only valid in terms of the outcomes it achieves. In relation to parental involvement, the outcomes are evident in the friendly, relaxed relationships, founded upon mutual trust, understanding and respect, which enable and support exciting and adventurous happenings in a school. Where such relationships exist, parental involvement is not regarded as a separate aspect of the managerial task: it is, as indeed, it should be, the natural way of life in a caring, educative community.

References

Coulson, A A (1984), *The Managerial Behaviour of Primary School Heads*, N E Wales Institute of Higher Education.

Davies, E (1980a), 'Primary School Records', in Burgess, T and Adams, E (Eds) *Outcomes of Education*, Macmillan.

Davies E (1980b), 'Primary School Self-Portraits', in *Where* No 160, ACE.

Davies, E (1984), 'The Role of the Headteacher in the Management of Change', in Skilbeck, M (Ed) *Readings in School-Based Curriculum Development*, Harper and Row.

Davies, E (1985), 'Parental Involvement in School Policy Making', in *Educational Management and Administration*, Vol ll, No 2.

Davies, E (1986), 'The Changing Role of Parents, Governors and Teachers', in *Educational Management and Administration*, Vol 14, No 2.

DES (1985), *The Curriculum from 5 to 16*, HMSO.

Gray, H and Coulson, A A (1982). 'Teacher Education, Management and the Facilitation of Change, in *Educational Change and Development*, Vol 4 No 1.

Griffiths, A and Hamilton, G (1984), *Parent, Teacher, Child – Working Together in Children's Learning*, Methuen.

Macbeth, A (1984) *The Child Between – A report on school-family relations in the countries of the European Community*. Studies Collection, Education Series No 13 Publ. Office for Official Publications of the European Communities, Luxembourg.

Merson, M W and Campbell, R J (1974). 'Community Education: Instruction for Inequality', in Golby, M et al (Eds) *Curriculum Design*, Croom Helm.

Mintzberg, H (1973), *The Nature of Managerial Work*, Harper and Row.

Nisbet, J (1975), 'Innovation – Bandwagon or Hearse?' in Harris, A et al (Eds) *Curriculum Innovation*, Croom Helm.

Peters, T J and Waterman, R H (1982), *In Search of Excellence*, Harper and Row.

Stevens, C (1984), 'All Parents as a Resource for Education', in Harber, C et al (Eds) *Alternative Educational Futures*, Holt, Rinehart and Winston.

16 School-focused training for governors

Barbara Bullivant

In English and Welsh schools today, decisions about the management of the school are no longer the headteacher's sole prerogative, guided by local education authority policies. To an increasing extent, the Department of Education and Science interprets and transmits the policies decided by the Secretary of State; staff expect to participate, financial constraints limit action, and new technologies impose their own demands. Now, too, the governors have a large share in decisions about policies and practices within the school.

The Board of Governors stands between the school and the outside world, of the school, but not in it, an extension of the local authority, but not entirely its agent. For the most part, governors are lay people, part appointed and part elected, who should play a considerable part in the life of the school, and their main contacts with the school are likely to be the key managers, the head and senior staff.

Governors have considerable legal powers vis-a-vis the schools, and these have been extended by the Education Reform Act of 1988. Governors are being encouraged to use their powers, as they have not always done in the past.

If they are to carry out their responsibilities properly, they must be knowledgeable. The acquisition of the necessary skills and knowledge may be best organised through training, and I hope to show how and why this might best be organised on a school-focused basis.

At the present time, there are few models for a structured training course for governors within the schools they govern, and these are even rarer in primary than in secondary schools. Help is available, but it will need commitment and skill to introduce such training. It is unlikely that any finance will be made available, and little time, other than that which staff, and the governors themselves, are willing to give.

However, the rewards for such efforts are likely to be worthwhile, not only for the governors, who will learn what the task entails, and to know their schools, but also for the head and staff, the pupils and parents, and the local community. These rewards may be intangible – better interviews, more committed governors, better public relations, or they may be material – improved resources, faster repairs, even additional pairs of hands to help. School-focused training can help to turn a collection of people meeting formally once a term into 'a cross-section of the friends every school should have' – friends, moreover, who may be well-placed, and committed, to working, with staff, for the good of their school.

Why have governors?

'Do we need governors?' This was an early question considered by the Taylor Committee, set up in 1975 by the Secretary of State, to enquire into school government. The 1944 Education Act had laid down a system of governors for secondary schools, and managers for primary schools, and a set of Model Articles, describing their powers and duties, had been issued shortly thereafter. With some honourable exceptions, the system had few obvious results. By the mid-1960s, however, parents had begun to organise themselves, and they saw the Boards as a way of channelling and legitimising their wish to have a real part in their children's education, at a decision-making level, without party political commitment. From this interest came the National Association of Governors and Managers, founded in 1970, which seeks the reform of school government, among its other objects.

The British system has always required some sort of public accountability for the spending of public money. It would be too great a burden on elected councillors alone to monitor every school, and the growing interest of the whole community in education needed legitimate expression.

The Taylor Committee, in its Report *A New Partnership for Our Schools*, (DES, 1977) recognised both the 'public accountability' function and the 'community interest' function which governors could fulfil and their recommendations on composition included the local authority, elected parents, elected school staff and a community element, each comprising one quarter of Boards.

The 1988 Education Reform Act has, to some extent, used this formula.

Who are governors

The 1980 Education Act required LEAs to establish, by 1985, individual boards, with elected parents and teachers, for their schools, and the 1986 Act required that boards should comprise only these, plus LEA appointed governors and some co-opted people from the local community, who must include a representative of the local business community, if that community is not adequately represented. Primary schools in an area with a minor local authority must have a representative of that authority; Church schools have some Foundation governors; Special schools have a governor nominated by an appropriate Voluntary body; headteachers may choose whether or not to be governors, but are entitled to attend all meetings. No other categories of governors are now permitted, although governors may use their co-optative places to bring in, for example, a representative of the non-teaching staff, but not a pupil.

Although, in the past, LEAs have often used their places on Boards to appoint on a non-party political basis, the reduction in the number of LEA places is likely to mean that LEA governors are now nominated by political parties, although they may not be elected councillors.

Powers and duties of governors

Although the Education Acts of 1980 and 1986 gave governors some new tasks, these acts were mainly concerned with the composition and legal framework of boards.

The 1988 Education Reform Act includes much more about the powers and duties of governors. Some provisions already operate; others are being phased in. When all the legislation is in operation, the functions of governors will encompass most aspects of school management.

The following list covers many of the areas on which governors may be expected to make decisions:

- the allocation of the school budget. This will be delegated to them in schools with over 200 pupils, and perhaps in others. Most of the money required for running the school, including the cost of wages and salaries, will be included, but not capital spending, major repairs and some specialised services;

- the appointment, promotion and recommendation for dismissal of all staff;
- cover for most staff absences;
- equipment and supplies;
- the use of the premises by others;
- internal maintenance, repair, decoration and cleaning of premises;
- putting certain services out to tender;
- the aims of the school;
- aspects of the curriculum;
- the school day, and occasional holidays;
- staff and pupil discipline procedures and appeals;
- out-of-school trips by pupils;
- charges for school activities;
- provision for those with Special Educational Needs (1981 Act);
- receiving and commenting on reports by HM Inspectors of Schools;
- requirements under Health and Safety, Equal Opportunities and Race Relations legislation;
- whether to apply for grant maintained status.

Governors are expected to monitor the performance of the school, and may be called upon to assess teacher performance. Each year, the governors must prepare and circulate an Annual Report to parents about their work, and hold an Annual Meeting of Parents. They are also involved in the preparation of the school's brochure for parents.

Central to all the duties of governors is their main duty. The Model Articles, drawn up after the 1944 Education Act, state:

The Local Education Authority shall determine the general educational character of the school, and its place in the local educational system. Subject thereto, the governors shall have the general direction of the conduct and curriculum of the school.

Some Articles use 'oversight' in place of 'direction', but the Model Articles go on to say:

All proposals and reports affecting the conduct and curriculum of the school shall be submitted formally to the governors.

The day-to-day management of the school is in the hands of the headteacher, but full consultation between the head and the Chairman of the Governors is also required by the Model Articles.

Governors may delegate some of their tasks to sub-committees, which may allow other governors to learn the skills of chairing. A sub-committee may then make recommendations to the whole board. Action delegated to a sub-committee, or to one person (Head, Chair) must be reported on at a subsequent board meeting.

Skills governors need

In order to carry out their duties, governors need a range of skills. On appointment, governors may be unfamiliar with modern educational principles and practices. They may never have entered a school since their own school-days, and they may have unpleasant memories of those days. Some will be unfamiliar with committee practice. A few may have, if not axes to grind, at least theories of their own to test, and may regard the Governing Body as the ideal sounding Board. It is unlikely that all the governors will know each other initially, and yet, if they are to act corporately, it is important that they are welded into a cohesive group. An experienced Chair and a helpful Clerk and head can do much to initiate new governors into 'the way we work'. Each school will have its own practices and traditions, even coteries, which the new governor may find it hard to penetrate or understand. A good Chair can help those who are new and, perhaps, diffident, to settle into the work of the governors meeting, and will encourage them to contribute. At the same time, the Chair has to ensure that no one governor, or interest group, dominates, and that no one feels left out of the discussions.

It has been said that it takes up to a year before a new governor feels sufficiently competent to make a worthwhile contribution.

Quite apart from the skills they require, governors need basic information about the system of school government. Some form of basic training is not only desirable, but is perceived to be desirable, and yet there is no requirement on them to obtain training, and the LEA is only required to see that 'such training as the authority consider necessary' is provided, although this must be free.

Training options for governors

Even the training which is available may be rudimentary or inappropriate. It may be devised by those who are not at the 'sharp end' in education: it may be riddled with psychological concepts and considerations which are quite unsuited to the wide range of people now serving as governors. It may be very general, not taking account of the differences of policy and practice in different LEAs. Even training provided on an area-wide basis, and related to local conditions, is inevitably unable to deal with the particular situations of individual schools.

The Open University has produced a new introductory pack, which comprises a 30 minute video, workbook and guide. Every LEA will have a copy, which schools may be able to borrow – or buy their own. Other training material which can be used by groups or individuals is listed at the end of this chapter.

Many LEAs run courses, either alone, or in conjunction with some educational institution – a University Extra-Mural Department or local College. The Workers Educational Association, local branches of CASE (Campaign for the Advancement of State Education) and local Parent-Teacher Federations have all run courses, as have the Cooperative movement and the political parties. NAGM (National Association of Governors and Managers) has been organising governor training since 1972, and has produced packs which anyone may use to run training, much of it based on primary schools, and including simulation material. AGIT keeps a register of courses, books, videos etc.

Who take up training options?

Some governors will resist the idea of attending a training course, provided centrally. They may be unwilling to commit the amount of time required, or unable to do so because of other duties. Not all training courses have been free of charge, and, if held at a distance, travelling costs may be a consideration. Some may have philosophical objections to training, like the parent-governor who said 'I was elected as a typical parent. If I attend training, I shall know more than other parents, and so will no longer be typical'! Or the objection may be to those who are providing the training. The Chairman of a large Primary School Board, who had not attended a training course, advised his fellow governors against doing so, saying 'They will be trying to tell you what to think.' In fact, some of the governors did attend the course. Far from being told 'what to think', they found the information provided useful and stimulating, and at future meetings of the Board were able to correct the Chairman, as a result, of what they had learned.

A report, published in September 1985, on '*School Governors – a strategy to meet the need for training*', (Taylor, 1985) included the results of a survey undertaken in South Norfolk, which explored not only what governors wanted to know and the preferred patterns of training which might be offered, but also, how many governors would be willing to attend. For primary schools, the figure was over 80 per cent, even though only 71 per cent believed that training would improve their effectiveness.

Do all governors need training?

Headteachers and staff may know their own school, and the world of education, but may be unfamiliar with some aspects of local policy and future plans for education in the area. Councillors and other LEA nominees may be familiar with policies, but may not have been into schools recently, and may know only what they read in the local Press about conditions in schools. Parents and other 'non-authority' governors may be very well aware of their needs for training.

Informal training in the school

There are draw-backs, as indicated above, to training provided in a centre. Although it gives governors an opportunity to discuss with the governors of other schools, and to hear speakers from the LEA, it is not so closely related to a governor's own school as he might wish, and will include some material which is not relevant to his needs. Even to consider a governor's responsibility for 'conduct and curriculum' can best be discussed in terms of the particular school. It is this which causes most concern to governors them-selves. While it is their duty to be satisfied that all is well, some will hesitate to ask questions on a report – or even to ask for a report – because they fear to tread on professional toes. These fears may be interpreted by the staff of the school as indifference, and a 'prod' may be necessary.

The head of a First School tackled the problem in a forthright manner. 'You have all been members of this governing body for three years' she said, 'but in all that time no one has asked how we teach children to read, nor what our success rate is.' As a result that governing body started its learning process. At each subsequent meeting, half an hour was set aside, and the head, or another member of staff, talked about an area of the curriculum, followed by questions and discussion. The interest shown by the governors led to an invitation for them to attend a parents' meeting, at which the adults present all received a lesson as it would be taught to the children. This proved to be a popular exercise, and was repeated with music and science as topics.

The curriculum is, of course, more than the subject taught. A junior school arranged for its governors to be briefed on the pre-paratory work which went on before a class visit to a farm. There was also a follow-up, when governors saw the work produced as a result of the visit. Governors were impressed by the amount of work which went into – and came out of – the visit, and asked whether one or two of their number could go along on future visits of this kind.

The head of a middle school, which made a feature of displaying children's work around the building, grew tired of inviting governors to 'come and see our displays'. With the agreement of the Chairman, the next agenda for the governors meeting included an item 'to examine displays within the school, and the need for more display space'. Several members of staff were on hand to conduct small groups of governors round the displays, and to explain the work on show.

All these are informal ways of educating governors, which could be matched by examples from many schools. As with all Adult Education, it is necessary to arouse interest, to be flexible in response to questions, and to allow governors to discuss topics of interest, and to find out more for themselves.

But is this sufficient to ensure that governors are fully informed about their role and duties, and gain skills? Some governing bodies have organised training for themselves on a formal basis, and more might be willing to do so if both the need were perceived, and the willingness to meet the need were provided.

Why should the school provide training for its governors?

When we consider the duties and responsibilities which governors have, it is apparent that they have a considerable influence on the school, and in particular, on the staff. If the aims and objects of the school have to be agreed with the governors, if they interview and recommend for appointment, and if they may also have a role in the disciplinary proceedings so far as staff and pupils are concerned, it is obvious that they need to know about the school, its staff and pupils, in order to act responsibly. Many teachers object to being interviewed by 'the butcher, the baker and the electricity-meter reader', but that is the system now in use, and it is better that the school has had, and has taken, the opportunity of seeing that the governors are well informed. If local rumours affect a school, if numbers are declining, if an HMI report contains some adverse criticism, governors who know their school, its policies and practices, who are in contact with the staff, and who are used to working together, will be in a much better position to defend the school than if these things are sprung upon them without their having adequate preparation for dealing with them. Governors who have experienced a cold school on a Monday morning, or seen the roof leaking on a wet Friday, will put more conviction into their requests for improvements, and be more active in following up delays in repairs. So to some extent, it is enlightened self-interest on the part of the school to become involved in training governors.

Dare I suggest that there is more to it than that? Sometimes, staff do not know what the local opinion of the school is. Sometimes, outsiders can be aware of problems which the school is having, or unwittingly causing. And school's staff can sometimes become insular, and need to discuss their work with others in order to develop a wider view. One school, for example, believing itself to be in line with the best modern practice, taught only metric measure. The governors pointed out that, at home, mum still used imperial measure for her recipes, and employers among them pointed out that local firms could not afford to go metric. The result was that the school taught both systems of measurement after that.

It is desirable that the school staff should be in agreement with any school-focused training for governors, since their help with the training is invaluable. Even if they are not prepared to be involved, it is still possible to arrange the training, though it may be less easy to focus on all aspects of the school, and throw a greater burden onto the head.

Setting up the training

It is easy to decide that there will be training, to start, and then to lose impetus and the attention of governors. Any training should be planned in advance, and discussed with the governors. Their wishes and needs should be built into the programme, and unless they are asked, their needs may not emerge. The study undertaken in South Norfolk, (Taylor, 1985) and referred to above found that the main topics on which primary school governors felt they needed training were, in order of importance, as follows:

- Duties and responsibilities of governors;
- interviewing and appointing staff;
- organisation and management of the school;
- the curriculum;
- school buildings and premises;
- teacher services – function and role;
- school and local community
- special educational needs and the 1981 Act;
- finance and education;
- administration of the service, nationally and locally;
- conduct of governors meetings;
- external examinations and GCSE

These topics were placed in rank order from a list of suggestions by governors, and there may be other topics, or extensions of the above topics, which could be included. For example, governors of Voluntary Schools, especially Aided Schools, could express a need for understanding the role of the Foundation.

If it is agreed to start training, the planning should be a first priority. The danger is that a decision to have training is taken at one meeting, and a planning committee is set up, which reports back at the next meeting, receives further guidance from the governors, reports back again at a third meeting, and training does not get under way until the fourth meeting, by which time a year may have passed. It is useful to have a small planning group – perhaps head, Chair and a parent governor, with assistance from the Clerk or attending LEA officer when possible. If an initial meeting, at which the proposition is discussed, can give some idea of the pattern of training which would be acceptable and which governors would be prepared to commit themselves to, then the planning group can come back with a programme all ready to go. It will depend on the governors themselves whether the training is to be taken in small doses of half an hour or so at each regular meeting, or whether they are prepared to set aside a day or half day, perhaps once a term, for training.

The planning group should ascertain whether the governors want any 'outside' speakers to join them, and if so, arrange the invitations in good time. The Chair of the Education Committee, or the Chief Education Officer, may not be willing or able to attend, but there may be another councillor or officer, able to explain local policies, who is willing to come for one meeting. Although the training is to be school-focused, the school does not exist in a vacuum, and the way in which it is affected by, and relates to, the outside educational world, can be important to understand.

The planning group may also wish to call on the talents of governors themselves. The head and staff governors are obvious people to help, but there may be other governors who could make a contribution. Or each of the governors could be asked to undertake a small piece of work which illuminates some aspect of the school, and report the results to their colleagues.

Using existing materials

There are now available several different courses and sets of material suitable for adaptation to particular needs. Many of these use stimulations, and this is material which can easily be constructed by the planning group for use in their own situation. Training arranged by NAGM relies heavily on simulations, and the materials produced by them have been obtained by many schools and groups of governors.

Simulations are an excellent way of training in some of the techniques governors need to acquire. They can help to develop confidence, as people learn in a non-threatening atmosphere, where the results do not 'matter', in the way that they might in a 'real' situation. They can also be very entertaining, which helps to retain interest and commitment to training. I do not suggest that all the training should be by simulation. Governors need basic information, before they start to put their knowledge into practice, even in a 'pretend' situation.

Devising simulations

The simplest simulation exercise is mounted by taking an old agenda and head's report, and working through them, as though in a real governors meeting. So the Chair, Clerk, head and others play their real-life roles. At the end of each item, or other appropriate time, there is an opportunity to stop and ask questions, or make comments, which governors might have hesitated to do during a real session. For example, one may say 'It is interesting to read about all the out-of-school visits children have made, but why are they all reported to us?' This gives the head an opportunity to explain that he is reporting action under delegated powers from the governors; that if the powers were not delegated, the governors would have to agree every out-of-school visit in advance.

As a variant, when governors are a little more secure in their role, and know one another better, some changes of role can be tried. This helps governors to see things from a different point of view, to realise how difficult is the job of the head, the teacher, the parent or the Education Committee member.

One area of their work which many governors feel nervous about is the appointment of staff. A simulation exercise here may need more 'setting-up', but can be very rewarding. It may mean the devising of several papers – the job description or advertisement of a post in the school, several sets of application forms from mythical teachers, and finding people willing to play the roles of these mythical interviewees. It is much easier to learn about interviewing in a situation like this, where mistakes will not affect the school, or the staff member, than in a real situation. The planning group may wish to supply a list of questions for governors to consider asking, or of points to look out for. If the simulation also includes 'confidential reports' on the candidates, this, too, can be helpful, as governors learn to understand what is not said, as well as what is written. A great deal of work may be needed to set up this simulation, but governors will learn far more from it (even if only a few are involved in the interview, and the rest watch from the side-lines) than they will from reading a book or listening to a talk on interviewing. It is obviously best if a reasonable length of time is set aside for this exercise, and different groups of governors could interview each candidate. Then the whole group could decide which of the candidates they would have appointed in a real-life interview.

The danger inherent in simulations of this kind within a school is that some staff – even the head – may feel under stress, or threatened, by them. But they can have an excellent effect in welding the governors together, and in increasing their sense of commitment. There are other situations which can also be used as a basis for simulation, such as an appeal against suspension by a pupil, but these are likely to occur only very rarely in primary schools. However, if school appraisal is to be a function of the governors, some training in this field would be helpful.

Who initiates the idea of training?

The initial suggestion of school-focused training may come from any member of the Board, but is unlikely to get very far unless the headteacher is in favour. The head and Chair may wish to discuss the suggestion first, and perhaps ask the Clerk (if an LEA Officer) or perhaps the vicar or priest (if a Voluntary School) before widening the discussion to all the governors. If possible, it is desirable that all the governors wish to be involved, so the initiator may need to have powers of persuasion, and persistence.

When to train

Governors may not take kindly to extra meetings arranged on snowy winter nights, or summer evenings when they would prefer to be in the garden. Training ought to be started as early as possible in the life of a Board, and should not last so long that everyone becomes bored with it. The membership of Boards changes from time to time as for example, when new parents are elected, and it could be confusing and depressing for new members to come into the middle of a three-year exercise. If governors are willing to give up some extra time, it would be better to complete the training within one term, perhaps repeating it after a year or two for the benefit of newcomers, and as a refresher course for others. Some governors may wish to attend locally provided courses instead of a school-based course, so it may be better to avoid holding in-school training at the same time as a local course is running. Governors may be attracted to the school training because nothing else is available. They may also find it an excellent basis from which to go on to an area-based course, or as an extension of what they have learned on an area-based course. So the planning group should try to obtain a picture of what training, if any, governors have already had, and of their intentions on training, and tailor the school-focused course to fit the governors, as well as the school.

After the training

Most courses of training can benefit from the comments and suggestions of those who have taken part. It is good practice to find out how governors have benefitted (or otherwise) from the training; what they found particularly useful; what could have been left out. If the staff of the school have been involved – in talking to governors and answering their questions, or in simulations, – their views could also be sought.

If these views are collected soon after the training, and collated, they will form a valuable guide for the next planning group brave enough to try again.

Benefits of the training

For individual governors, the benefits of training may be seen in terms of increased knowledge, greater ability to communicate, less apprehension about participating, and a greater understanding of the institution they govern.

For the Board as a whole, there is the likelihood of better decisions, based on greater knowledge, knowing each others strengths and weaknesses, and what each member can contribute to the work of the Board, and to the school, and greater commitment to the school.

Where to find help

Some sources of help have already been mentioned; others are given at the chapter end. Borrow material from the LEA if possible. Some courses are expensive to buy, but NAGM has a number of training packages available at reasonable cost. Guides designed for individual study can be easily adapted for groups and for particular schools. For example, it is possible to work through a book of this kind, a chapter at a time, seeing where it is appropriate for the school. Guides of this kind must cover the provisions of the 1988 Act to be worth studying, and more such guides appear all the time. There are now also a number of training videos available, and it may be possible to borrow some of these from the LEA. If the LEA is a member of AGIT, the list of available training material may possibly be borrowed from the LEA.

Other bodies which may have useful material available include the National Association of Head Teachers, the National Union of Teachers, and other teacher-organisations, CASE, political parties, Industry Matters, and local area-based training schemes, whose lecturers may be able to point to locally produced materials, which will fit into a school-based scheme of training.

Conclusion

School-focused training can be a help to the governors and the school. A good head is probably the best training agent, since he knows about education in practice, and relates it to the school. The head, too, may find the training beneficial, for pertinent questions requiring answers concentrate the mind, and after a course of school-focused training, the governors should be aware of the questions to ask, and be able to evaluate the answers they receive.

References

DES (1977), *A New Partnership for our Schools (The Taylor Report)*, HMSO.

Taylor, G F (1985), *School Governors; A Strategy to meet the Need for Training*, Norfolk Education Department.

Further Reading

ACE (1989), *ACE Governors Handbook*, Advisory Centre for Education.

Bullivant, B (1988), *You are the Governor*, Bedford Square Press.

Harding, P (1987), *A Guide to Governing Schools*, Paul Chapman.

Hill, D & Spinks, J (1989), *Financial Delegation and Local Management of Schools*, Paul Chapman.

Mahoney, T (1988), *Governing Schools: Powers, Issues and Practice*, Macmillan.

Sallis, J (1988), *Schools, Parents and Governors*, Routledge.

Training materials

BBC, *Getting Started* (audio cassette and booklet).

Focus in Education, *LMS: Lessons from Norfolk* (video based on the experience of four secondary schools).

Focus in Education, *On being a School Governor* (three videos – the role of the governor, shortlisting and interviewing, interpreting the headteacher's report).

Forum Television, *Spending Power* (video and booklet on LMS and finance).

NAGM, *Basic Training Kit, Special Schools Kit, Meetings Skills, Selection and Interviewing, Appointing a Headteacher, Training for Chairs* (simulation material and notes).

Open University, *Governing Schools in the 90s: Into Action* (video, workbook and guide).

Organisations

Advisory Centre for Education (ACE), 18 Victoria Park Square, London E2 9PB.

Action on Governor Information and Training (AGIT), c/o CEDC, Briton Road, Coventry CV2 4LF.

BBC Governor Training Project, PO Box 50, Wetherby, Yorkshire LS23 7EZ.

Focus in Education Ltd, 65 High Street, Hampton Hill, Middlesex TW12 1NH.

National Association of Governors and Managers, 4 Hammersmith Terrace, London W6 9TS.

17 Marketing schools

Michael P Brunt

Generally, educationalists resent the intrusion of the concepts of competition and marketing into their world otherwise untainted by such base considerations. For some, competition is considered *infra dignitatem*, while marketing is considered a bit of a joke, something to which really important, professional services do not demean themselves (McCloy, 1985). For others, professional ethics demand that schools and teachers ought to eschew competition in favour of collaboration in the common interest. They see the profit motive as incompatible with a public service, dedicated to altruism. Some suspicion may be traced back to the days when the market was regarded as the place set aside for people to deceive each other (Frain, 1981). The intellectual has never been kindly disposed toward the marketplace. For him/her it is a place of vulgar people and base motives (Stigler, 1963). Others regard the analogies of industrial marketing as far-fetched and unhelpful in the context of a non-profit-making activity. Yet others argue that expert and trained professionals know what kind of education to provide and are unwilling to respond to the passing whims of governments, employers or the public. 'The professionals know best,' they say. Ironically, those same educationists who reject the notion of marketing in the context of schooling may see it as being perfectly legitimate for parents to exercise their rights and responsibilities for providing and obtaining the best possible educational experiences for their children by buying, for example, 'educational' toys. Indeed, this practice is widely applauded. Why, then, is it not recognised that those same parents are exercising their same market-place rights and responsibilities when 'buying in' schooling for their children?

It is the thesis of this chapter that concepts borrowed from the art and science of marketing may be adopted as analogies useful to our understanding of relationships between schools, children, their parents and society and in defining appropriate responses to the unabating demands made of schools and to the increasing competition among providing institutions. An analogy may be drawn from the definition of marketing:

> Marketing involves balancing the company needs for profit against the benefits required by consumers so as to maximise long term earnings per share. (Davidson, 1975)

There is a considerable resistance to treating children as a product to be finished off and to the equation of schooling to the activities of a porcelain factory: but it is not necessary to draw a strict equation, it is sufficient to draw a parallel.

> Marketing a school involves balancing society's needs for a cultured population against the immediate demands of parents, providers and consumers so as to maximise the school's contribution to the well-being of society at large.

The contribution of schools to society is made by means of the school's curriculum, defined as the sum of the experiences, directly or indirectly, overtly or discretely, deliberately or fortuitously, presented by the school to the children.

Implicit in this parellel is the recognition of the difficulty of defining who is the client or customer or consumer of the education service (Douglas, 1985). The primary consumers or clients are the pupils themselves who will eventually make direct use of their education for personal ends, the secondary consumers are their parents, future employers and society, who perceive the advantages of having a better behaved household, a more skilled workforce and more cultured neighbours. This chapter makes no attempt to define whose desires and interests should predominate in any conflict of values. Sometimes there will be irreconcilable differences. I have argued elsewhere that these should be mediated through the school's governing body (Brunt, 1985a and 1985b). It is central to the argument that the adoption of a marketing orientation and its attendant attitudes, value systems and management techniques is a necessary precondition for recognising such disputes and therefore for resolving them.

The marketing orientation to education received its apotheosis during the 1980's by having two Education Acts devoted almost entirely to it, the Education Act, 1980, and the Education Reform Act, 1988. The former had as its *leitmotif*, its prevailing theme, the pursuit of the dominance of the consumer and the operation of free market economics within the education service. It established the conditions for greater competition among schools by strictly delimiting the circumstances in which admission to a school may be refused (Education Act, 1980, Sections 6 and 7). It also encouraged competition among neighbouring LEAs by allowing parents to send their children of compulsory school age across LEA boundaries (ibid, Section 31). It encouraged competition between the public and private sectors in the form of the Assisted Places Scheme (ibid, Sections 17 and 18). This Act also obliges competing LEAs to describe their policies, their processes and their products in a pre-scribed form, in order that the potential consumer can make sounder judgements about the relative merits and demerits of the competing commodities (ibid, Section 8, and Education (School Information Regulations, 1981, SI 1981/630). The Education Act, 1980, was designed to meet growing pressure from parents for more involvement in school life. The vast majority of schools have responded to that pressure by opening to parents first their gates, then their doors and more recently by removing the palisades about the secret garden of the curriculum. the image of the interfering parent is being replaced by that of a parent as helper and partner in the education of his/her children. However, that there is still a resistance to parental involvement is evidenced by the demand made by the National Confederation of Parent Teacher Associ-ations that parents be given a statutory right to establish a home-school association (Hammond, 1985). The statutory framework of the 1980 Act would, of course, have been both ineffective and unnecessary, had not demographic change, falling enrolments, changed the seller's market of underprovision into the buyer's market of excess capacity, thus making competition among pro-viders between and within the public and private sectors inevitable.

The 1980 Act has therefore created two of the classical conditions in which marketing can become important. It has provided the context for competition among schools and the requirement that the customer should be provided with the information on which to base a sound choice. When this is combined with a fall in the demand for places caused by a falling birth rate, we have the classic conditions necessary for competition.

The Education Reform Act, 1988, has taken the marketing orien-tation several logical strides further. Individual institutions are to become profit centres able to compete for trade, with the artificial barriers to competition (the planned admission limits of the Edu-cation Act, 1980) set aside so that schools must admit up to their building capacity, if there are sufficient applicants. Popular schools will become the (usually unwilling) agents of putting their neigh-bours out of business.

Another key strand is the breakdown of local government's vir-tual monopoly on the provision of schooling and its absolute mon-opoly on the provision of fee-free schooling. No longer (paraphrasing Ford's slogan 'You can have any colour car as long as it's black') will one be able to say of the education service: 'You can have any school as long as it's LEA-maintained'. Now there will be City Technology Colleges, CTCs for the Arts and Grant-Maintained schools alongside the current range of LEA schools. All this is consistent with the notion that excellence is achieved, not by the intervention of governments, but by the combined effects of enlightened consumers exercising informed choice in a varied and competitive market place. It is also consistent with the prediction put forward by several commentators that the Education Reform Act, 1988, is but a staging post towards the introduction of a voucher system involving both the public and private sectors.

Another of the classical conditions necessary for competition is an increase in the opportunities for product differentiation. The abolition of the Schools Council and the introduction of the National Curriculum envisaged in the Education Reform Act, 1988, run counter to the free market mentality. The latter, however, offers a product specification with which all schools' provision may be compared and the national testing arrangements provide a yardstick against which the performance of schools will be measured.

It would be a mistake, however, to concentrate exclusively on the use of marketing as a means of promoting competition among educational institutions, marketing concepts can be useful in establishing strategies for improving the market standing of the education service generally in its competition for an increasing share of the public purse. Indeed, since the mid-1970s, the education service's public relations team has scored several own goals (William Tyndale, the Great Debate, disruption caused by the pay dispute, the Honeyford Saga, the Poundswick dispute) and has left the impression in the public mind that schools are inadequately equipped, understaffed, badly housed, indisciplined, incompetent in inculcating basic skills, irrelevant to the needs of the industrial and economic society and peopled by reactionary communist bureaucrats (Beare, 1985). It follows from this disturbing summary of education's corporate image that schools do themselves and the service they represent inestimable damage if they base their competition with other schools on the demerits of their competitors rather than on their own merits.

Professor Ted Wragg (Wragg, 1989) rightly emphasises the difficulties inherent in non-aggression pacts among neighbouring schools, as the silence leaves the press with only rumour and scandal on which to base its copy. Far better for heads in a locality to work in concert in providing, each in turn, press releases and features highlighting the excellence of the service provided in our schools.

To ensure that the analogy between the marketing of a school and the marketing of a product should not be extended beyond the bounds of reason, it is necessary to distinguish between social marketing and business marketing in three dimensions.

1 Business marketers try to meet the needs and wants of markets: social marketers try to change their attitudes or behaviours.

2 Business marketers aim to make a profit through serving the interests of the market; social marketers aim to serve the interests of the market without personal profit.

3 Business marketers market products and services through the medium of ideas: social marketers market the ideas themselves rather than products or services. (Kotler, 1975)

The first process undertaken by the Marketing Director is the four-step marketing planning process:

1(a) Gathering relevant information about the external environment and about the organisation's internal resources.

1(b) Identifying the organisational strengths and weaknesses vis-à-vis the external market and opportunities and competitive threats facing the organisation.

2 Laying down the marketing objectives of the organisation based on the results of the first two steps above.

3(a) Laying down strategies for achieving the objectives.

3(b) Laying down programmes for implementing the strategies to include timing, responsibilities and costs.

4 Measuring the progress towards achievement of the objectives, reviewing and amending the plan as necessary. (Wills et al, 1975)

Phase one of the marketing planning process, therefore, will entail identifying the potential customers and defining the characteristics, educational background, attitude sets, etc, which enable them to be broken down into sub-groups. This 'market segmentation' can be useful when targeting any promotional activities. Since the school's offerings are unlikely to appeal equally to all people, segmentation of the market makes it possible for the school's offerings are unlikely to appeal equally to all people, segmentation of the market makes it possible for the school's characteristics to be presented accurately and attractively to people in ways which are relevant to them.

In many areas, the school's market has already been strictly delimited by geographical factors or the policy of the LEA, but it has been shown that parents are willing to move house to be in the catchment area of a favoured school (Guratsky, 1982). The market is therefore not as rigorously delimited as might appear at first sight.

In order comprehensively to pursue the analysis of one's potential consumers, it should be remembered that consumers, when they purchase a commodity do not purchase the object *per se*, but the benefits, immediate or long-term, which it potentially provides. Black and Decker, for example, made its fortune not because potential customers wanted 8 millimetre drills but because people wanted to have the wherewithal to make 8 millimetre holes; from which it follows that if there had been developed a more cost-effective means of making holes, Black and Decker would develop that product or lose out on its market. Similarly, then, children do not want schooling, *per se*, but the benefits which it provides immediately or in the longer term. This distinction is helpful when schools decide what characteristics might make them more attractive to a potential client group. These characteristics are the criteria on the basis of which customers make their choices.

Choice criteria may be functional or non-functional. Functional criteria relate to the physical properties of a product eg the number of miles to the gallon performed by a car. Non-functional criteria relate to the connotations evoked in the customer by the product eg its style, image and tone. Functional criteria adopted in the selection of schools may vary widely from the perceived success rate of the school in achieving a desired educational outcome for its pupils, to the length of the school day. The market standing of a primary school serving an area with a large proportion of parents desiring selective secondary education for their children will clearly depend upon the school's success or otherwise in achieving that ambition, and a proportionate (or disproportionate) amount of time may therefore need to be devoted to the achievement of that aim. Some schools serve children a high proportion of whose parents are both away from home throughout the school day. In such cases, without abrogating their responsibilities for poviding a curriculum suited to the long-term needs of the children and of society, schools will need to have regard to the advantages of extending the length of the school day, and their market standing will be disproportionately affected by any disruption of school dinners during an industrial dispute or by the abandonment or curtailment of after-school activities.

The more qualitative educational considerations are difficult to apply justly to schools as functional criteria of success. Nonetheless, parents continue to rely on such measures as selective school pass rates as a criterion for choosing a school. By contrast, parents who understand the shortcomings of that approach may be influenced to adopt a basically non-functional criterion such as the presence or absence of a uniform because of its associations with the school's style, tone or image. In the words of Curtis (1984):

the less tangible the product, the more powerfully and persistently the judgement about it gets shaped by the packaging.

For this reason, headteachers may need to adopt visual symbols like logos, mottos, monograms and colour schemes to enhance the public image of the school.

Having identified one's potential customers and the criteria, functional or non-functional, which they may adopt in choosing the school, headteachers adopting the marketing approach should determine who are their potential competitors in the market place. In a prosperous area, the local preparatory school may pose a real threat to the school's continued viability. In most areas, particularly in urban locations where schools are relatively accessible, the neighbouring school with its newly appointed dynamic headteacher is the potential competitor. In some areas of the inner cities, there may be a demand for provision sensitive to the tenets of different cultures and religions, and consequently education at home or at the local mosque may be considered by the potential clients (or their parents) to be a real alternative. In other cases there may be a tradition of rejection of schooling, posing a real threat to the school's effectiveness. In all such cases, the headteacher should identify the characteristics of the potential competitor (be it the preparatory school, the neighbouring county school, the mosque or no school at all) which make it attractive to its clients or their parents. Those characteristics might be, in the case of the preparatory school, for example, its very separateness or its freedom from disruption during pay disputes or its perceived excellence in providing for gifted children or the range of extra-curricular activities or some combination of these and other factors. In the case of competition from the local mosque, there may well be a reluctance on the part of parents to allow girls and boys to be educated in the same school, or to take swimming lessons at the same time. The assessment of the competition is rarely as clear-cut, simple and starkly depicted as these few examples. Usually there are more subtle nuances of choice in operation.

Having defined one's competitors in a certain market place, one decides whether the school is able to compete in that sector, remembering that there may be some characteristics of the competition (for example its selectivity, its separateness or its single-sex provision) which cannot be emulated.

Next, one makes a judgement about whether one wishes to compete for that sector of the market and risk alienating a different sector of the community. Stripped of its racial and emotional overtones, the Bradford, Drummond Middle School, Ray Honeyford affair could readily be viewed as a headteacher's conscious decision to concentrate on one sector of the market to the exclusion of the other.

This approach, the analysis of the potential consumers and competition and appropriate responses thereto, has been described as the SWOT (Strengths, Weaknesses, Opportunities, Threats) technique. (Wills, 1975). It involves an analysis of the school's internal strengths and weaknesses and the external opportunities and threats. The outcome of that analysis will be an initial position statement or marketing audit. It should include a strategy for building on the school's strengths, for eliminating its weaknesses, for taking advantage of the opportunities and for neutralising the threats.

The position statement or marketing audit is the first of four analyses which the marketing approach demands. It poses the question: 'Where is the school now?' it should be followed by:

- Question No 2. 'where do you want to get to?': Aims and Objectives;
- Question No 3. 'how do you propose to get there?': Strategy and Tactics;
- Question No 4. 'how will you know when you have arrived?': Performance Appraisal.

The position statement is rather like the assessment of the product mix in the marketing context and it falls to the headteacher periodically in the light of assessments of the requirements of the potential consumers or in the light of increased competition or changes in the social or economic context to make subtle changes to the curriculum provided in order the better to cater for the special characteristic of the market in which the school is operating. For this purpose, the headteacher will need to engage in a continuing process of acquiring information on the consumers, their satisfaction with the provision, the changed provision which might better suit their needs and the size and share of the market for which the school is likely to be catering, so that the school will be able to take advantage of, and not be threatened by, environmental social, economic and demographic change.

Aims and objectives

'Cheshire Puss, would you like to tell me which way I ought to walk from here?'

That depends on where you want to get to,' said the cat.
'I don't care where,' said Alice.
'Then it doesn't matter which way you walk,' said the cat.
'So long as I get somewhere,' said Alice as an explanation.

'Oh you're bound to do that,' said the cat, 'if only you walk long enough.'

This quotation from *Alice in Wonderland* exemplifies as well as any the importance of defining the purpose of the school's activity and the destination for which it is heading. Too many schools are run on the principles of Christopher Columbus:

- when he set out, he did not know where he was going:
- when he arrived, he did not know where he was:
- when he got back, he did not know where he had been:
- and all this done on public money.

What is clear from the Peters and Waterman's (1982) study of excellent marketing practice in US industry as being an important facet of preparing a school for its market place is the adoption of a definite belief system and the commitment in practice to its implementation. The value system should not just be transmitted in writing but should pervade the whole culture of the institution , in its stories, anecdotes and activities. If good behaviour, consideration for others, academic achievement and the work ethic not only find reflection in the daily act of worship but pervade the school's daily dealings and sayings, then the spin-offs will percolate as far as the parents, whose commitment will, in turn, be enhanced. Peters and Austin (1985) in their analysis of the common characteristics of outstanding companies operating in the business marketplace emphasise the importance of clarity and determination of purpose, advocating that businessmen, to be successful, have to know where they are going, have to have the ability to state that direction clearly and concisely and have to care about that purpose with passion. In short, they have to have a vision. The importance of the substance of that vision is a different issue from that of communicating it in all one's dealings with consistency and fervour.

According to Peters and Waterman, the value system is to be expressed in terms of qualitative rather than quantitative variables and should be underpinned by a firm belief in the dignity of individuals, be they workers or customers. Peters and Austin (1985), likewise, quoting Sara Lightfoot, show that these attitudes should be transmitted in practice throughout the organisation and that therefore attention should be paid to the need for teachers to have adult interaction, support, reward and criticism. If it is true in industry that only by treating people as adults can they in turn learn to treat their colleagues and customers with dignity in mature, selfless relationships, how much more apposite is that observation in the context of the school and its pupils.

When a school wholeheartedly adopts the marketing concept as a way of regulating its business, it bases its actions on the fundamental belief that in every phase of its operations, the organisation must bring itself into mutually satisfactory relationships with the users of its services. This pattern of mutually satisfactory relationships is often termed user-orientation or market-orientation; that is the proposition that a school should face outward towards the wants and needs of its users and not inwards towards what it likes doing or what it is experienced in doing (Frain, 1981).

A further corollary of this marketing approach is the commitment to listen intently to, and act upon, customer requirements, suggestions and complaints. The excellent companies studied in Peters and Waterman (1982) and Peters and Austin (1985).

- provide structured opportunities for customers to complain;
- expect the most senior members of staff to listen in to those complaints;
- actively seek information on customer satisfaction;
- put both compliments and complaints on public display;
- disseminate and implement the recommendations.

Schools, like companies, therefore, break down into two groups. The first, the most typical, views the complaint as an evil to be survived and forgotten. The second views the complaint as an opportunity to improve working practices and foster and improve public relations, working on the knowledge that each dissatisfied complainant has several scores of acquaintances, most of whom will, no doubt, hear of his disaffection, and pass it on, in sensationalised form, to their neighbours. Unfortunately, the opposite attitude, that of excessive sensitivity to complaints, has traditionally been associated with the education service, which relies on a technician-like arrogance that the product will sell itself.

It is implicit in the advocacy of a marketing approach to managing schools that one is sensitive to the needs of children and the demands of parents and society, from which it follows that it is unnecessary, impossible and undesirable to lay down a single rigid definition of the curriculum applicable to the widely differing social, economic and cultural environments and to children with widely disparate abilities, aptitudes and motivations. Such rigidity is incompatible with the increasing necessity for responsiveness to change and flexibility of delivery required of schools. In defining curricular aims and objectives, it is also implicit in the marketing approach that the school should give extensive consideration to the needs of the direct and indirect consumers, pupils, parents, potential employers and future neighbours. Relevant changes which need to be taken into account include declining enrolments, new technology, changes in the structure of the family, the growth of leisure, the decline of heavy industry, the rise of high-technology industry and the multi-ethnic nature of society. Consequently, the curriculum should provide pupils with the knowledge, conceptual understanding, skills, attitudes and personal qualities necessary for the individual's future effective participation in and contribution towards his home, his work, his leisure, the social, economic and political environment and personal relationships. These considerations should be a direct and primary focus of the school's aims and purposes, rather than a casual indirect spin-off of the academic curriculum. (Hewlett, 1985).

Strategy and tactics

The third strand to the marketing approach has to do with resources, obtaining them and deploying them. For a headteacher, obtaining from an unwilling LEA an adequate supply of staff, hardware and consumables (or in these days of Local Management Schemes, an adequate budget) is a primary activity. In the words of Charles Tandy, founder of the Tandy Corporation, (quoted in Peters and Austin, 1985): 'You can't sell goods from an empty wagon.'

However, the headteacher must avoid leaving the impression that the school is failing for want of resources or that it will fail if it does not receive more resources. Parents will not send their children to a failing school, LEA members and officers will not wish to invest in failure. Who wants to shop with an organisation of which one requires a long-term service, if its proprietors dress it up as bordering on bankruptcy? Far better to base one's arguments for increased resources on evidence of previous success with limited means.

Resource acquisition may be an important consideration, but resource disposition is crucial – it is the equivalent of the product mix in the marketing context. If the school's aims and objectives speak loftily of positive discrimination and in practice the remedial class is perpetually banished to the mobile hut, all the senior staff are men and English as a Second Language is first to be withdrawn whenever any member of staff is absent, the whole ostensible value system is discovered as a sham, with disastrous consequences for morale. The balance of resource disposition is a policy issue which requires to be clearly laid down and must accord with the thrust of the school's belief system.

There are four key variables in the strategy and tactics of marketing, namely product, place, price and promotion. An analysis of the nature of the product or service which is to be provided will give insight into the additional specialist qualifications and personal attributes, recruitment methods and training requirements of the personnel to be employed. An analysis of the place in the context of marketing a school would appear at first sight to be redundant, as the location of the school is a given fact over which the headteacher has no control; but on closer examination it can be imagined that some marketing activities located other than at the school – community-based charitable ventures, surveys conducted in the locality, displays and exhibitions in local museums and shopping centres and the activities of home-school liaison teachers – are both valid and relevant educational activities and have spin-offs for the market standing of the school. It must be recognised that headteachers are not often provided with the figures on which to base an analysis of the price (in, for example, teacher or other staffing time) of entering certain markets. The assessment of the opportunity costs of one course of action as against another is usually addressed superficially and intuitively, if at all. This is largely attributable to the longstanding practice among LEAs of allowing very little or no discretion to their headteachers in exchanging one kind of resource for another, but the pioneering work of Knight (1977), and Humphrey and Thomas (1983a and 1983b) and changes in practice in Cambridgeshire (see Audrey Stenner's chapter in this book) and Solihull, for example, have served as models for the Local Management provisions of the Education Reform Act, 1988, giving headteachers increasing flexibility in determining the balance of the resources which are allocated to pursuing various policy initiatives. Pricing policy will become increasingly important. As to promotion, schools continue to be coy about adopting strategies for selling themselves on their services to their potential customers, an attitude which is founded on a professional ethic now abandoned by the legal profession. If the analogy of schools competing in the market-place continues to be valid, it will not be long before headteachers need to examine the choice of communications media for an active promotion strategy together with the nature of the message to be transmitted. For the time being at least, the message will probably continue to be rather indiscriminately targetted and based on a public relations type of strategy as described below.

Performance appraisal

The fourth strand to the marketing approach is performance appraisal – how do we know when we have arrived? The difficulty with answering this question is probably founded in the fact that education is both the journey and the arrival, both a process and a product. The usual thrust of school performance measures has been to concentrate on the latter to the exclusion of the former. Pupil achievement, concentrating solely on areas in which outcomes can be measured, has been paramount. In the secondary domain, the average number of O-level passes per pupil, sometimes crudely related to the nature of the pupil intake of the school, has been king. The fact that these examinations were devised to measure pupil performance and not school effectiveness has largely been overlooked, as has the corollary that if one adds a Grade A in Physics to a Grade C in Woodwork O-level and a Grade 1 CSE in European Studies, a total of three is a less than adequate summary statistic. Likewise in the primary sector, intelligence quotients, verbal reasoning test scores and mathematics results have been summarised as the outcome of primary education, ignoring the factors over which the school has no control and ignoring the fact that to attempt to summarise standarised test scores of, for example, 130, 120 and 75 by an average figure of 110 is a statistically invalid operation. Other difficulties with performance appraisal based on pupil achievement are the absence of agreed input-output measures and the amount of 'noise' in the system, that is the change in the school's performance which is beyond the school's control. The testing arrangements incorporated into the 1988 Act attempt to make good the absence of agreed measures of output, but make no attempt to account for differences in the nature of the schools' inputs.

Academics invent a new measure of school effectiveness every week using the most sophisticated statistical techniques of multiple linear regression analysis, cluster analysis and analysis of variance, with the result that most of the debate and discussion surrounds the validity of the measures rather than the excellence of the children's performance which is what one is attempting to monitor.

Such measures of school effectiveness as are used should be few in number and simple of application: their shortcomings should be recognised from the outset. The workd 'satisficing' has been used to describe the real world process of reaching a satisfactory but avowedly imperfect solution to a complex issue. Much more satisfactory than pupil performance measures as a yardstick of school success, despite being often disparaged as 'soft' data not validated by quasi-scientific enquiry, are measures of customer satisfaction. It matters but little if Johnny has achieved scores of 130s throughout on standardised tests, if the range of his experiences at primary school has totally alienated him from any future committed participation in secondary education. Fortunately, such cases are extremely rare, but their absence is not born of any commitment on the part of the education service to the measurement of consumer satisfaction. One 'soft' source of data on the strength (or absence) of consumer satisfaction is for the headteacher to spend a substantial part of the school day with one (randomly selected) child. It will not be altogether difficult for the headteacher's sensitive observation to discern the whole range of pupil emotion from joy through puzzlement, boredom, frustration, loneliness and fear to anger at receiving less than the 10 minutes of individual attention from the teacher which is the most that the average child in a primary school can hope for in a day. A range of carefully constructed questions will soon reveal that the 'customer' has constructive remarks to make about the quality of the fare provided for him/her. This technique is widely used by school inspectors. Even a small number of such visits, is rigorously acted upon and used as the basis of small but significant improvements in the quality of the child's working day, can make a substantial contribution to the teachers' performance and the children's self-esteem. Peters and Waterman (op cit) and Peters and Austin (op cit) both refer to this technique as Management by Walking About. It can be, in the school setting, as fruitful a source of small items of potential improvement and as creative of a climate of respect for the pursuit of the objective of consumer satisfaction as it has been shown to be in the pursuit of excellence in the industrial setting. However, it is recognised that teachers vest a great measure of professional pride in their classroom performance. It would therefore be an essential preliminary to such an approach that there should have been created within the school a climate of trust, collegiality, self-confidence and commitment to excellence.

The measures which could readily be used may not be perfect, but most of them have the distinct advantage of having been available for years, so that real comparison of progress over time can be made, for example:

– attendance rates;
– proportion of the children in the immediate area opting for the school;
– proportion of parents involved in school activities;
– proportion of children smiling;
– number of letters of appreciation received.

It should be noted:

1 That these measures have largely to do with 'customer satisfaction' rather than pupil performance.
2 That they cannot reasonably be used as a basis for comparison with other schools in different circumstances but can be used to monitor one school's progress over the years.
3 That no attempt has been made to find the best possible measures,

but, in the context of a real-world complex environment, they may be the best measures possible.

These measures are to be contrasted with the highly sophisticated measuring tools which academics attempt to devise to measure pupil or school performance and to which they attribute spurious statistical validity, which process has been equated elsewhere with the weighing of mules in Texas.

If they want to weigh a mule in Texas, first they tie the back legs together, then they tie the front legs together, then they tie the front legs to the back legs. Then they look around for a big plank which they balance on a fulcrum, then they place the mule on one end of the plank before looking high and low for a boulder that will exactly balance the mule. When at last they have found such a boulder, they guess the weight of the boulder.

Readers whose patience has permitted them to read thus far will probably be surprised that advertising has not featured more prominently in the discussion. They will be more surprised to learn that advertising has nothing to do with marketing. Advertising is a subset of selling, which is a product-led activity, whereas marketing is a consumer-dominated approach. it is attempting to assume that a product which has been so excellently honed by the processes described above will, in effect, advertise and sell itself. In the words of Ralph Waldo Emerson:

> If a man write a better book, preach a better sermon or make a better mousetrap, though he build his house in the woods, the world will make a beaten path to his door.

But it is never safe to assume that you are providing a service with inbuilt acceptability. For this reason, proper attention must be given to marketing communications, which is not the same as advertising. Generally, the information booklets available for parents prior to their children's admission are attractively presented and give, in language readily accessible to the average parent, simple information about practical considerations like admission arrangements, school hours and holiday dates, dinner money, dress requirements and sickness arrangements. Other documents provide the technical curricular information required by the Education Act, 1980 (Section 8).

An effective school brochure should have regard to the following factors:

– What are the benfits of attending your school as they might be seen from the viewpoint of the potential customer? What are his/her needs?
– What sector of the market is the leaflet aimed at? It may be necessary to provide different leaflets for different market segments.
– Attract attention, adopt a house style and/or logo.

- Arouse interest and create a desire for the benefits promised by the school; be enthusiastic.
- Promote action on the part of the reader by getting him/her to seek more information or enrol his/her child.
- Layouts should be simple and attractive.

The booklet's contents should embrace:

1 A description of the benefits provided by the school.
2 A description, in layman's terms, of what pupils will learn.
3 A statement of the teaching and learning methods.
4 An indication of the later progression available as a result of the benefits to be obtained at the school.
5 The school's credentials and the quality of the staff.
6 A re-statement of the important benefits of attending the school.

Public relations practice is the deliberate, planned and sustained effort to establish and maintain mutual understanding between the schools and its public. The key word here is 'mutual'. Too many of the communications emanating from schools are one-sided. Prize days, open days, parents' evenings, information on curricular aims and objectives, school reports, brochures and letters contain a welter of information for, instructions to and requests for money from parents. If the marketing mentality is adopted, however, then there will pervade these documents and meetings a sense of openness and willingness to listen to and act upon the views and aspirations of individual parents.

Despite the best preparation and preventative action, unfortunate incidents beyond the control of the headteacher and his staff can occasionally do untold harm to the market standing of the school by being recounted in lurid detail in the press. The damage will be minimised if sound relationships have been established in advance by providing regular positive copy and invitations to social events. Any items which then appear in the local press should serve as free publicity and marketing material. Local and national newspapers, radio and television welcome ready-made news items, particularly those with a distinct personal interest line. Consequently, the focus should not be on the advertisement of a particular course but on using a personal storyline, the particular success of an individual pupil, for example, as a means of obtaining for the school an association with that success. Care should be taken to obtain the necessary permissions from parents and the Local Educational Authority and to avoid political issues. A good press release should have the following characteristics:

- a good headline attracting immediate interest;
- a local people-centred angle;

- a first paragraph stating who the story is about, what it is about and why, when and where it has happened or will happen (the five Ws);
- brevity;
- one or more quotable quotes from a named individual;
- a photograph showing relevant (local or well-known) people; and
- a contact telephone number.

Its layout should include wide margins, double spacing, a dateline and explanatory notes. Other useful forms of publicity for the school include letters to the press, calls to local phone-in programmes, interviews and feature articles.

The school's communications should reflect its marketing strategy. In defining it, the headteacher will need to address the following questions which serve as a summary of the main points of this chapter:

1 How accurate is the school's position statement?

2 How lucid and visionary is the school's document of aims and objectives?

3 How relevant are those aims to the needs and demands of the various consumer groups?

4 Does the school have a value system which pervades its very ethos?

5 Does the concept of the worth and dignity of the individual pervade the value system?

6 Are all the school's personnel committed to the development of those aims and objectives?

7 How accepting of, and responsive to, criticism is the school's staff?

8 How attractive and inviting is the school building?

9 Does the school have a house style, logo, motto, image?

10 How easy or difficult is it to make contact with the school?

11 What criteria has the school adopted in measuring its effectiveness in achieving its own objectives?

12 Are the measurements in terms of consumer satisfaction?

13 Are the school brochures effectively designed for each of the market segments and written in terms readily comprehensible to the layman?

14 What arrangements have been made to provide the media with frequent and positive copy about the school?

References

Beare, H (1985), Education's Corporate Image, in *Educational Management and Administration*, Vol 14 No 2.

Brunt, M P (1985a), Marketing the Primary School: Working through the Governors: Part 1, in *Education 3–13* Vol 13 No 1.

Brunt, M P (1985b), Marketing the Primary School: Working through the Governors: Part II, in *Education 3–13* Vol 13 No 2.

Curtis, J H R (1984), *Marketing Further Education*: Coombe Lodge Working Paper.

Davidson, J H (1975), *Offensive Marketing: or how to make your competitors followers*, Penguin.

Davies, P & Scribbins, K (1985), *Marketing Further and Higher Education*, Longman.

Douglas, B (1985), Consumerism, Control and the Evaluation of the Professional, in *Educational Management and Administration*, Vol 14 No 2.

Frain, J (1981), *Introduction to Marketing*, Macdonald and Evans.

Guratsky, S P (1982), *Owner-occupation and the Allocation of Comprehensive School Places: the case of Walsall*, Centre for Urban and Regional Studies.

Hammond, J (1985), Re-assessing roles – Teachers, Parents and Governors, in *Educational Management and Administration*, Vol 14 No 2.

Hewlett, M (1985), A Curriculum for Consumers, in *Educational Management and Administration*, Vol 14 No 2.

Humphrey, C & Thomas, H (1983a), Making Efficient Use of Scarce Resources, in *Education*, Vol 162 No 7.

Humphrey, C & Thomas, H (1983b), Counting the Cost of an Experimental Scheme, in *Education* Vol 162 No 8.

Knight, B A A (1977), *The Cost of Running a School*, Scottish Centre for Studies in School Administration.

Kotler, P (1975), *Marketing for Non-Profit Organisations*, Prentice Hall.

McCloy, R (1985), Week by Week, in *Education*, Vol 166 No 6.

Peters, T J & Austin, N (1985), *A Passion for Excellence: The Leadership Difference*, Collins.

Peters, T J & Waterman, R H (1982), *In Search of Excellence: Lessons from America's Best-Run Companies*, Harper and Row.

Stigler, G S (1963), *The Intellectual and the Market Place*, Institute of Economic Affairs Occasional Paper.

Wills, G et al (1975), *Introducing Marketing*, Pan.

Wragg, E (1989), 'The Hot Dinner Ladies', in *The Teacher* 20 March 1988.

Further reading

Cawthray, B (1982), *Putting it Together: Marketing and Advertising*, Bristol Polytechnic Management Learning Productions.

Cuthbert, R (1979), *The Marketing Function in Education Management*, Further Education Staff College.

Kotler, P (1980), *Marketing Management – Analysis, Planning and Control*, Prentice Hall.

18 Caring and curriculum: the management of continuity

John Thorpe

It would be difficult to find anyone who would argue with the idea of continuity in education, entailing as it does commonsense notions of progress and development. In this light, those who would consider how planning and preparation may build on what the child has already experienced and ask questions about whether or not the various parts of the educational experience fit together to make a coherent whole. This is not always an easy task, for children make progress at different rates and in different directions, and so those concerned to manage continuity must also ask how to prevent arbitrary divisions in the total organisation of the education system from cutting across or destroying the continuous educational progress of each child. As Dean (1980) puts it:

> . . . we need to make the curve of continuity a smooth one from teacher to teacher, class to class and school to school.

The manager of continuity must also acknowledge that the context in which we as educators now all operate, presents him with a situation of sharp discontinuity. Recent legislation has served to impose an 'official' version of continuity in some respects quite different in focus from previously accepted and desirable professional practice. This exemplifies the distinction made by Richardson (1973) between 'the "caring" and "demanding" sides of the educational task'. It concerns on the one hand what happens to *children* as they face the various changes in their educational lives, whether teachers, classes or schools, and on the other what happens to children's *learning* as they make those changes. The 'official' focus now is most clearly on the 'demanding' side of our task.

There are also difficulties which must be faced concerning both the particular *view of management* and its relationship to the *task of teaching*. It encompasses notions of '*professionalism*', '*autonomy*' and '*power*' and demands the consideration of '*continuity in practice*'. If we consider management to be about the achievement of some purpose, usually coordination and co-operation towards the attainment of a particular goal, then we must also consider the notion of '*consensus*' and how this fits with institutionalised divisions of schooling.

In looking at educational settings, Johnson and Brookes (1979) distinguish between 'management' and 'instruction', a useful distinction which will reappear in several forms in this chapter. It raises here the sometimes thorny question of the relationship of 'policy' and 'practice' which leads in the end to the notion of 'control' and, as we shall see, there is a certain duality in this notion of control, both sides of which will be considered here. The very issue of continuity itself raises interesting questions about the nature of educational provision in the new context in which we find ourselves and we very quickly begin to ask about the implications for our practice as we move swiftly towards an increasingly centralised system of education. This newer kind of centralised policy making leads us initially to identify what is called here '*the official rhetoric of continuity*' as the changes envisaged take shape and then to consider the reality of '*an imposed continuity*' as the legal requirements have been made clear.

The other side of this issue of control though, and one which we must not lose sight of, is of course what happens in practice. The point at which curriculum continuity is most seriously threatened is where children change teachers, classes or perhaps most importantly, change schools. How teachers manage these changes becomes generalised in what we might call their '*conventional wisdom of continuity*'. However, the focus of this conventional wisdom seems at first glance to be not the curriculum but rather *children's welfare*. Those who would manage continuity may well be now led to ask how this conventional wisdom will adapt itself to the newer requirements.

Managing then is about getting things done, making things happen, things you want to happen. However, good management is also about evaluating what actually happens, because sometimes other things happen which you don't want to happen. This enables the manager to identify some of the barriers to what he is trying to achieve. Later in this chapter then we shall consider continuity in practice first of all by asking questions about the teacher's conventional wisdom of continuity – is it just about children's welfare? Evaluating continuity in practice also involves looking critically at interprofessional relationships, for this is its very basis and we will seek to identify those barriers to real professional co-operation which in turn create curriculum discontinuity. And what about those who experience discontinuity? Evaluating practice, it is believed here, involves taking seriously the views of our pupils, those who inhabit the management-instructional interface and who, through constant interaction and negotiation, in no small part shape it.

Together these elements, the official rhetoric/reality and conventional wisdom of continuity and the issues raised by the evaluation of practice, it is suggested form the baseline from which any consideration of the management of continuity must begin.

The official rhetoric of continuity

Official statements about 'continuity' go back a long way. *The Hadow Report* (1931) asserted that:

> ... the process of education from the age of 5 to the end of the secondary stage should be envisaged as a coherent whole, that there should be no sharp division between infant, junior and post primary stages, and that the transition from any one stage to the succeeding stage should be as smooth and gradual as possible.

This encompassing view though, hints at a duality in the notion of continuity that in later versions becomes even more apparent. By the time of the *Plowden Report* (DES, 1967) it was seen fit to assert that 'learning is a continuous process from birth' whilst also pointing out the need to avoid strain at the points of transfer from one class to another and from one school to another. It is here that we see emerging the duality which reflects the 'caring – demanding' dimensions or 'tutorial – teaching' functions noted by Richardson above. However, as I shall show in this chapter, it is the latter of these embodied in notions of *curriculum continuity* that became by far the most prominent concern in the multitude of official documents published during the 1980's and which made increasingly insistent 'demands' for its professional consideration. In a sense, these have now been overtaken as we move into a new 'era', one in which we must face squarely the far reaching implications and 'requirements' of the Education Reform Act.

The 'caring' dimension though has not always been absent from the official rhetoric of continuity. Perhaps its epitome is embodied in that familiar sentence from the *Plowden Report* (DES, 1967) 'At the heart of the educational process lies the child.' Our 'caring' as teachers begins with the very first change the child encounters, the entry into school. *The Plowden Report* sees continuity here in terms of:

> It ought not to be just a matter of bringing a child to school, but of placing him in a *cooperative undertaking* in which mother and teacher both have parts to play.
>
> (my emphasis)

and indicates how this caring for the child makes real demands on teachers:

> . . . welcoming a child is more than a matter of reserving proper time to attend to him. It is the *quality of the welcome and the imaginative insight given to it which counts.*
>
> (my emphasis)

Similarly 'caring' about children as they move on to secondary school the Report suggests must ensure that

> . . . if change is to stimulate and not dishearten, it must be *carefully prepared and not too sudden.*
>
> (my emphasis)

Without question however, the last decade or so has seen a much more direct 'official' focus on the *demanding* side of the educational task, particularly on curriculum continuity. Perhaps since the Great Debate brought issues of curriculum into public debate, but certainly since the *HMI Primary Survey* (1978) identified the differential success of the 'considerable efforts . . . made to ease children's *transition* from one school to the next' with the fact that *curriculum continuity* was 'largely overlooked', has this trend gained in momentum. The report on *Local Authority Arrangements for the School Curriculum* (DES, 1979) remarked on the great variety of ways in which schools were tackling issues of continuity but also noticed too the discrepancy between what the LEAs said was going on and what the Primary Survey the year before had found was going on. Again the distinction is made between 'transition' and 'continuity'. In the HMI discussion paper *A View of the Curriculum* (DES, 1980) the concern was being made increasingly explicit:

> The variety of age ranges found in schools and the numerous points of transfer which now co-exist argue urgently for more thought to be given to curricular continuity and progression.

and so too its focus:

> . . . schools as a whole need to shape their policies and to plan the content of work with awareness of what has preceded.

But this document also makes the vital distinction between a *vertical continuity*, that between different ages and stages, and a *horizontal continuity*, between schools in the same stage:

> Between primary schools and the schools which receive their pupils there needs to be not only communication about individuals but also consultation about aspects of the curriculum. Similar consultation is also necessary between the primary schools of an area . . . It is . . . important to try to ensure that comparable expectations are being established about the range of experience and performance of pupils at a given stage.

The message is restated in *The School Curriculum* (DES, 1981):

> Authorities and schools need to ensure continuity in pupils' programmes both within and between the primary and secondary phases, whether this involves direct transfer from primary to secondary schools or transition through middle schools.

and then extended:

> Records should be kept and transmitted with this end in view.

This message is repeated again and again in the various publications of the Curriculum Matters series. Incidentally, each one in the series on *Aspects of the Curriculum 5–16* is prefaced with the remark: 'It is essential that this document should be read as a whole.'

Each of these documents emphasises that 'continuity and progression should be ensured from one class or teacher to another and from one school to another' (DES, 1985c) and that to ensure it requires 'adequate curricular liaison between contributory and receiving schools' (DES, 1984). The authors of *Science 5–16: A Statement of Policy* (DES, 1985d) can state that:

> Under present circumstances few secondary schools can rely on any degree of common experience in science on the part of their new pupils. Continuity between schools is, in practice, far too often ignored.

whilst those of *English from 5–16* (DES, 1984) are much more explicitly prescriptive:

> There should be agreement between the schools about what pupils should be expected to have learnt and experienced by the time they transfer.

In *Better Schools* (DES, 1985b) it is noted that, not only is there no agreement *between* schools, but also within them for as they say

> . . . there is little evidence of agreed curriculum policies directly influencing the school as a whole.

The message can be no more easily found than neatly packaged in this paragraph from *The Curriculum from 5–16* (DES, 1985a):

> There is, therefore, a need for *unity of purpose* throughout the 5–16 span. That unity needs also to apply across the school system as a whole if the desired range and quality of experience and learning are to have a more assured place than they do now across the country, in LEAs, in individual schools and above all, in what is offered to individual pupils.

A National Curriculum: from rhetoric to reality?

A brief examination of DES/HMI publications through the first half of the decade then reveals the emerging elements of the official rhetoric of continuity. Since this chapter was first written we have of course witnessed two significant pieces of legislation, the Education Acts of 1986 and 1988, both of which have served to strengthen considerably the curricular focus of the official view of continuity. The first of these (Education No. 2 Act, 1986) provided a framework of responsibility for the curriculum involving the LEAs, school governors and headteachers, with each given a clearly defined role. Although advances were made at this stage towards enhancing the possibility of continuity between the schools within authorities by requiring each LEA to formulate a written curriculum policy and send it to all their schools and governors who, in the light of which, were in turn required to formulate and make public their school curriculum policy, clearly the government had in mind a rather less casual or 'localised' approach.

This 'nationalised' approach has been unfolded for us over the two years since the appearance of the *National Curriculum 5–16 consultation document* (DES, 1987a) and has been made ever more clear through the variety of documents since. Moreover it is now embedded in statute, the Education Reform Act 1988. The consultation document (DES, 1987a) acknowledges first that:

> Many LEAs and schools have made important advances towards achieving a good curriculum for pupils aged 5–16, which offers progression, continuity and coherence between its different stages.

but then complains that progress has been, 'variable, uncertain and slow' and indicates that the Government wished 'to move ahead at a faster pace'. This document also clearly indicates their aims;

> Pupils should be entitled to the same opportunities wherever they go to school and standards of attainment must be raised throughout England and Wales.

the achievement of these aims it is thought will be reached by a 'national curriculum' which will on the one hand ensure that:

... all pupils, regardless of sex, ethnic origin and geographical location, (should) have access to broadly the same good and relevant curriculum and programmes of study which include the key content, skills and processes which they need to learn ...

while at the same time:

It will also help children's progression within and between primary and secondary education (and on to further and higher education) and will help to secure the continuity and coherence which is too often lacking in what they are taught.

Above all though, the move away from possible localised solutions is emphasised as the Government's conclusions are stressed:

... consistent improvement in standards can be guaranteed only within a national framework for the secular curriculum.

We now have in place a National Curriculum comprising of specified foundation subjects, attainment targets and programmes of study. One of the pivotal strategies in the attempt to raise standards within this national framework is the setting up of assessment arrangements for each of the four key stages, for as the Task Group on Assessment and Testing Report (DES, 1987b) asserts:

Promoting children's learning is a principal aim of schools. Assessment lies at the heart of this process. It can provide a framework in which educational objectives may be set, and pupils progress charted and expressed. It can yield a basis for planning the next educational steps in response to children's needs. By facilitating dialogue between teachers, it can enhance professional skills and help the school as a whole to strengthen learning across the curriculum and throughout its age range.

The most recent official statement (NCC, 1989) summarises the stage we have now reached:

The National Curriculum will provide teachers with clear objectives for their teaching; children with identifiable targets for their learning; parents with accurate, accessible information about what their children can be expected to know, understand and be able to do, and what they actually achieve. The result will be higher expectations and more effective progression and continuity throughout the years of full-time education.

This now poses huge questions for those who would consider the management of continuity at whatever level of the system. The reality to be found out there in the real world of schools it would seem has been quite different from the one now 'legally' envisaged. Those of us who are, or have been practitioners, know from experience how much thought and effort, time and activity is directed at helping children move smoothly and successfully from one school to another. But this is our 'caring' function which can itself present us with a stiff managerial task. When we consider the implications of the newer rhetoric which asserts how much better we have been as practitioners at addressing the 'welfare' aspects of continuity than the curricular ones (DES, 1985a) and the newly imposed 'reality' requiring our focus on the 'demanding' side of our task, the curriculum it would seem that we are facing a situation of genuine hysteresis. The management task has now become monumental.

The following sections of this chapter then will look at the management of continuity from these two perspectives, hopefully considering how we may move towards bridging the gap between a rhetoric which now requires the focus on curriculum and the reality it acknowledges of the effective caring for pupils as they undergo traumatic changes in their educational lives.

Managing continuity 1: towards a conventional wisdom

The distinction noted in the official rhetoric of continuity between 'transition' and 'continuity' instructs us to look carefully at what happens in schools. If asked most teachers would, of course, display considerable agreement about what would consist of good practice in managing continuity – how it should be organised and who should benefit – so much so that we may refer to it as the practitioners 'conventional wisdom' of continuity. In this conventional wisdom, certain changes the child must go through in the course of his educational life are considered to be events of such importance and the source of so much possible trauma that they have to be carefully managed. Each change of class, change of teacher, the move into the Juniors, may represent such an event, but for the primary teacher, the two most critical changes are those the child undergoes when first entering the school and then transferring to Secondary school.

The entry into school is perhaps the single most stressful event of the life of each child up to the age five and parents, teachers and schools work very hard to alleviate the stress. Ghaye and Pascal (1988) reporting on a pilot research project suggest a threefold differentiation of potentially stressful activities as children start school. They refer to these as '*separations*', when children have to leave parents, family, and the familiarity of home as part of a new daily routine; '*transitions*', as children move from one activity to another, one part of the classroom or school to another during the day; and '*incorporations*', as children are engaged in those activities which lead them to become part of a new and less familiar social group. This differentiation can help us to think carefully about particular strategies for overcoming possible difficulties and how the continuity from home to school might be successfully managed. A brief consideration of the ways in which this is accomplished reveals that there are both problems and strategies for overcoming them which are general problems of 'continuity' rather than being age-specific. In thinking about these I want to consider what we may think of as three 'management' strategies in particular – 'liaison', 'transition' and 'induction'. The first of these, 'liaison' might be thought of as the stage of *communication* where first contacts are made and the exchange of information about the school and teachers and the child and his home takes place. The various activities which may result from this kind of strategy would go a long way to meeting the need for what Blatchford et al. (1982) call 'the continuity of environmental demands' ensuring that, . . . the demands of one stage must be compatible with those of the next'.

When I was a headteacher we tried to meet this most important requirement by sending out to parents of children approaching school age, along with a letter of welcome, a booklet of ideas and suggestions about appropriate ways to help prepare children for school, but which also incorporated information about the school and its ways of going about its business. This was also supplemented by an invitation to parents to come into school for an informal chat with myself and the child's first teacher, when we encouraged parents to tell us as much as possible about their children. We tried to establish, as early as possible, a relationship which we saw as a 'partnership', working together to do the utmost for the good of the child. Looking back it was perhaps too much a one-sided arrangement, typical of the 'child-school incorporation process' noted by Ghaye and Pascal (1988), a one way process in which the child adjusts to the school. As a true 'partnership' it might have been much more, enabling us to overcome more speedily some of those inevitable difficulties which can occur as parents sometimes try to help their children in ways not always entirely appropriate. As the *House of Commons Education, Science and Arts Committee Report* (1988) suggests, parents should be made perfectly clear of 'the dangers of trying to introduce a formal kind of teaching and learning at too early an age'. One way in which problems of this kind may come to light at an early stage might be through home visiting. Reception teachers may find out a great deal more about the children they are about to welcome into school by visiting them at home and just as importantly, in the same way, parents might more effectively understand what the school was trying to achieve and their teaching methods. How much better if communication with parents as partners can sometimes be accomplished on their own ground rather than always the teachers. As Cleave et al. (1982) recommend:

... gaps in understanding might be bridged if parents and staff could have more insights into each other's worlds, both of which are inhabited by the child.

Activities to prepare the way and ease the *transition* from home to school may constitute a second management strategy. There is of course in many areas institutionally organised 'transition' in the form of nursery schools or classes, which must be the ideal we would aim for, whereas in other places playgroups or other voluntary self-help groups fulfil this valuable function more informally. These first pre-school contacts outside the home are vitally important and we should not underestimate the contribution made by those who have the responsibility for guiding the child through this stage, for as Blatchford et al. (1982) put it:

This is a serious responsibility, not least because first experiences may set up an enduring pattern that will structure the child's reactions to settings he will encounter later in his life.

The informally organised playgroup serves another very valuable function too in that it encourages parental participation in the transition from home to school. Parents can be involved in planning, preparing and supervising relevant activities for children, which may help them to understand and appreciate the constraints under which teachers also operate once their child is at school. At the playgroup too, parents are in control, they decide on when and how often their own children will attend, perhaps increasing attendance as the time for school approaches. Teachers can overcome the lack of formal contact that may exist between the school and the nursery by visiting the children in the playgroup before they come into school. Some schools like that at Castleton in North Yorkshire find that they have the space for the playgroup children approaching school age to spend time in a spare room on a number of occasions before they actually start school.

As children actually enter school and how this is made easier and smoother enables us to consider a third strategy, the management of *induction*. Many schools make very great efforts to ensure that children coming to school for the first time are made welcome, feel secure and happy. There are many ways of doing this. During my time as Headteacher we evolved our practice over a period of twelve months, during which time we involved parents in discussion and practical trial of ways for children to enter school. Each intake of children during three terms had a slightly different induction

period, each one modified after parents were invited into school
to consider successes and failures. Together we arrived at our
school policy. As part of the gradual process of taking children into
school we tried to engage their parents, establishing a relationship
based on trust, a partnership caring for the child in an atmosphere
where parents were always welcome and teachers always
interested.

An important way of thinking about minimising the difference
between home and school is that referred to by Cleave et al. (1982)
as 'continuity of scale'. These writers make practical suggestions
about the ways in which the environment the child first encounters
at school can be managed. They recommend

> a secure base of appropriate scale . . . a child orientated setting
> a gradual extension of the range of new territory and the careful organis-
> ation of space the young child's needs
> familiarity with the school before he starts will give the child an idea of
> what to expect . . .

This concern with 'scale' and the kinds of 'relationships' tied up
with it have therefore significant implications for the way in which
daily events like assembly, playtime and dinner-time are organised
and we should consider them carefully if 'induction' is to be managed effectively.

If we now turn to the other end of children's primary school
experience, we find them facing transfer to secondary school, and
here we may see similar strategies used to manage the changeover
from one stage to the next. In many ways these strategies have
already been 'rehearsed' at the point of entry into the primary
school and as I shall try to show initially, their focus is ostensibly
children's 'welfare'. Later in this chapter I shall discuss the view
that this is not in fact the case and the implications this has for the
management of continuity. I don't want to dwell on it here but
when we consider the first of the strategies noted above, liaison,
we perhaps get a hint of later arguments. Any successful *liaison* is
about good communication and obviously this occurs at the teacher
level. It may be that communication passes only between headteachers, or between headteachers and heads of year, or alternatively
schools may have teachers with specially designated responsibility
for primary-secondary liaison. Liaison might operate formally
through specifically organised meetings or informally through a
telephone call. The essence of its success though as a management
strategy lies in the establishment of effective lines of communication. Liaison between primary and secondary schools over the
transfer of pupils then will involve the *communication of information* about those pupils. As we shall see later on though, it is

the content of this information which is crucial, whether in fact it contains only personal details, with perhaps the odd test result thrown in, or whether it contains a more useful curriculum profile. Liaison as the communication of information also occurs as the secondary school makes itself known to parents through meetings and open evenings in both feeder primary schools and secondary schools themselves, publicity materials, brochures and as the secondary school teachers make themselves and their ways known to their future pupils in their final year in primary school. The recently completed *Secondary Transfer Project* (ILEA, 1987, 1988) however found that many schools were not making the most of the opportunity of transfer to secondary school to build a positive relationship between parents and their children's new teachers and recommended that schools give more attention to finding ways of welcoming parents into the process of their children's secondary education.

Activities organised to ease the *transition* from primary school to secondary school may seem more immediately concerned with children's welfare in the way that it is seen as a preparation for things to come. This may take the form of anything from a range of joint activities for fourth year junior and first year secondary pupils to short preliminary visits to the secondary school for new entrants to have a look around. There may be a succession of planned visits or even a full working day actually in the secondary school for future pupils. Writers such as Dutch and McCall (1974) have described the possibility of a transition department within the secondary school while David (1988) reports on how one secondary school actually went some way towards this by converting two spare rooms into primary style classrooms with noted benefits not only for the children coming into the school who found something familiar but also for the teachers involved who found themselves with an opportunity to explore different ways of working. In their interesting final report to the SSRC (Secondary Schools Research Council) on *The Adaptation of Pupils to Secondary Schools*, Woods and Measor (1982) describe a particular scheme they had observed in which children made two visits to their new secondary school during which they experienced some lesson situations. They were treated to a play by teachers in the English department and magical experiments in the Science laboratory, both of which, as they were intended to, helped create a certain excitement and expectancy.

In this rural and relatively isolated part of North Yorkshire, where children face a lengthy train and coach journey to their new secondary school, their primary school teachers try to ensure that part of the transition the children make is that they become much more familiar with other children from neighbouring villages who will also be transferring to the secondary school. Preliminary visits are made to the new school in order to familiarise the children with their new surroundings, and these are made at the same time as the other children of the same age from neighbouring villages.

The management of *induction* or 'getting them in' is now extensively covered in a growing literature on pastoral care – a fact in itself, which emphasises its 'welfare' focus (Hamblin, 1978; Baldwin and Wells, 1979). For instance Leslie Button (1981) in his book on *Group Tutoring for the Form Teacher* suggests a detailed programme covering the whole first year in secondary school. His programme would include a fair amount of time – the first day – all day during the first week – 35 minutes or one period on each day – and then 35 minutes or one period each week + 15 minutes on each of two other days. He goes on to suggest a number of themes which might be covered in this time:

- the pupils place in school
- building up a caring community
- relationships, the self and social skills
- communication skills
- school work and study skills
- academic guidance and careers education
- health and hygiene education
- personal interests

This kind of tutorial programme is designed, of course, to enable the tutor responsible time and opportunity to get to know so very much better the children in his group, in fact, in a way rather more like the primary school teachers the children have just left. Woods and Measor (1982) are also convinced of the value of 'carefully devised and programmed induction schemes'. Although their emphasis is slightly different to that of Button, they too make recommendations which we would do well to note. Among them are:

> a *sponsorship scheme* in which 2nd (or 5th/6th) year pupils take responsibility for new first year pupils during the first day, especially in informal periods of the day
> *homework skills* should be taught
> *rules and the rationality behind them* should be made very clear

Other writers, like Cox (1984), have noted that in general too little time is given over to implementing effective schemes, largely because of the demands of other priorities during the year, while the rather different approach reported by Brice (1984) goes some way to overcome this. Known as *The Gateway Project* it involves an induction period during the first week of the summer holidays when new first year pupils are given the opportunity to a week in the school on their own with their new teachers affording them the opportunity to settle into the school on their own. However we would also do well to heed the advice of Walton (1983) who suggests that '*induction demands extremely careful and skilled management*'.

This focus on two major changes the child undergoes in his educational life, the entry into primary school and the transfer to secondary school enables us to examine activities which support what were suggested as three possible management strategies: liaison, transition and induction. Taken together these activities shape what we might refer to as the teacher's conventional wisdom of continuity and, as we can see, its basis seems to a large extent to be about children's welfare. In other words, it seems to concentrate on the caring side of the educational task. In a subsequent section I want to examine this rather more carefully and ask questions about its implications for the management of continuity and the purposes it serves, but first I want to consider the other demanding side of the educational task and in particular to ask if the possible strategies we have identified in a 'welfare' context can be applied to the management of curriculum continuity.

Managing continuity 2: towards curriculum continuity:

It is appropriate to look back to a report as significant as the *Cockroft Report* (DES, 1982) and to notice how it saw fit to comment on much of what was accepted as good practice in terms of the transfer of children from one school to another, that schools:

... while making a major contribution to ease of transfer from a pastoral and social point of view, we do not always pay as much attention as we would wish to ensuring continuity of mathematical development.

This is the nettle which those who would manage continuity perhaps never quite grasped and which in no small measure has contributed to the seeming desire of central government to overlay a framework of continuity in the form of a National Curriculum. True, it was a task which over recent years had grown in complexity with the increasing number of possible transfers a child may have to make during his educational career. These may include playgroup, nursery, infant school, first school, junior school, middle school, lower school upper school, high school, 6th form college. It was a situation which had led HMI (1980) to comment that:

The variety of age ranges found in schools and the numerous points of transfer which now coexist argue urgently for more thought to be given to curricular continuity and progression . . . (and) more effort to establish and maintain continuity and coherence in what children learn and are expected to achieve.

And more recently (DES, 1985) they gave notice of possible ways of achieving this continuity *within* schools they say, by 'clear curricular policies which all the staff have been involved in developing' and while accepting that between schools continuity was more difficult to achieve, they insisted that it was nevertheless possible 'to arrive at some important agreed objectives' made easier by the existence of LEA policies. Times change though and the desire to engage in professional debate has weakened: we now have a 'national' policy.

We might consider how our three strategies may yet help us towards the effective managment of continuity. In the final report of the LEA Development Centre Project on *Continuity in Education (Junior to Secondary)*, Neal (1975) suggests that continuity in the curriculum is dependent on effective liaison between schools. This report also identifies some of the difficulties in establishing such effective liaison procedures, like staffing ratios, distances between schools, the large number of feeder primary schools to each secondary school and the general lack of sympathy between primary and secondary school but then goes on to make a number of recommendations to overcome them. Its view is similar to that of the *Bullock Report* (1975) of the same year, that '*effective liaison is a priority need.*' Marland (1977) however, warned that exhortations to create closer liaison can be 'romantic vaguenesses' in reality difficult to achieve. He too acknowledged that much liaison between schools has a pastoral focus and that little is achieved to establish a 'functional continuity'. How then might this be achieved? The manager of continuity might consider two ways forward. The first involves keeping *effective records*, a much neglected aspect of our professionalism when compared to with other comparable groups like social workers or doctors. Teachers tend to carry around in their heads a great store of information about their pupils but the real test comes when others need to take over, whether it be in the same school, in the next class or in another school. For the teacher taking a child for the first time, as the *Bullock Report* (DES, 1975) says:

> There is no substitute for first hand knowledge of the children and of the kind of learning situation in which they have been involved.

But as Cockroft (1982) also notes, this is not an easy task 'to record concisely on paper'. All too often it results in what Bullock refers to as 'shadowy assessments' containing no more than an 'intimation of a child's earlier education'. The demand for more detailed record keeping then has always been there. In the area of language for instance, Marland (1977) listed four clear requirements:

- A language 'profile', that is a description of each pupil's language use.
- Standardised reading data, measured by the same tests throughout the group of schools, preferably in the form of informal reading inventories or diagnostic test data.
- Titles of books read.
- Samples of various kinds of writing by the pupil.

This kind of detail could be similarly replicated for other areas of the curriculum. As we begin to work out the implications of implementing the requirements of the National Curriculum we might reflect that this area of record keeping is one which requires our most urgent attention. How long we might otherwise speculate before we are handed standardised forms of records? However the crucial point for the manager of continuity is contained in what Marland (1977) goes on to say about records, that 'knowledge of schools or of individual pupils is not in itself enough unless it leads to *action*'. This indicates a second possible way forward, for a prerequisite of action according to HMI (DES, 1980) is 'not only communication about individuals, but also *consultation* about aspects of the curriculum'. In this way then groups of schools, through effective liaison procedures involving consultations about curriculum and detailed records of each child's work, could create a broadly agreed policy addressing problems of continuity.

Such an agreed policy would have implications for the management of transition since it would have to acknowledge what the Schools Council (1972) in a much more recently sounding turn of phrase once referred to as 'the single sweep of total education'. Such a policy too would have to address some of the pedagogical as well as curricular implications of continuity as teachers begin to tackle the requirements of the recent changes. In the also distant words of the *Plowden Report* (1967), teachers would 'need to know each others work', and in so doing may then be more able to translate into action the kind of *philosophy of continuity* embodied in the recent legislation. Curriculum planning and schemes of work would then have to take into full account both previous and future stages in the child's development. Teaching methods and learning materials may then be selected with careful reference to what had gone before and to what would follow as children's real needs are identified and tackled at each stage of their development.

Examples of how this might work out in practice occurred in this part of North Yorkshire recently when a working group of primary headteachers along with the secondary school head of art, organised an exhibition of examples of children's art work from all the feeder primary schools, the two lower schools and the upper school in the Whitby area. The aim was not to display samples of excellence but rather to show *stages of development*. The display, which filled the upper school hall, was open to the public and aroused much interest. The organisers eventually produced a booklet describing these stages of development (Liddle et al., 1985) which was distributed among all the participating schools. The teachers involved were so pleased with the idea that it has since been repeated in the area of science. The real success of the projects though is reflected in the working together of teachers of all age groups in the common purpose of investigating the stages of development, in particular curriculum areas, of children from the age of 4 to 18.

Cleave et al. (1982) suggest other strategies which may help to minimise curricular discontinuity for the child:

- recognise readiness for more complex tasks
- supply appropriate resources
- allow for changing physical demands of a new school
- organise activities in the new setting which are already familiar
- gradually expand new materials and activities
- encourage parental support

Although these writers were considering in particular the child's move from home to school, I think these sensible strategies could have application over every transition between stages in the child's educational life.

The acceptance of a philosophy of continuity would also have implications for the management of induction. There would be less repetition of work already done as children move into the secondary school, less of the tendency to 'start again'. This would, of course, be more likely to be the case where groups of feeder primary schools and their secondary school had got together to consider common approaches and to identify broadly agreed goals. Such an approach would go some way towards meeting the need for what Richards (1982) calls 'curriculum consistency' by which he means:

> . . . the opportunity for *all* pupils to be introduced to some of the major concepts, skills, rules and underlying generalisations associated with established ways of knowing (both theoretical and practical) in our society.

The National Curriculum now provides a framework of what every child can expect to experience but it does still require the variety of teachers involved in each child's journey through school to be involved in discussion *at every level* aimed at establishing a broad common understanding about content and the pedagogical implications of its delivery at the various stages.

Induction then involves building on the experiences children have already had and also making headway to overcome those other external or subcultural factors which may mitigate against successful continuity, for example the deep seated gender differences noted by Woods and Measor (1985) in attitudes towards maths and science and by Catton (1985) towards craft design technology (CDT). the Education Reform Act goes some way to providing more equality of opportunity for previously disadvantaged groups, like girls in these areas, but this opportunity now needs careful management if these gains are not to be lost. The agenda has been set for us, we need now to act on it.

Although it is therefore possible to identify to a certain degree 'liaison', 'transition' and 'induction' as possible components of planned curriculum continuity, we must also be aware of the rather more limited success in the implementation of these as management strategies. The new legislation requires a curriculum that is 'balanced and broadly based' and this is already in place. It also sets out a series of attainment targets and programmes of study which span the years of compulsory education. The management of continuity over these years as children pass through the various institutionalised stages could certainly be enhanced if those involved have clearly articulated strategies with which to approach their task. The fact that they haven't in the past leads us to look at those hidden or unintentional consequences of action, what Stillman (1985) refers to as 'resulting transitions' and consider the evaluation of continuity in practice.

Managing continuity 3: towards an evaluation of practice:

A not so conventional wisdom

One of the immediate effects of looking at aspects of the organisation of transfer like the welfare of children or curriculum continuity is that it can deflect attention away from what Galton (1983a) suggests is a much more important concern, 'the effect on pupils of teachers'. For despite the very considerable efforts which go into caring for children as they transfer between schools, such changes can be seriously traumatic. Galton asks us to look for reasons within ourselves as to why we treat children in schools the way we do, for he says:

> ... only when we do this will we make the discovery that the gap between what we ideally would like to do and what in practice we actually do has similar origins whether we are primary, secondary or teachers in higher education.

Galton (1983b) suggests that rather than teachers changing their particular teaching styles to suit the needs of children, as might be inferred from the welfare focus of the teacher's conventional wisdom, it is rather more the case of children having to adapt themselves to meet the demands made on them by new teachers. Moreover it is a situation which starts early. In her excellent study, Willes (1983) shows how children from their very first days in school learn how to become pupils:

> It seems beyond dispute that teachers start with a thoroughly internalised set of expectations about the interaction in classrooms and the role relations that the interaction reflects and reinforces.

In reporting a small empirical study, Ribbins (1981) uncovers other intentions behind pastoral arrangements, clear indication that transfer could be managed 'to serve other functions than those of the needs of children'. He found that programmes of induction in secondary schools were seen by some teachers as the opportunity first of all to attract 'really good children' to the school, a blatant kind of impression management, and secondly to identify children with problems and *problem* children. Willes (1983) sees this kind of activity deriving from the teacher's 'custodial' rather than 'educative' function, that which is often overlooked in educational discussion, '*the obligation to control* a number of pupils. Ribbins (1981) concludes of some induction activities:

> ... that the main interests being served by these events are often those of the school and its teachers rather than those of the child.

This conclusion might direct the manager of continuity to consider the context of activities or strategies designed to promote such continuity with great care because it might seem much more complex than 'conventional wisdom' might indicate. In particular it instructs him to consider very carefully whose interests are being served by such activities and strategies.

Professionalism and curriculum discontinuity

Curriculum continuity coupled with effective record keeping is also often discussed from a 'teacher' perspective, usually in terms of the opportunity it affords for increasing the 'professionalism' of teachers. One of the very real barriers to so called professionalism and thus to real continuity is seen as the difficulty encountered in getting teachers to work co-operatively. But this shows the confusion which surrounds the use of the term 'professionalism', for barriers to continuity may be erected by teachers seeking to defend what they see as their professionalism, the maintenance of their autonomy, their own conception of self. Within schools this autonomy can be a difficult task for the manager to counter given the preponderance of class teaching reinforced as it is by architectural determinism, while between schools the difficulties are even greater. This is especially the case between primary and secondary school, where great differences between teacher's views of professionalism may be found. The term 'profession' encompasses the notion that the basis of practice is a body of knowledge about that practice acquired through professional training. The class teacher – subject teacher differentiation may thus point up the contrasting focus of the professionalism of primary and secondary teachers, the former rooted in pedagogical relationships with children, the latter in subject specialism. Neither will the recent changes in teacher training overcome these opposing identities at all quickly.

Of course, to take this argument too far would be simplistic, but it does cut across another important issue for the manager of continuity to consider. He must be careful not to confuse continuity in the curriculum with *progression*. In certain senses, parts of the curriculum may seem to be continuous like a historical project, elements appear to follow on as part of a seemingly logical framework. Progression, however, directs attention much more clearly at the level of children, those who experience the curriculum. The class teacher seems to be in a good position to ensure continuity, both in a horizontal or integrative sense, like language or maths across the curriculum *and* progression, whereas this has to be more carefully managed when the child is taught by a number of subject specialists.

In some areas of the curriculum there exists a fairly clearly defined hierarchy of skills which some children master more quickly than others. Perhaps we should also consider then whether the organisation of individual learning found in many primary classrooms enables the teacher to manage progression more effectively compared with specialist subject teaching, which might be dictated more by organisational constraints, resulting in children having mastered certain skills being forced into needless repetition waiting for others to catch up. This can be especially true as children move into secondary school from a number of contributory primary schools. Above all though, it is important that limiting ideas about professionalism must not be allowed to get in the way of continuity and progression, particularly as we have seen, as children move from primary to secondary school. As the Blackburn Project (COPE, undated) found of primary and secondary teachers who benefitted from the sharing of expertise and resources in science, the most important factor relating to success was the *attitudes* of the teachers involved. It is a view also expressed by Gorwood (1986) who says:

> Unless genuine attempts are made to understand how other schools function, it is difficult to achieve the degree of openness needed to progress towards continuity.

It is the question of attitude then which those who wish to ensure effective continuity must tackle first. For Ginnever (1986), this is best initiated at headteacher level, for as he says:

> . . . discussions between headteachers across the sectors is a minefield . . . Yet it is at headteacher level that discussions have to begin . . . They have the power to bring about change, but for it to work they must see it as desirable.

Responding to practice: children's views

An important aspect of any evaluation of practice must be the inclusion of the views of the participants. In most writing about evaluation there appears a grave imbalance attached to the views of children compared with teachers, as Meighan (1978) points out:

> . . . existing definitions of the situation appear to take teaching as more important than learning, the teacher's activity as more central than the pupil's . . . *despite the official rhetoric of educational writing and debate that makes claims for the pupil's welfare as the central focus.*

The transfer of children from primary to secondary school provides a most instructive example of the contrast between the formal (or intended) and informal (or unintended) consequences of organisation. Measor and Woods (1983) stress the importance of this informal aspect saying:

> Above all, it is in the interaction between identities and formal and informal cultures, that pupil transfer and other status passages have to be understood.

Those who would consider continuity in educational contexts would therefore do well to heed Hargreaves (1982) advice:

> Teachers and adults become blind to the hidden curriculum because that is not what schooling is officially supposed to be about. We believe our own grown-up propaganda. One needs the eyes of a child or a stranger to see.

A number of studies now exist which begin to detail the pupil's view of transfer, particularly to secondary school. Brown and Armstrong (1986) reveal how surprised they were by the range of worries that children expressed before transfer while Walton (1983) comments how so often these problems that children experience go unrecognised by teachers. Smith (1985) suggests that thinking about the size of the secondary school is what causes most problems for children, and their parents, and he is led to make twenty-one recommendations to ease their worries in the lead up to transfer. the ILEA Secondary Transfer Project (1987) found that difficulties in adapting to secondary school had a curricular dimension, in particular they found that poor readers settled less well than others. Similarly my own study of children's views of primary-secondary transfer (Thorp, 1980 and 1983) revealed that the most significant cause for concern among children was the threat to existing identities of imposed banding labels. Woods and Measor's (1982) larger scale study led them to see the threat to identity or self image in more general terms:

> All the paraphernalia supporting one's conception of self would have to be constructed anew – private spaces, reputations (for example as a fighter) appearances, and, most importantly, friends.

Elsewhere Woods (1987) also attempts to consider the child's experience of transfer from infants to junior school, and in comparison indicates how at this younger age, children's anxieties are on the whole 'more immediate and more localised' and significantly, 'more susceptible to conventional treatment'. Observing how a group of seven year olds adapted to their junior school Woods (1987) notes:

> The move from infant to junior is a considerable transition for young children to make. They have experience of only a small range of teaching approaches. Their adaptability, as yet, is limited. It is not surprising that, at the beginning of their junior career when first exposed to this new approach they were, for a time, in a kind of limbo. They had lost the stern external controls of the old . . . without, as yet, having developed the internal ones of the new. At the beginning of the year, therefore, this class were a noisy, rather undisciplined group, its members bursting and vying with each other at times for individual attention and with very limited powers of application.

Their activity at this stage is mostly directed towards the teacher but is not according to Woods 'attended by the same kind of developments as in puberty', as in the later secondary school transfer.

It is that relationship between formally organised structures within the schools and the informal groups or subcultures which either respond to them or are created and sustained by them, which we find at the transfer to secondary school stage, that I find most disturbing. Here we find the activity surrounding the ideas of liaison, transition and induction in a quite different light which we might describe as the 'informal management of continuity'. Liaison at this informal level would include communication among children about the impending change of school, the spread of rumours, myths and exaggerated scare-mongering about new teachers and older children. According to Measor and Woods (1983) these activities are functional in that they 'prepare the pupil emotionally as well as socially for a quite profound change to the new world of the upper school'. Transition is seen as a distinct phase overlapping both primary and secondary schools, a pre-adolescent state of flux, the ritual preparation for teenage, and the passage through it as a 'status passage'. Delamont (1983) for instance, indicates how pupils seem to select roles for themselves during this passage and adopt strategies to accomplish them. And induction then involves the ceremonies of initiation into a variety of subcultures, either pro or anti-school, and the appropriation of associated 'styles'.

Those who have looked closely at this informal level of activity are left with no doubts that it is a passage of some vitality and significance, which, in a sense, both teachers and older pupils are competing to define for the passagees. Teachers might say they are anxious to avert the possible discontinuity that some subcultural values might inflict, while children might see it rather as the natural continuity of growth towards adolescence. It is most sympathetically described by Measor and Woods (1984):

> The root difficulty for teachers is that while they accept their roles as elders witnessing the pupils ritual progress through the transition, some of the progress interferes with the continuities thought desirable in the formal passage . . .

and the dilemma for the management of continuity made clear.

Managing continuity 4: into the new ERA

The first section of this chapter traces the development of thinking about 'continuity' and tries to show how the framework which the National Curriculum provides has grown out of an earlier official rhetoric and into legislation in the Education Reform Act. The consequences of this Act are indeed potentially far reaching and may affect fundamental changes in the way the children of this country are educated. Education has never had such a high profile as thinking at every level has been touched. The most recent official publication (NCC, 1989) talks about 'higher expectations' and these are everywhere but whether its claim that 'more effective progression and continuity' will result, remains to be seen. At a simple level, the 'framework' provided by the Act may well work *but* there are some wider issues which those who would manage the kind of continuity envisaged must address as they begin to take account of the new context in which we all now operate. These seem to encompass two broad and closely related areas.

Choice and continuity

The introduction of 'open enrolment' appears to guarantee parental choice and who would argue with their right to choose their children's school? We might however consider the possible discontinuity which could result from the exercise of this choice. The freedom to choose, in theory, means that parents can now move their children to whichever school they want, provided there are places available. There are also implications here for who is actually able to make such choice, given the constraints of transport and finance. Inevitably though this will mean that some 'popular' schools will be full, others will be less full and when the effects of per capita funding are felt, some very 'unpopular' ones likely to close. The full implications of the kinds of restrictions on choice this is likely to lead to is at the moment unclear, but in each instance problems are posed for those who are trying to manage continuity, problems born of uncertainty. The government on the other hand seem to be hoping that this 'market-place' strategy for removing surplus places as rolls fall will prove an effective mechanism to control what the schools are doing. Schools must now compete for clients and we can only speculate on the effect this will have on the curriculum in both popular and unpopular schools as their 'managers' struggle with their changing circumstances. It's a situation likely to cause the worst kind of uncertainty, and one of which the Association of County Councils, in its response to the National Curriculum consultation document, (see Havilland, 1988) commented:

> If parents are to have real opportunities to make choices it is essential that they should be able to do so within a system which operates fairly, efficiently and openly, and which can safeguard the features which led to the choice in the first place.

It seems impossible however for schools to remain unchanged by the uncertainty engendered in this present situation. How do those who would manage continuity plan for the future amid such uncertainty. Indeed, how far does the need to 'compete' with other schools in the market place inhibit thinking about continuity which is so essentially cooperative? And how far will the 'insularity' which competition between schools will inevitably bring in the future, lead to real disincentives to exercising choice as parents continue to be frustrated by the absence of guarantees against the kinds of unnecessary repetition of work or missing out of important key steps in learning as children actually make the move from one school to another.

Testing and discontinuity

One of the central features of the new National Curriculum is to be the national testing arrangements it proposes at the key stages of 7, 11 and 14. Perhaps more than any other, it is this aspect of the new legislation which has attracted most criticism from educators who might wonder how much notice has been taken of the large body of reearch which has shown the destructive results of 'labelling' children. It was the realisation of the effects of streaming, informed by this research, which led to the removal of the old 11+ test. Currently however, we seem to be putting the clock back rather a long way. Typical of the objections to the kind of 'competition' which the Act has brought back is that of the British Association for Counselling (see Havilland, 1988):

> We question the atmosphere of competition that will be engendered by national testing. Competition can be helpful, it can motivate, but competition where a large number of our children will be less than average (statistically this has to be the case) will lead to young people who believe themselves to be less than average people. It will demotivate them and lead to a withdrawal and lessened confidence.

It seems that all those in-school processes which have been identified as contributing to pupil disaffection, particularly the labelling effects of streaming, are likely to be intensified as a result of the proposed testing programme.

These questions which arise out of thinking, albeit briefly, about some of the implications of two broad issues 'choice' and 'testing' provide the context in which any consideration of continuity must now be considered. On the one hand the imposition of a centrally controlled National Curriculum and the desire to give choice to parents over their children's schooling seems somewhat paradoxical, a case of giving more choice about less. It has however weakened professional control over the curriculum and provided a mechanism of accountability. What is more giving choice to the consumers, parents, forces schools into the kind of competitive market place situation which compels them to abandon the kind of co-operation so essential to the achievement of real continuity, itself embedded in the idea of a national curriculum framework.

And on the other hand, the return to mass testing, one of the ways in which it is intended to both inform parental choice and impose a kind of continuity on the system brings with it the now well documented detrimental side effects on children.

The new context is by no means a straightforward one and is further complicated by the seeming unfairness which characterises the way in which it is likely to work out in practice. This poses a number of difficult questions for those who would now consider continuity, among the most fundamental of them is that of Sallis (1988) who asks:

> How can we reconcile choice for parents with equal opportunity for children, given that the desire for choice arises from, feeds on and perpetuates inequality

How indeed might the needs of our children in terms of continuity be served by such competition both within and between schools?

Conclusion

In this chapter I have tried to show that thinking about 'continuity' occurs at different levels which involves the identification of an 'official rhetoric/reality' and a 'teacher's conventional wisdom' of continuity. However a consideration of 'continuity in practice' reveals the significant differences of emphasis between them. The official rhetoric was thought to be mainly concerned with 'curriculum continuity' or what might be called the 'demanding' side of the educational task. This is further strengthened by the official 'framework of continuity' contained in the recent legislation for a National Curriculum. The teacher's conventional wisdom on the other hand seemed to be about children's welfare, or the 'caring' side of the educational task. For whatever reason a critical look at practice seems to indicate how much better teachers are at the caring side than the demanding one.

In looking at issues of continuity there are marked differences in emphases as children get older. For younger children continuity would seem to be less of a problem. The predominant classteacher role might embody both the caring and demanding side of the educational task and movement between classes may very often be in one primary school under the management of one headteacher. As children get older the functions of caring and demanding diversify and after the crossing of the 'great divide' between primary and secondary schools are very often shared between complementary roles of 'academic' and 'pastoral' staff. There are those who argue that such a differentiation is a useful one, for they argue that as children grow towards adolescence then *discontinuity* can serve a useful function. Measor and Woods (1984) for instance suggest that

> . . . it would be a mistake to aim for an entirely smooth continuous transition . . . the trauma associated with a sharp break is functional.

Another part of this discontinuity which may also be functional is the 'split' of the caring and demanding or pastoral and academic roles as children enter the secondary school. Best and Ribbins (1983) take issue with those who argue that these two functions should be combined by showing how the needs of the child, the development of 'autonomy, rationality, sensitivity and the like', must be considered alongside the differences in *relationships* between 'the child and the teacher as instructor, carer and disciplinarian'. As children grow and need *different* relationships with adults in school, so too should schools seek to develop those appropriate relationships, a situation not always possible suggest Best and Ribbins, 'where teachers are wearing more than one hat'. This becomes especially important to remember for as children grow in their need for greater *independence*, the increasingly 'product' orientated curriculum of the later years seems to demand greater *dependency*. As we arrive at the stage where we begin to appreciate that children need these different kinds of relationships as they develop fully, or 'educationally', we find that our attention is being focussed for us very much more sharply on just the one, the demanding, the curriculum side of our task. It would seem that the requirements embodied in the Education Reform Act are attempting to change the common-sense way in which we think about our job. The changes that this has brought has meant a shift in the balance of power over the curriculum with the result that, as teachers, we have been removed from certain levels of decision-making about the curriculum. The need now is for us to resist being deflected from our other professional responsibility, that of 'caring' for children. This has become even more important as we enter an era which promises a far greater emphasis on the 'product' of our enterprise and we must therefore not allow ourselves to be what Apple and Teitelbaum (1986) call 'de-skilled' in this area of 'care'. It is here that those who would manage continuity may find their greatest task, because now we must learn how to manage both the worst excesses of 'choice' and their effects on already disadvantaged groups and the worst excesses of 'testing' and their effects on all children.

However the manager of continuity who wishes to retain a view of the child at the centre of the educational stage will remember the words of Richardson (1973) who insists that:

> Being an educator – in the broadest sense of the term – involves both making demands on and caring about the person.

and realise that 'continuity' is not about one thing or the other, but a *unity of both caring and curriculum.* As Dean (1980) so rightly points out:

> Continuity is what is or is not experienced by the individual child.

and it is the totality of that experience which should be considered by the manager of continuity as he strives for the fine balance between the demands of a rhetoric which sees children as human resources and his commitment to practice which insists on treating children as human beings.

References

Apple, M & Teitelbaum, K (1986) 'Are teachers losing control of their skills and curriculum' in *Journal of Curriculum Studies*, Vol 18 No 2.

Baldwin, J & Wells, H (1979) *Active Tutorial Work: The First Year* Blackwell.

Best, R & Ribbins, P (1983) 'Rethinking the pastoral-academic split', in *Pastoral Care*, Vol 1 No 1.

Blatchford, P, Battle, S & Mays, J (1982) *The First Transition: Home to Pre-school* NFER/Nelson

Blythe, A & Derricott, R (1985) 'Continuities and discontinuities in the primary curriculum', in *Curriculum* Vol 6 No 2.

Board of Education (1931) *The Primary School The Hadow Report* HMSO

Brown, J & Armstrong, H (1986) *Transfer from junior to secondary the child's perspective*, in: M. Youngman ed (1986) op. cit.

Brice, C (1984) *The Gateway Project at Holloway School, Islington*, in B. Gorwood ed (1984) op. cit.

Button, L (1981) *Group Tutoring for the Form Teacher 1. Lower Secondary School* Hodder & Stoughton

Catton, J (1985) *Ways and Means: the Craft Design and Technology Education of Girls* SCDC/Longman

Cleave, S, Jowett, J & Bate, M (1982) *And So to School: a Study of Continuity from Pre-School to Infant School* NFER/Nelson

COPE (undated) *Primary-Secondary Liaison: the Blackburn Project* Scottish Committee on Home-School Relations

Cox, T (1984) *Transfer from primary to secondary school – a primary school view* in: B. Gorwood ed (1984) op. cit.

David, H (1988) *Junior partners: bridging the secondary transfer gap* T.E.S. 14.10.88.

Dean, J, (1980) 'Continuity' in: C. Richards ed. (1980) *Primary Education: Issues for the Eighties* A & C Black

Delamont, S (1983) *The ethnography of transfer* in: M. Galton and J. Willcocks eds (1983) op cit.

DES (1967) *Children and their Primary Schools The Plowden Report* HMSO

DES (1975) *A Language for Life: The Bullock Report* HMSO

DES (1978) *Primary Education in England A Survey by HMI* HMSO

DES (1979) *Local Authority Arrangements for the School Curriculum* Report on Circular 14/77, HMSO

DES (1980) *A View of the Curriculum* HMI Series: Matters for Discussion, HMSO

DES (1981) *The School Curriculum* HMSO

DES (1982) *Mathematics Counts The Cockroft Report* HMSO

DES (1984) *English from 5 to 16* Curriculum Matters 1, HMSO

DES (1985a) *The Curriculum from 5 to 16* Curriculum Matters 2, HMSO

DES (1985b) *Better Schools* HMSO

DES (1985c) *Mathematics from 5 to 16* Curriculum Matters 3, HMSO

DES (1985d) *Science: a Statement of Policy* HMSO

DES (1987a) *The National Curriculum 5–16 a consultation document* HMSO

DES (1987b) *National Curriculum Task Group on Assessment and Testing* A Report, HMSO

DES (1989) *National Curriculum: from Policy to Practice* HMSO

Dutch, R. D. (1974) 'Transition to secondary: an experiment in a Scottish comprehensive school' in *British Journal of Educational Psychology*, No 44.

Galton, M (1983a) 'Changing schools – changing teachers' in: L. A. Smith ed. *Changing schools: the problem of transition* Report of the proceedings of the March Education Conference, Goldsmiths College

Galton, M (1983b) *Problems of Transition* in: M. Galton and S. Willcocks eds (1983) op cit.

Galton, M & Willcocks, J (1983) *Moving from the Primary Classroom* R.K.P.

Ghaye, A. & Pascal C. (1988) 'Four year-old children in reception classrooms: participant perceptions and practice' in *Educational Studies* Vol 14 No 2.

Ginnever, S (1986) *Liaison and curriculum continuity* in: M. Youngman ed (1986) op cit.

Gorwood, B. (1984) *Intermediate Schooling* Aspects of Education No 32, University of Hull.

Gorwood, B. (1986) *School Transfer and Curriculum Continuity* Croom Helm

Hamblin, D (1978) *The Teacher and Pastoral Care* Blackwell

Hargreaves, D. (1982) *The Challenge for the Comprehensive School* R.K.P.

Havilland, J. ed (1988) *Take Care Mr Baker* Fourth Estate

House of Commons (1988) *Educational Provision for the Under Fives* First Report of Education, Science and Arts Committee, HMSO

ILEA (1987) *The first year at secondary school: general curricular and pastoral* Secondary Transfer Project Bulletin 11.

ILEA (1987) *Pupils adjustment to secondary school* Secondary Transfer Project Bulletin 16.

Johnson, M. & Brooks, H (1979) 'Conceptualising classroom management' in: D. C. Duke ed. *Classroom Management* 78th Yearbook of N.S.S.E. University of Chicago

Liddle, A. J. R. et al. (1985) *Art and Craft in the Primary School* Mimeo

Marland, M. (1977) *Language Across the Curriculum* Heinemann

Measor, L. & Woods, P. (1983) 'The interpretation of pupil myths' in: M. Hammersley ed. *The Ethnography of Schooling* Nafferton

Measor, L. & Woods, P. (1984) *Changing Schools: Pupils Perspectives on Transfer to a Comprehensive* Open University Press

Meighan, R. (1978) 'A pupil's eye view of teaching performance' in *Educational Review* Vol 30 No 2.

N.C.C. (1989) *An Introduction to the National Curriculum* National Curriculum Council

Neal, P. D. (1975) *Continuity in Education: Junior to Secondary* E.D.C. Project 5 Final Report City of Birmingham Education Dept.

Ribbins, P. (1981) 'What kinds of conferences do teachers really need to help them meet their pastoral responsibilities?' in *West Midlands Journal of Pastoral Care* Vol 1 No 2.

Richards, C. (1982) 'Curriculum consistency' in: C. Richards ed. *New Directions on Primary Education* Falmer

Richardson, E. (1973) *The Teacher, the School and the Task of Management* Heinemann

Sallis, J. (1988) *Schools, Parents and Governors: a New Approach to Accountability* Routledge

Schools Council (1972) *Education in the Middle Years* Working Paper No 42, Evans

Smith, J (1985) *Transferring to secondary school* Home and School Council

Stillman, A. (1985) 'Curriculum continuity: some problems and solutions from a research perspective' in J. Castle and I. Lawrence eds *Policies for Curricular Continuity* West London Institute of Higher Education

Thorp, J. (1980) *From Primary School to Secondary School: the Subcultural Context of a Status Passage* Unpublished B. Phil Dissertation University of Birmingham

Thorp, J. (1983) 'Evaluating practice: pupil's views of transfer from the primary school to the secondary school in *Pastoral Care* Vol 1 No 1.

Thorp, J. (1988) 'Starting school: thinking about our practice' in *Rumpus* No 22 Winter

Walton, S. (1983) 'Junior to secondary: towards an easy transition' in *School Organisation* Vol 3 No 1.

Willes, M. (1983) *Children into Pupils: a Study of Language in Early Schooling* R.K.P.

Woods, P. (1987) 'Becoming a junior: pupil development following transfer from intants' in A. Pollard ed. *Children and their Primary Schools A New Perspective* Falmer

Woods, P. & Measor, L. (1982) *The adaptation of pupils to secondary school* Final Report S.S.R.C.

Youngman, M. ed. (1986) *Mid-schooling Transfer: Problems and Proposals* NFER/Nelson

19 Enrichment through Federation

Pat Williams

'The Quality of School Education concerns everyone'
– Better Schools 1985

At a time when primary schools are struggling to respond to ever increasing demands and expectations, when the advocacy and excitement of reform so typical of the 1960s and early 1970s has given way to the appraisal of policy and practice of the 1980s, it is important that primary schools should not under value the progress they have made and the expertise the have developed in planning and delivering an intellectually challenging and appropriate curriculum. In school-based inservice, and individually, teachers have worked to develop a deeper understanding of the subject matter of the curriculum and of children's learning. This has been essential as they have tried to respond to the expectations of a wider, more relevant and differentiated curriculum and in turn this has necessitated a greater degree of inter professional consultation. What is essential now is that these efforts are not lost and that individual schools and authorities encourage the development of more clearly articulated frameworks for coordinating individual efforts. The challenges of the 1980s can be met: the resources are there within the profession but what is necessary is a new professional vision, one which encourages the school, the headteacher, the teachers to see themselves as part of a larger professional network whose aim is support, whose concern is quality.

1978 saw the beginning of a decline in the overall school population as a result of which many primary schools are now in the process of establishing for themselves a new identity at a smaller size. The term 'small school' has differing connotations. Many schools have spare space and use it most creatively and effectively but it is appreciated as a mixed blessing when the number of staff in the building is sadly depleted. It is particularly ironic that this reduction in size should come at a time when the demands being made on the primary teacher are such that a reasonably sized professional group would facilitate response.

A primary teacher today will be expected to play an active and informed part in the definition and development of curriculum. In order that they may more skilfully match work to children's needs they will need to have greater understanding of curriculum content and enhanced judgement in terms of expectations of pupil performance. The requirements of the National Curriculum will create a framework for such curriculum planning but will still require professional expertise if it is to be appropriately and effectively delivered. Each teacher will need to become more familiar with the ways in which Information Technology and Design Technology can contribute to the primary curriculum. Most schools consider the involvement of parents desirable but their effective use requires considerable planning and organisation.

As a group, a school staff can work together to face these challenges. Within the group there will be opportunities for the development of professional leadership and for the recognition of different professional hierarchies as the expertise of individual members of staff is made available to the group. Perhaps most important is the stimulus of professional discussion, the challenging of ideas and the possibility of sharing responsibility for the implemenation of ideas. In the one form entry primary school, this discussion and activity takes place against the background of a limited level of resources and of restricted possible organisations.

For the small rural school not only is this professional group even more severely curtailed, resources will be less and the organisational possibilities narrower when two or three teachers must cover the 5-11 range. The teacher in the small rural school will face the same pressures as those in the larger urban schools but may also:

– experience a degree of geographical isolation;
– have less resources;
– have less prospect of internal promotion;
– have a wider role definition;
– work with a wider vertical grouping:
– teach the same group for 3 or 4 years.

This is not to say that size alone ensures success but to suggest that professional support of a particular kind is essential today and that increased peripatetic staff or capitation will only provide part of the answer. To remain educationally viable small schools must use their own strengths, identify their own needs and be willing to share their expertise. In the many attempts which have been made to support small schools three objectives repeatedly occur:

- to reduce their isolation;
- to create flexibility;
- to enable them to act as a mutual resource.

It is these ideas which have led to the development of a pattern of Federations amongst the small rural schools in Berkshire. Groups of small schools were identified on a geographical basis and were offered a peripatetic teacher with specialist skills and group funding. An adviser was to act as leader and initiator in the early stages but it was envisaged that the group would eventually be responsible for its own direction. From the outset it was established that each Federation should be considered on its own in the light of local personnel, resources, needs and aspirations. This was an important principle as it has allowed Federations to develop distinctive identities which encourage a feeling of ownership amongst the member schools.

Six Federations have come into existence since 1979 and are seen as serving a variety of purposes, enabling the small school to:

- operate from a position of greater strength (resources, staffing etc);
- minimise the disadvantages of professional isolation;
- widen the children's horizons;
- overcome problems of distance from libraries, museums and other such centres;
- increase teacher liaison and contact;
- provide relevant in-service training for teachers;
- foster cooperative ventures;
- widen and develop the curriculum:
- maintain stimulation within the wide age-range often found in a single class;
- create and identify a unit which the LEA could support in a more realistic, positive and creative way.

Wherever possible these groupings were around a secondary school, but the strength of this link varies. In one Federation, grouped around the Downs Secondary School, the link is extremely close as it draws virtually 100 per cent of its children from the Federation schools. The headteacher of the secondary school is a member of the Federation and senior members of staff regularly attend Federation meetings. Sports days and musical events take place at the secondary school and a member of staff will, on occasions, join the primary school journey. In other areas the link is less close as even a small schol may send children to two or three Secondary schools.

In all cases, however, the grouping has enabled the small rural schools to benefit more effectively from outside support. This support already existed, from the comprehensive school, the Advisory Service and the LEA but fragmented between a large number of small schools its potential was limited. For the secondary school it becomes possible to consider sharing resources and facilities or to offer specialist expertise, whilst for the Advisory Service, the pastoral and coordinating role of the Advisor and the support role of the Advisory teacher are considerably enhanced as more frequent contacts are possible. In the present climate of increasing expectations and reducing financial support it is more important than ever that support should be cost effective – in educational terms! Resourcing and staffing on a group basis provides the LEA with a realistic mechanism for responding to the needs of the small schools.

As the Federations have developed it has been possible to identify four stages in their development.

Informal

This first stage involves rather tentative approaches in order to establish procedures, together with anxiety about autonomy.

Time was necessary for schools to appreciate the benefits of 'togetherness'. At first contacts were on a fairly casual level, a joint sports day, visiting other schools for concerts, using the finance available to play a more active part in the normal activities of the area. Teachers were brought together to share experiences, but these were often on the basis of work done in one school but shown to another. The schools were part of a group, doing things alongside each other rather than with each other. Headteacher meetings became a regular event and the benefits of sharing experiences with colleagues in a similar situation were quickly appreciated. Fears about loss of autonomy or of external direction gradually subsided.

Identity

During this stage the framework is used as an organisational device and formal contacts are established. Trust develops at headteacher level.

At this point the Federation began to acquire a rather higher profile and formality. As might be expected the administrative and organisational advantages of the grouping were exploited as school journeys became a possibility and such events as Music Festivals were organised as a whole group. Joint inservice courses developed; the impossibility of school based giving way to the practical reality of Federation based. Other schools and teachers became familiar as courses and events were held where the school's resource was appropriate. Experiments were made in bulk purchasing and a Federation identity emerged.

The Downs Federation were able at this stage to mount a joint primary/secondary Conference to look at areas of shared concern and to establish joint working parties. The Conference produced a series of recommendations. Of the two examples given much has been implemented.

Handwriting

1 That the Federation should seek to achieve a degree of uniformity in the policies of schools towards handwriting and presentation skills.
2 That schools should seek more positive approaches in helping children with handwriting difficulties.
3 That a working party be established as soon as possible to look at all aspects of handwriting and presentation skills, and that examples of children's work should be collected for this purpose. Membership of the working party should contain representation of all schools.

The exchange of teachers and materials

1 That the regular exchange of teachers and materials be a central part of the Federation's activities.
2 That primary and secondary schools exchange teaching staff on a one-day observation basis, and that similar exchanges between Primary schools also take place.
3 That it should become normal practice for a primary and secondary teacher to exchange roles for one week at least in every school year.
4 That all schools make lists of the equipment they are prepared to lend to other schools eg audio-visual equipment, science materials, etc, and that a named teacher should coordinate this exercise.

Realisation

This third stage is typified by more spontaneous groupings, more involvement of class teachers, more cross groupings of children and Federation identity acknowledged.

The Federations had begun to build up shared resources such as science materials, a PA system, and musical instruments. Although activities had brought together staff and children from the member schools, attempts were now made to more directly involve teachers in the Federation. Not only did schools now share school journeys but follow up work was undertaken as a joint exercise and the resultant exhibition of work was a Federation Exhibition. Entries to a locl show were Federation entries. At headteacher interviews governors were quick to explain to candidates the benefits of Federation: a much more flexible attitude developed to the sharing of Federation resources and various patterns of co-operation developed, from all schools being involved, to two infant teachers coming together to work in their schools combining for games and PE on a regular basis. Individual schools began to take initiatives which they saw as for the benefit of the Federation. Two schools separately developed Nature Trails which are available to the rest of the Federation whilst another school planned a programme of work introducing children to the computer and then invited other schools to come and see it and use it for themselves. Having taken from the Federation, schools are now beginning to identify ways in which they can contribute.

Adventure

At this stage confidence and security is displayed and schools rely on each other for support. Federation is seen as a reality by parents and governors.

The more well established of the Federations are now moving into the exciting stage of genuine commitment to sharing and actively exploring ways in which they can release the expertise in their own schools for the benefit of others. The exchange of teachers is occurring and appointments are made with exchange in mind. Children are being brought together to work on projects planned by a number of schools with support teachers and compensation is made for restrictions imposed by limited peer groups or physical facilities. Joint parent teacher meetings have been held and a governing body elicited the support of other governing bodies in the Federation over a matter of joint concern. More and more frequently the Federation is being seen as a relevant and flexible mutual resource. Joint curriculum planning exercises are being undertaken.

As the Adventure stage of the Federation develops the concern must be to find ways to release the potential within the member schools and to make it available to the group in some manageable way. An attempt to do this will be made in the coming year by allowing each school in the Federation X number of supply days each year. The school may use these to free a teacher.

- to work alongside another teacher in their own school;
- to work alongside another teacher/teachers in a Federation school.

Some of the days may be pooled to release one teacher for a longer period to run inservice for the Federation or coordinate a project. It is hoped that this will create for the headteacher of the smaller school the opportunity to vary organisation that is enjoyed by the larger school. It will be within the headteacher's control and can be used therefore to respond quickly and easily to the needs of the individual school.

As all of the headteachers concerned have a considerable teaching commitment this support staff may be used to release them not to do administration but so that they can work alongside their own member of staff, standing outside their classroom role to see their school in action.

Federations have made considerable use of the statutory INSET days to make available the skills of individual teachers to the whole Federation. A series of workshops have been offered within a Federation so that teachers may choose the most appropriate activity. It is increasingly being appreciated that a Federation activity need not involve everyone each time but can target selected small groups eg the infant teacher from each school.

All of these initiatives represent a move away from the traditional role of the school as self sufficient. Schools are becoming willing to rely on each other as they appreciate that this can be done without sacrificing their individual identity. Such changes take place slowly but a new professional vision is emerging. A move in this direction has been given considerable impetus by the recent Educational Support Grants designed to enrich and strengthen the curriculum offered in rural primary schools.

The notion of facilitating and self enrichment underlies many of the ESG submissions. Extra resources are seen as an opportunity to release time and expertise within a group of schools so that they can more effectively identify and meet their own needs. Twin threads of concern repeatedly emerge and are clearly stated in the Dorset submission:

- the quality of learning experiences for the children;
- the professional development of the teachers with the provision of some new career opportunities.

Using the resources provided by the grant, Dorset have established two projects the 'Dorchester project' which comprises 10 first schools and the 'Cranborne Chase project' which has 11 First Schools. The management and staffing of the project have been drawn from the member schools, directly creating career and staff development opportunities.

One headteacher is to be seconded each year from the group to take responsibility for the coordination of the project and this post will rotate around the member schools. The headteacher vacancy will be filled by the deputy or scale 2 creating a further vacancy which could bring in a newly qualified teacher. A scale 2 teacher is also seconded from the schools to develop a particular aspect of the curriculum across the cluster of schools. The planning for this post has been carefully undertaken.

The post exists for four terms enabling the teacher to spend a term on preparation, personal inservice and planning of the programme for the year. Again this new post creates the opportunity for a new appointment.

Perhaps one of the most interesting aspects of the two projects is the secondment of a scale 2 teacher to develop a parent education/preschool/school programme. This directly reflects the particular difficulty experienced by many small rural infant schools, that of the child entering school who finds it difficult to take advantage of all that is offered because of their isolated play experience and the few opportunities they have had to be with other young children. Playgroups have done much to help these children but some, not all children, have access to playgroups. The brightly painted 'Play and Learn' van travels around the area. It is equipped with toys, books, games, musical instruments and many pre-reading and pre-number activities. The project teacher meets and guides parents in the ways in which they can help their children before they come to school. She will visit the parents at home but also has a regular programme of visits where the van is stationed at a school or playgroup and parents come to borrow materials and discuss their child's needs, progress etc. Parents are shown how they can actively prepare their child for school by helping them to develop concepts of shape and colour, to note differences and to develop pre-number and pre-reading skills. Advice is supported by offering appropriate resources which are bright, attractive and can be varied as the parent visits the van.

The projects are based in a member school having an office supported by a full time secretary/ancillary helper. There is a strong sense of identity within the project teams and an excitement stimulated by the variety of professional contracts they enjoy. The commitment is clear however. The success of the project will be judged by what it leaves behind in the schools. Support cannot be continual. The project aims to create a network which will allow schools

to come together with some sense of purpose and gradually learn
to depend on each other and value their shared potential. The aims
of the projects quite clearly have 'togetherness' as their theme:

1 To develop co-operation between schools in relation to curriculum
planning and implementation.
2 To enhance the quality of learning experiences for the children
through the enrichment of the curriculum and shared learning opportunities with their peers in other schools.
3 To provide support for the teachers who are trying to cover the
curriculum by sharing expertise, exchange teaching and shared curriculum leadership.
4 To increase the confidence of teachers in small schools by providing
a forum where they can share their ideas and concerns with more adults.
The stimulation and raised expectations which arise from group thinking
are likely to enhance the self-image of the teachers.
5 To encourage teachers to look more critically at what they are doing
to be clear in their intentions and the manner in which they communicate, and moderate their practice in respect of the experience and views
of other colleagues.
6 To reinforce the value of liaison and continuity as joint curriculum
planning develops. Common understanding should lead to common
policies of assessment and record keeping.
7 To provide a structured home/school link, particularly for the isolated
homes. This would concentrate on helping parents to help their children
and counteract some of the effects of rural deprivation.
8 To supplement the available resources which can be shared.
9 To provide a programme of inservice training which will support the
work of the schools involved in the project at all levels and foster the
professional development of the teachers involved.
(Dorset LEA – ESG Rural Schools submission)

The projects provide a formal structure which in their own way
make demands on the small schools. At the same time, however,
they clearly indicate a way in which schools can enhance their own
provision and it is their ownership of the project which will generate
change.

Establishing a group identity takes time and the Wiltshire ESG
project has sought to build on the activities which had already
developed between schools. Two clusters have been established.
One around Marlborough links twenty-five schools which feed one
comprehensive school. Another around Downton, Salisbury brings
together ten schools. These, however, because of the existence of
the 11+ do not relate just to one secondary school. The aim of
the project is to extend the areas and range of the curriculum. A
coordinator has been appointed for each group whose role is very
much that of enabler and facilitator. This coordinator is appointed
for the length of the project.

Resources available to the groups include supply cover, funds for the transport of children, finance for inservice and clerical assistance. A temporary classroom has been made available for each group and this is to serve as a base for the project. It will act as a classroom when bringing groups of children together or as a teachers' centre for staff from the project schools. Features such as a base for the project help schools to develop a sense of group identity. To further this sense of corporate identity a series of workshops will bring together teachers from the group schools and a headteacher conference will seek to evaluate the progress of the project. Using a day closure it is hoped to bring together nearly all the teachers in the member schools.

The emphasis is again on helping schools to help themselves and Federation projects are quite clearly confident of the expertise and enthusiasm which is waiting to be released. It is hard to over estimate the constraints a small school experiences in a rural situation with only two or three members of staff. This is not to devalue the contribution any one person may make but rather to emphasise that the limited opportunities for flexibility within affect also its ability to respond and relate to other schools. The provision of supply cover, funds to transport children, an expectation of shared commitment adequately resourced, lifts some of the pressures on the small school leaving it more able to function in a wider context.

As Federated groups of schools had existed for some time in Berkshire the ESG submission was intended not only to build on the experience the schools already had of working together but to complement and extend the provision made by the Authority. Three main ideas lay behind to submission:

1 That many children in small schools experience a peer isolation and that they seldom have the opportunity to work in the size of peer group they will encounter at Secondary school.
2 That there was a need to help small schools in the writing of curriculum guidelines – the task for two teachers was simply too heavy.
3 A conviction that teachers working alongside each other was perhaps one of the most effective and appropriate inservice approaches.

To this end it was planned to appoint a team of four scale 3 teachers each of whom could work with one Federation in an identified curriculum area. Each Federation was asked to consult its member schools and to identify a curriculum area in which they would welcome support and an opportunity to share joint ventures for both children and staff. It was envisaged that the scale 3 posts would work in the following way:

– to support and develop curriculum;
– to work alongside teachers to develop good practice;

- to assist in school based inservice;
- to work with Federations to develop curriculum guidelines;
- to provide workshops which will bring together children of a similar age enabling them to work together in a group larger than is normally possible;
- to promote liaison between subject department at Secondary level and feeder schools.

In the first year of the grant all four Federations chose to work in the areas of Science/CDT/Computers. The Curriculum Support Teacher worked closely with the headteachers of their Federation and responded to the suggestions of that group. Very different patterns of organisation emerged in the way Federations wished to use their teachers' time. In some cases the teacher worked with one age band across all the schools, whilst others booked time for a school. It was difficult initially to establish the role of this teacher. It was not simply a peripatetic one as there were expectations of leadership and decision making in the job description that had to be reconciled with the traditional pattern of leadership of a school. Establishing an acceptable image and defining the job of the Curriculum Support Teacher was the subject of much debate within the team at their regular meetings.

Previous funding by the Authority had encouraged joint ventures but the grant now enabled the Federations to bring children together to work on a more regular basis. Whole and half day workshops provided a wider social network for the children who worked together on common topics. The Support teachers could introduce new materials which were then made available to the schools. Children coming to the workshops were accompanied by their teacher and it was possible to have three or four teachers working together, often in the school hall with all the opportunities for discussion that such a day provides.

Rather more slow has been the opportunity to bring teachers together after school to consider and plan the development of curriculum guidelines but even here discussions are under way.

As envisaged in the submission the role of the Curriculum Support Teacher was intended to provide a challenging career opportunity. The posts allow the holders to make use of expertise they already possess by working alongside other teachers. It also demands however a degree of management skill in the handling of funds for resources and transport, developing curriculum initiatives and the use of time. There is also the need to establish a person credibility and the ability to be accepted by and work within a variety of school organisations. It is only if schools accept a wider professional context than their own school that such posts will develop their full potential. They are not intended to challenge the autonomy of the head and yet to be fully effective within the Federation they must not only develop what is there but also initiate.

The ultimate goal was always for the Federations to become self supporting in their quest for curriculum enrichment. Most recently the use of the ESG has been varied in three Federations as they expressed a wish to appoint a Coordinator, a headteacher from within the Federation, to actively exploit their own resources.

One Federation, although it still meets as a group of ten schools works mostly in much smaller clusters of two or three schools.

Even without the benefits of the ESG, pilot projects have explored the benefits of Federation. The Small Schools Project which began as an experiment in 1982 in Nottinghamshire has provided curriculum support for more than fifty small schools, each with fewer than 108 pupils. The Federated groups are small, usually four or five schools. Having identified a curriculum area to which they wish to give particular attention a 'consultant teacher' is appointed. This is a teacher with a particular expertise seconded from their own schools for one or two terms to work alongside the teachers in the Federation schools. The focus may be on curriculum development but other benefits are clearly identified – the network between schools has been strengthened, the schools greatly appreciated 'a new face' and staff enjoyed the stimulation of joint planning and evaluation of the work with the consultant teacher. The investment of 1,000 extra teaching days was relatively small. The exercise was not to seek to plug gaps but to stimulate a school and group response to identified needs.

Federations of small schools exist across the country in many forms. They are obviously not the only answer to the problems faced by small schools, but allowing schools to plan as a group rather than as isolated units can make better use of existing resources.

> Such an approach has little place for those who are determined to be kings in their own castles. It takes courage and a sense of dedication to expose ones difficulties and problems to the informed scrutiny of another professional. Yet where such openness can be achieved it provides a strong network of support for heads of small schools where there are only one or two other members of staff to provide the necessary cut and thrust of professional discussion. (Joyce and Ron Cave, 1982)

For many schools a Federation has offered the opportunity to enrich their performance in a variety of ways.

Headteacher

For the headteacher the Federation can offer an extension of his role and an increase in status. As part of a larger unit the headteacher will be involved in decision making at a different and perhaps more complex level. His authority and views may well be challenged far more openly by his fellow headteachers than by his staff and there will be increased opportunities for organising and planning. The loneliness of the headteacher position is often spoken of and many headteachers experience genuine difficulty in self evaluation since they so seldom see other schools in action. The close contact with other headteachers in the Federation and the opportunities which will naturally arise to visit other schools in the cause of Federation activities should provide many headteachers with practical opportunities to compare and contrast their own performance and help them in evaluating themselves and their schools.

Teacher

Through Federation the classteacher too can experience a reduction in professional isolation. Meeting, working and sharing with teachers from other schools can challenge them to look at their own situation in a new light and yet there is the reassurance that these teachers also work within the constraints of a small school. Federation based inservice will allow the teacher to explore curriculum developments and teaching methods and pursue professional development within an appropriately informed context.

Children

Within the small school organisation it will frequently be necessary for a child to remain with the same teacher for a number of years. Any way in which the Federation can increase stimulation for the teacher will directly affect the opportunities for the child. Perhaps more directly the Federation can facilitate a wider peer group social network for the child and through this to some extent ease the transition to Secondary school. Federating may also expose the child to contact with a larger number of adults in both formal and informal settings.

Resources

In terms of both people and material resources, small schools operating as a group offer opportunities for flexibility and efficiency of use that are not available to them as individual units. This after all is the educational evaluation of resource – quantity alone is no indicator of quality.

Curriculum

The ERA has established in law the principle that each pupil should have a broad and a balanced curriculum which is also relevant to his or her particular needs. Each school will be required to deliver the National Curriculum, three core subjects of English, Maths and Science and the foundation subjects, technology, history, geography, music, art and PE. All schools will need to be involved in the debate of how they will deliver this National Curriculum, but given the complexity of the debate it is not reasonable to suggest that small schools will benefit from coming together on these issues. In the last resort, decisions will have to be made which relate to each individual school but much worthwhile discussion can take place within the Federation which in no way inhibits a school's decisions – it should rather serve to inform them. In terms of curriculum support staffing too the Federation can facilitate matters by identifying a unit which the LEA can realistically support and by providing a mechanism which enables it to use the expertise it already possesses.

Governors and parents

As the Federation identity develops, governors and parents are quick to realise its potential for supporting the small school. It can increase their confidence in the school's ability to meet the challenges of the present times and help them to appreciate the professional strengths and skills of teachers in a wider context. As people concerned with the well being of the school it is reassuring to meet and share with others who have similar concerns.

A recent local newspaper headline read 'Schools' governors will work together – Although governors were mindful of the competitive nature of future developments regarding local management of schools, they were strongly in favour of the idea that the Federation should be a mutually supportive organisation'. (Newbury Weekly News, 1989)

Throughout, the concern has been to show the way in which Federation can enrich the role of the small school. This is not to suggest that the small school is all problems. It possesses a spontaneity and atmosphere that is all its own and on which many larger institutions cast longing glances. At a time when all schools are feeling under pressure the small school finds that there are simply not enough people and hours in the day to respond to all the challenges being thrown out. But it is still master of its own fate and Federation is only a way of using the school's strengths to support itself.

Enrichment through Federation is not only for small schools. Wherever professional support is necessary schools can benefit from coming together. For many years schools have been rightly proud of the autonomy they enjoy. Sharing experiences with others need not destroy individuality. Common concerns can be met by individual responses. As the task of the individual teacher in delivering an appropriate curriculum becomes increasingly complex support must come from within the profession, from those who appreciate the difficulties, share the same ideals and have the same commitment. That means your colleagues, your area, your neighbourhood schools – it can mean Federation.

References

Cave, J & R (1982), 'Strategies for Supporting Small Schools', in *Education 3–13*, Vol 10, No 1.
DES (1985), *Better Schools*, HMSO.
Newbury Weekly News *Schools' Governors will Work Together*, 30.3.89.

Further reading

Allway & Davis (1983), 'Turning Problems into Challenges', in *Education*, Vol 22, April 1983.
Anderson, K (1984), 'Week by Week', in *Education*, 17 August 1984.
Bayliss, S (1985), 'United They Stand – a Small Schools Success Story', in *Times Educational Supplement*, 15 February 1985.
Bell, A and Sigsworth, S (1987) *A Matter of Quality* The Falmer Press
Forward, W (1988) *Teaching in the Smaller School* Cambridge University Press 1988
Keast, D (1984), *Lets Be Positive*, University of Exeter School of Education.

20 The relationship between the headteacher and the Advisory Service

Brian Smith

In recent years, a great deal of emphasis has been placed upon the important role played by all the 'partners in education'. There is a genuine desire abroad to ensure that consultation takes place between all those involved and interested in education. The major aim, encapsulating the spirit of these consultations, is that young people are educated in such a way as to prepare them for adulthood in a world vastly different from that in which their parents grew u;. There are changing patterns in society, in working life and in family life, and the education system responds through a continual process of review, development and evaluation.

One of the important partnerships in the education service is that between the headteacher and the local authority Advisory Service, without which many objectives of the organisation and management of a school cannot be fully realised, and without which many of the aspects of interpretation and implementation of authority policy cannot be achieved.

There are many partners from outside the immediacy of the classroom who put forward new ideas, new projects and new materials all thoughtfully designed to help and support the classroom teacher. But these partners do not always have regard for the essential dissemination, provision of trial materials, evaluation and inservice training which needs to follow any initiative.

In recent years, there has been a spate of policy statements, discussion documents, inspection reports, surveys, analyses, and national and local government sponsored schemes, all purporting to represent the identified needs of pupils and teachers alike.

There is now the National Curriculum, embodied in the Education Reform Act 1988, which defines, as never before, the core and other foundation subjects, attainment targets, programmes of study and assessment arrangements to be undertaken by all pupils of compulsory school age. There are also demands, locally and nationally that the education service should demonstrate that the resources used are giving value for money: in other words accountability is to the fore. There is the Local Management of Schools, also embodied in the 1988 Act, which details the challenging new role to be played by headteachers under the Financial Delegation arrangements soon to be implemented in all County and Voluntary schools in each Local Education Authority. All of these nostrums are easy to propound and provide appropriate legislation, but creating the right atmosphere at the right time for these theories and requirements to be put into practice in widely differing schools is another thing altogether. This is where the Advisory Service needs to continue to play an important role. There should be an acknowledgement that the development of new techniques and the evaluation of the effects of change are time-consuming matters. When all in the education service respond to the challenges of planning for the future, rather than simply fighting for survival in the present plethora of legislation, then the requirements of young people will be more clearly identified, understood and implemented in stimulating and exciting environments.

Of course, questions should be asked about current practice and teachers will always value the many opportunities to exchange views and seek ways to answer these questions in a positive and challenging manner rather than seeing the need to adopt a defensive stance.

If the partners in education are working to the same end, then the sharing of experiences between teachers, officers and advisers ensures the development of secure professional relationships based upon mutual respect for each other's role.

This is particularly true of the relationship between the headteacher and the adviser and both will function more effectively when the role of each is agreed and accepted by the other.

The functions of the adviser

In this text the word adviser is used to identify the Local Authority Adviser and Inspector.

What are the functions of the adviser and how do they relate to and complement the functions of the headteacher? There are four main functions common to the vast majority of Local Authority Advisory Services. These are:

1 To monitor and evaluate the education service within the local authority.
2 To offer expert advice, both specialist and phase to all in the education service.
3 To support the individual classteacher, the groups within the school and the whole school, through counselling and the provision of inservice training.
4 To encourage and initiate educational innovation and development, through local, regional and national activities.

The extent to which these four functions are undertaken by the individual adviser and the amount of time devoted to each, varies according to the priorities determined by the chief adviser responsible for managing the advisory team. However, the control of these priorities does not always rest within the Advisory Service. Many issues either are the direct result of decisions taken for example by elected members, governing bodies and other education officers, or are determined by the timetables and schedules laid down by local and national projects. Nevertheless, all four functions should be covered by the whole advisory team if the Authority is to fulfil its overall responsibility for the development of its schools and colleges.

There is every possibility that a particular primary school may have visits from a number of advisers, each fulfilling a specific function. The mathematics adviser offers advise on approaches to number work. The pastoral adviser counsels the individual teacher about career prospects. The phase adviser assists in the evaluation of the organisation and management of the whole school. This requires a coordinated approach by the advisory team, in order to make sure that the total advice offered has a coherence and relevance for all working therein.

With this in mind, it is important that the working relationship between the headteacher and the school's pastoral adviser and his specialist colleagues is clearly defined, agreed and understood if the contribution made by each towards the enhancement of the learning environment for pupils and teachers alike is to be effective.

The role of the headteacher in the school and the role of the adviser in the Authority can be seen to be based on similar precepts and yet, in many respects, they are complementary to each other. The headteacher with a knowledge of the detailed workings of the school the strengths of the staff and the needs of the pupils can offer advice to colleagues in the school and, from one school's standpoint, to the Authority. The adviser, knowing the workings of the Authority the strengths of many of the teaching force and the needs of pupils from a wide range of schools, can offer advice to the Authority and to teachers in one particular school. Both roles need similar and yet complementary management skills. A more detailed consideration of the four functions of the adviser will help to elucidate the nature of the relationship between the headteacher and the Advisory Service.

Monitoring and evaluating the education service

In this function, a detailed and first-hand knowledge of each school and college needs to be gained through a series of visits ranging from:

– the formal procedures undertaken by a specialist team of advisers at a pre-arranged time, and resulting in the presentation of a written report. These give an evaluation of existing practice and propose recommendations for the future development of the school as a whole or of certain aspects of the school requiring immediate attention;

– through the specialist and phase advisers involvement in curriculum development and staff development when identified by the headteacher and/or the adviser;

– to the more regular contact of the pastoral adviser over a long period of time during which secure working relationships can be built up, through which the flow of information so vital to the education service can be channelled and through which the continuous development of the school can be stimulated.

Each of these types of visitation has its part to play in the monitoring and evaluation of any school.

From the advisory point of view, the only way this can be achieved is to have a team of well-qualified and experienced advisers led by a chief adviser, whose collective expertise covers all the identified needs of the Authority and whose general work in each school provides that up-to-date and locally significant picture of the management of the curriculum.

The balance between advice and inspection and between specialist and pastoral work is a delicate one and requires sensitive handling.

As the role of the Local Education Authority changes in the light of recent legislation, there is now a real danger that any change in emphasis to increase the more formal inspectorial function at the expense of the specialist, pastoral and development agent functions could be as potentially damaging to the relationships between schools and their advisers as would be the removal of the pastoral care systems set up in a school to respond to the curricular, personal and social needs of pupils and teachers alike.

This is not to say that advisers do not inspect schools, far from it, for advice cannot be given without the essential elements of observation, making judgments, monitoring progress, matching aims and objectives with responses from pupils, analysing staff deployment and the use of material resources, in other words, inspecting and evaluating the management strategies employed at all levels of responsibility. However an inspection should not be seen by the staff as a team of advisers engaged in the process of bringing the school into line. Inspection which generates discussion and debate, and produces action from the staff can be very beneficial. Inspection without follow-up is likely to have minimal effect upon the development of the school. Inspection without the possibility of the provision of additional resources, be they of personnel, inservice training or materials, is also likely to be non-productive. What must be avoided at all costs is an inspectorial system which creates an 'us and them' attitude between teachers and advisers.

The Secretary of State for Education and Science recently stressed the important future role to be played by the Local Authority Adviser/Inspector in undertaking 'inspection in all its forms'. This phrase identifies the variety of functions ranging from the formal in-depth inspection through to the developmental appraoch to curriculum initiatives, all of which will be required by the Advisory Services in the coming years.

Inspections without the co-operation and collaboration of the head teacher and staff are likely to be less effective. The purpose underlying the inspection needs to be understood by all involved so that the outcomes can be incorporated in the further development of the school. Whilst it is possible that an inspection ·can produce a positive response from a school in which the quality of the learning leaves much to be desired, it is equally likely that a more long-term strategy will need to be adopted involving a planned succession of visits by advisers each working to a brief agreed by the chief adviser.

Inspections alone will not supply responses to the demands of any educational reform based upon accountability, for it is the headteacher and the staff with their day-to-day knowledge of the school who ensure that the needs of the pupils are anticipated, the curriculum is developed, and the education processes are reviewed and evaluated. The senior management team and those teachers having responsibility for each curriculum area can adopt an advisory function towards their colleagues within the school and this can complement the work of the advisory team.

One practical consequence of the adoption of this approach is seen in a number of Authorities who initiate consultative visits and whole school evaluation. The consultative visit brings together the advisory team and the whole school staff. Whole school evaluation is generated by the involvement of the school staff who determine whether consultants external to the school should take part in the evaluation or subsequent inservice training.

The purpose of the consultative visit is:

- to encourage the development of self-evaluation techniques;
- to provide working documents to be used as guides for future initiatives;
- to provide information to assist the Authority in the determination of its policies.

The methods to be used during the consultative visit are usually outlined in a document prepared by the Authority and used by each member of the advisory team in consultation with the headteacher and with individual classteachers. Basic information about the school is gathered together by the pastoral adviser before the visit with a view to advisers and teachers starting the exercise from agreed standpoints. The senior phase adviser would normally lead the advisory team and at the completion of the exercise would produce the final report in consultation with the headteacher. Depending upon the size of school, the length of the visit can be up to three weeks. During this time each adviser works alongside individual teachers, has individual discussions with teachers and attends year group or curriculum development meetings. At the end of the visit detailed recommendations are made and, although comments are not made about individual teachers, every member of staff is aware of and has made a contribution to the recommendations in the final report. Whilst there may be disagreement about the emphasis placed upon a particular point and the school may wish to include its own interpretation in the report, in general, consultation and cooperation tend to produce a well motivated response by the staff to the issues raised. Perhaps the real value comes from the procedures and processes undertaken during this joint venture which will continue well after the visit has ended.

This type of exercise can be extremely time consuming and since it relies heavily upon the relationship between the teacher and the adviser, the team of advisers must be enabled to commit themselves to the programme of visits at the expense of all other calls upon their time. An attempt is usually made to follow-up the outcomes of the final report during the twelve months following the visit, which again can be demanding of advisers' time. The demands of the Education Reform Act and the developmental needs of schools can still be served using consultative visit techniques since these

should be seen as part of the 'inspection in all its forms' functions of advisers. It is to be hoped that the developmental needs of schools continue to be served using these techniques,
     In recent years schools and Authorities have developed their own methods for whole school evaluation. An increasing number of schools are basing these upon such initiatives as the School Curriculum Development Committee's project *Guidelines for Review and Internal Development in Schools* – (GRIDS), (McMahon et al 1984, revised 1988). This is a whole school approach involving every member of staff in:

 – the review of all aspects of the life of a school;
 – the establishment of groups of teachers able to determine priorities and to recommend action for development in the future;
 – the evaluation of the effects of any change taking place.

Such a method can only be successful if the headteacher is prepared;

 – to accept a team approach to decision making;
 – to create an open form of management structure;
 – to develop a strategy for staff development.

The procedures may require the involvement of external (to the school) consultants who might be the pastoral adviser, the specialist advisers and teacher trainers from institutes of higher education. The consultants are brought in at the behest of the staff who define the brief of these helpers. Any school engaged in the GRIDS programme can expect support from other schools in the project and from the Authority.
     The essential difference between inspections, consultative visits and the GRIDS method, lies in the degree to which the advisory team is engaged in the procedures. In the first two there is total involvement from the start whilst in the third the involvement is by invitation. In each of the methods described, the essential element for achieving successful outcomes is the mutual trust and respect which must be built into the relationship between the headteacher and the advisory service. If the headteacher is put on the defensive or if the adviser becomes prescriptive then the exercises are likely to have a minimal effect on the school. Whatever method or methods an Authority encourages, the benefits gained by an individual school will add to the general and specific information about the quality of education.
     How much better will these management techniques be received and acted upon by the teaching force when they can be identified with a healty professional relationship between the schools and the advisory servies. How much more readily will they come to a

successful conclusion in the learning activities of pupils when based upon such a partnership for monitoring and evaluating the education service.

Offering expert advice

This function concerns the giving of advice in the specialist areas of the curriculum and in the general organisation and management of the school. Specialist advisers need to demonstrate a working knowledge of classroom practice and of recent innovations and developments. They should be able to identify and satisfy the professional requirements of all teachers working within the specialist area. Advisers should be supported by specialist advisory teachers whose role relates to the translation of inservice training programmes into classroom practice. The combination of specialist advisers, advisory teachers and school teachers working together should provide the major source of specialist information and advice to the Authority. But this can only be of real benefit when under the direction and guidance of the chief adviser within the Authority and of the headteacher in the school. Otherwise a particular specialism might dominate the whole curriculum pattern of an Authority or school determined by the interest and enthusiasm of an individual rather than being seen to be an integral part of the whole.

Similarly advice on the organisation and management of a primary school can only be achieved through the expertise demonstrated by those advisers carrying a phase responsibility. Whilst experience in senior positions of responsibility in primary schools is a basic essential for primary phase advisers, this must be combined with an up-to-date knowledge of management techniques and strategies for curriculum development. Structures should therefore be set up:

– to facilitate the determination of realistic, feasible, challenging and attainable objectives or goals;
– to develop strategies for the acceptance and acknowledgement of line, lateral and functional responsibilities;
– to motivate the teaching and non-teaching staff to produce a good performance in all they do;
– to evaluate the processes and procedures for maintaining and improving standards;
– to establish a clear, concise, correct and complete communications network in the school and with external agencies.

Whatever the management structures set up, success will only follow if teachers know the part they are to play and then carry out those parts through all the learning experiences in which they are engaged with their pupils. Each post of responsibility should be well defined and each agreed objective should be reflected in the work of every teacher at some stage in their curriculum planning. However, it is generally accepted that structures will not produce effective school management unless set in a climate which encourages the development of fruitful relationships between teachers and pupils, between the school, its parents and the local community and between the school and the local authority.

Whilst the main thrust of advice is centred around the teaching force, others associated with a school may wish to seek advice. These can include parents, governors, elected members, the outside agencies who work with individual pupils and members of the local community. Now that Governing Bodies are assuming a higher profile in the management of schools, greater demands are likely to be made upon the time of advisers since they will be required to attend more meetings with Governors. Their detailed knowledge of the management of schools and their teaching and learning strategies will be in greater demand by a wider audience than at present.

Whatever the source of the enquiry, it is important that advisers are seen as people who are aware of the declared aims of the school, of the teaching strategies adopted therein, of all aspects of the curriculum, of the part played by specialist teachers and of the ethos which pervades all the learning processes. It is equally important for the adviser to be an independent evaluator capable of giving a dispassionate but professional view of the range of learning experiences going on in the school. The adviser needs to be recognised by others as someone who supports the initiatives undertaken by governing bodies, headteachers and their staff, thereby earning the title of 'critical friend'.

With regard to the offering of expert advice perhaps one of the most critical tasks undertaken by headteachers and advisers is in the area of selection and appointment of teachers. Upon such appointments depends the future development of the individual teacher, the specialist area of the curriculum, the pastoral care system and ultimately the overall management of the school. When a vacancy occurs, it would be so easy, in the short-term, to fulfil the responsibilities of the present postholder. In the final analysis this may in fact be the outcome when the vacancy is filled. However, a vacancy also gives the opportunity to review the present structure and to ask whether the existing teaching force is able to satisfy the changing needs of all pupils and then to ask whether different expertise and experience is required of the new member of staff. For example this could mean the replacement of a general class teacher by someone experienced in special educational needs or the establishment of computer education in the curriculum of all pupils. In other words, a vacancy can be one means whereby the school's policy for reviewing the curriculum can be implemented. In this case it is essential to define the role of the adviser in the process and to agree at what point the advice will be required to be given and to whom. Once again this stresses the importance of the school being 'known' by the advisory team. Only then can the individual adviser take an active part in discussing:

- the `need for a replacement, which might have to be argued in the light of Authority policy;
- the nature of the post to be advertised and the detailed job description;
- the quality of the applications received prior to the selection of candidates for long-listing and short-listing;
- the approach to be adopted when candidates visit the school;
- the nature and extent of questions to be asked at interview;
- the performance of each candidate at interview, followed by an opinion of the likely potential for the particular post;
- the help and support likely to be needed by the successful candidate prior to and subsequent upon taking up the appointment.

To be successful, it is essential for the adviser to offer advice which is relevant, up-to-date and precise. The credibility of the adviser is enhanced if headteachers and their staff can acknowledge that the advice given has been drawn from personal experience. This should not rely upon past experience but should be seen to be supplemented by a well-planned inservice training programme, for advisers using the knowledge, skills and concepts generated through local, regional and national contacts. The programme can be based within the Authority, using a planning series of seminars and working groups specific to that Authority and can be based upon courses, for example, set up by the National Association of Inspectors and Educational Advisers (NAIEA) which represents the vast majority of local authority advisers and inspectors and through which advisers can come together to share experiences and train together at regional and national level. In recent times NAIEA has been involved in the setting up and development of the Centre for Adviser and Inspector Development (CAID) in West Yorkshire which caters for both new and experienced advisers.

Here again, there are parallels for headteachers, through inservice training programmes instigated by their national associations and by the setting up of regional headship training units for both new and experienced headteachers.

Thus the inter-play between advisers and headteachers in the offering and provision of expert advice to colleagues and to the

Authority adds to the enhancement and further development of schools.

Supporting the individual teacher and the individual school

The support given by advisers is usually in response to specific requests at various stages in the professional development of individual teachers; for example probationary teachers, experienced teachers and newly appointed deputy headteachers all require encouragement and challenge. Once instigated these contacts must of necessity be demanding of time and energy, can never be rushed and will draw upon the counselling skills of the adviser. Initial discussions range around the areas of performance as a teacher, positions of responsibility and promotion prospects. Experience, identifiable strengths and potential are analysed in detail and evidence of flexibility and adaptability in approach is sought. Ultimately targets are agreed for the next 12 months with the promise of review at any point along the way. None of this can be achieved unless the adviser has had opportunities to observe the teacher working with pupils in the classroom.

Where this counselling is a recognised part of the school's policy for staff development and the adviser is seen as one of the essential elements in the procedures, then the effect of the actual support given is more than likely to bring about significant development in the individual teacher and hence in the school as a whole.

If the Authority has a policy for the training of staff tutors in each school, then the advisory service can expect to be brought into the staff development programme by the staff tutor, as a matter of course. Since the adviser is responsible for counselling many teachers, each with different needs, this function can be used to influence the nature and design of the Authority's inservice training plans.

Here again the complementary role of headteachers as counsellors to their own staff ensures that the counselling role of advisers is far more effective and the individual teacher will benefit from a joint approach. Most headteachers recognise that the independence of the advice given by the adviser goes hand-in-glove with their own opportunities in the day-to-day organisation and management of their school. At the present time, when declining pupil numbers and financial stringency create frustration and low morale amongst teachers, the headteacher and the adviser need to work closely together. Whilst it is important to help and support the individual, it is equally important to develop a strategy for staff deployment which reflects the strengths and potential of the teaching force, in an endeavour to offer all pupils a broad, balanced and coherent curriculum. By the same token advice given to a group of curriculum leaders or to the staff as a whole needs to be seen as being part of the school's policy for staff development.

Support given by advisers through inservice training can range from half-day specialist sessions, specific to one topic, through to the organisation of a three-day residential course. Opportunities can be offered for an in-depth study to be undertaken of a general theme or of current and relevant issues such as language development or spatial awareness. In addition, as a result of National Curriculum INSET programmes, advisers are increasingly, becoming involved in school-based inservice training which advantageously brings them into contact with teachers in the classroom situation. Advisers will set up and make contributions to an Authority working party or study group which can be centrally organised or can be based upon geographical groupings of schools. Similarly headteachers are drawn into these groups as contributors or participants, depending upon their expertise and experience. Headteachers and advisers work together on professional advisory bodies established to advise on the inservice training organised through teachers centres and institues of higher education, thereby making sure that there is a right balance and range of courses.

Advisers are actively involved in the Authority's secondment programme and, in conjunction with headteachers, encourage teachers to engage in one-term or one-year award-bearing or full-time research projects. Each secondment should be designed to satisfy the needs of the teacher, the school and the Authority. Using this system an Authority can benefit from its secondment policy provided the work of the teachers is fed back into the school and the Authority.

Advisers and headteachers share their experiences on regional and national courses organised, for example, by Her Majesty's Inspectors. Here the national perspective is brought to bear upon the development of management skills and specialist expertise required, for example, to develop in all pupils an awareness of the multi-cultural society in which they are living.

Thus whether an adviser is working with a single teacher, or the advisory team is working with headteachers and their staff, the processes of counselling and the provision of inservice training provide a motivating support service for the individual teacher and for the Authority.

Curriculum initiatives are always welcome and the teaching profession should always respond to them. Anyone responsible for the setting up of an initiative will bring forward recommendations for future development and will expect action on behalf of the pupils. The headteacher and the adviser jointly must make sure that preparation and planning time is provided in a stimulating environment within which the initiative can grow strongly. Time is also needed for consultation to take place with all those who might be affected by the resultant change. Time should also be provided for an evaluation to be undertaken into the effect of the change, once initiated.

Headteachers and advisers should provide opportunities for all those interested in education to become aware of new developments and the thinking behind them. Otherwise parents, governors and elected members might well ask why there is a need for change. If the change is well organised, well resourced and is seen to be effective and an improvement upon previous approaches, then confidence in the initiative will grow.

There is a responsibility on the part of the headteacher in school and the adviser in the Authority to make sure that decisions are made about time-scale, staffing and provisions of resources, if success is to be achieved. It is important also to inform interested people during the processes of change, and at a time when advantages are beginning to be seen, rather than when a *fait accompli* is presented at the end of the project.

Advisers should be given every opportunity to develop this fourth function since it would be so easy for them to be drawn into administrative type of work or be required to take over the responsibilities of other colleagues when vacancies occur, at the expense of development activities.

Conclusion

In considering these four functions of the adviser and relating them to the functions of the headteacher, an attempt has been made to identify the many areas of overlap and interdependence. Both strive to identify and use the strengths of the teaching force and to improve the quality of the learning experiences. Through such activities the reality of the partnership between the headteacher and the local authority adviser can be demonstrated.

Partnership demands teamwork and it is only when all team members pull together that progress is made. In the recent past, discussions about teachers' conditions of service and the teachers' action in support of a pay claim have produced tensions of a type not previously experienced in the profession. A great deal of time and patience was needed on the part of headteachers and advisers to relieve any strains experienced. Whole school strategies will have to be developed continually if the current performance of teachers and advisers is to be recognised and built upon. A climate should be created in which headteachers and their advisory colleagues can acquire new skills as a matter of course and in which the development of new relationships between pupils, teachers, parents, governors and elected members can be fostered.

To conclude: it should be possible to explore the many challenges of the Education Reform Act 1988 by adopting a positive approach, particularly at a time when the functions of advisers and headteachers are under scrutiny. The professional partnership between the two should be further developed so that the combined and complementary functions can be of lasting benefit to the education of young people. This will only be possible if headteachers and the advisory service are given the strength and quality of teams to maintain the high standards expected of their united service to education.

Reference

GRIDS (1988) *Primary School Handbook (Second Edition)*, Longman for SCDC.

21 Employer/employee relationships: a former chief education officer's viewpoint

Derek Esp

I have been asked to write this chapter 'from a chief education officer's standpoint'. One CEO cannot speak for all 104 (soon to be 117) CEO's in England and Wales. This is an individual contribution, open to challenge by other CEO's of longer standing or greater wisdom.

I have also been asked to consider the headteacher as employee. The head is also the employer's 'agent' and this makes the head's role as difficult as that of the CEO. Both head and CEO are the focus of public criticism if the school or an individual teacher fails to deliver 'standards' and 'effective' schooling. In one sense, therefore, CEOs and heads stand or fall together as the observed custodians of public and individual hopes and aspirations for the nation's children. The trouble is that public expectations are often confused and sometimes conflicting. Our response will often be like that of God in the poem:

> God heard the embattled nations sing and shout
> 'Gotte straffe England', and 'God save the King',
> God this, God that and God the other thing,
> 'Good God,' said God, 'I've got my work cut out.'

There are plenty of people prepared to tell us what should be done. The Better Schools paper (DES, 1985) began with the statement:

The quality of school education concerns everyone. What is achieved by those who provide it, and by the pupils for whom it is provided, has lasting effects on the prosperity and well-being of each individual citizen and of the whole nation.

This places a heavy load on the shoulders of the head of Little Rumbling in the Bog County Primary School. Thankfully the paper goes on to recognise that the schools have had to cope with conflicting views about how their objectives and actions should develop in the face of changing demands.

There has been neither clarity nor agreement about priorities among the many aims they set for themselves and those which others set for them. The Education Reform Act (1988) now establishes clear guidelines in terms of content and attainment targets. There are signs that there will be freedom within these national guidelines. A combination of a clear national framework and freedom for individual teacher initiative could provide a helpful working 'climate' for headteachers.

In this chapter I shall attempt to describe 'the employer', outline some of my expectations of the head as employee and, finally, describe some ways in which the CEO and headteacher can help each other.

The employer

Power and authority in education is to be found in many places. It is exercised by headteachers, by Local Education Authorities, by the Secretary of State for Education and Science and by Parliament. The Local Education Authority works within a changing framework of legislation and national administration. The Education Reform Act (1988) makes fundamental changes to the role of the LEA. It should encourage LEAs to set frameworks within which schools will be free to manage their own affairs and deliver the requirements of the National Curriculum within the approved budget. The role of the LEA politician is likely to be considerably diminished. The role of the CEO will change. He will be less of a team captain and more like a team coach standing on the touchline and hopefully encouraging and supporting the real players on the pitch – the headteachers. The effective LEA will have to ensure that the National Curriculum is delivered, that attainment targets are achieved and that budgets are not overspent. There will be sanctions for 'defaulters' but even here governors will be able to appeal to the Secretary of State. The CEO will have the task of creating a clear framework within which schools can work. The LEA will have to provide an effective monitoring service and will secure support and training for staff in schools. The new emphasis on the strategic role of the LEA should release schools from the pettyfogging restrictions inherent in the working practices of a minority of LEAs. There will still be tensions between the LEA desiring to meet the need for resources at an adequate level and the various restrictions imposed by government departments. The community charge, legislation on competitive tendering and other requirements may provide a turbulent climate for LEAs at a time when they will be reorganising their managerial and administrative arrangements to fulfil their new duties. The Education Reform Act will not automatically create a more even distribution of resources, opportunities and standards of provision across the country. Indeed, the emergence of Grant Maintained Schools and City Technology Colleges may lead to even greater variations in resource allocation.

The LEAs are very varied. The size, urban or rural nature of an LEA and its historical development of political administrative systems, can alter various aspects of employer/employee relationships. For example, within LEAs of similar size, there may be different committee structures, greater or lesser intensity of party politics, and a different degree of corporate involvement by other central departments in the management of the education service. The whole balance of influences and relationships between members (councillors) and officers of the LEA, can have considerable influence on employer/employee relationships.

Each LEA has its own management style. This will influence relationships between the school and the LEA office. There are some LEAs where there is less willingness to trust heads to manage the schools; others where there is willingness, officially at least, to give more autonomy to schools.

Local Management of Schools will force the hand of those authorities which have held a tight rein on schools but there will be some pockets of resistancwe where elected members and officers may find it painful to adapt to the post ERA world of relatively autonomous schools.

The school can only be relatively autonomous because it has to work within the rules and guidelines laid down by external authority. The debate on the autonomous school in the Netherlands concluded that 'public authorities must impose the right conditions for the development of the autonomous school' (Dutch Catholic Schools Council Conference, 1979). This attitude contrasts greatly with an attitude I encountered in another LEA, where the then Chairman of the Education Committee said that he needed to keep a tight rein on schools because he did not trust education officers, advisers, heads, governors or teachers! Where is your employer on this continuum? Perhaps your CEO believes in autonomy, but the message has not yet reached the parts that other beers cannot reach. Many ideas get lost in the bureaucratic machinery and the helter skelter of busy education departments. In the words of David Streatfield of EMIE, who has studied the reading habits of education officers, 'many reports get flushed through the system without touching a single mind'.

A recent report (Audit Commission, 1985), identifies examples of successful action and practice in local authorities. It provides a useful check list for employees and others to assess the Authority in terms of public image and responsiveness. Try some questions on this check-list on your LEA:

    – What impression is gained by people who try to contact the Authority? Rate the Authority on each of the following:

Figure 21.1 – A checklist to measure L.E.A. responsiveness

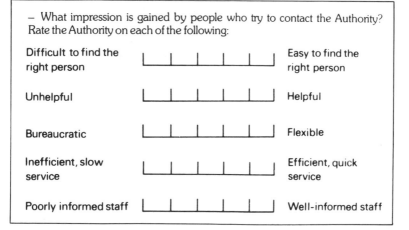

If the public and the head of the school find the contacts unhelpful and inefficient, what price employer/employee relationships? You can also use this publication to check your employer's approach to you, the employee:

    – Do employees have pride in their Authority and enjoy working for the council?
    – How satisfactory are working conditions?
    – Do staff feel wellinformed and appreciated?
    – Is delegation accompanied by greater accountability and recognition?
    – Do staff respect chief officers and have their own opinions listened to and respected?

Obviously national events, such as industrial action, ministerial statements and other external factors, will have an impact on morale. I am indicating, however, that it is important for the head, as employee, to analyse the attitude, style and effectiveness of the employer in order to understand what employer and employee need to do in order to improve their joint efforts to serve the children well.

The changes being implemented now are a true test of the ability of the LEA to be responsive and positive in its attitude to the delegation of management responsibility to schools.

Great expectations: a CEO's of the primary school head

In the past few years I have studied the selection and training of headteachers. Numerous people have told me how different primary school headship is from Secondary School headship. I am not so sure. I accept the 'POST' project attempt to define the tasks of the Secondary head. The roles of 'leading professional' and 'chief executive' are intertwined and both vital to the exercise for effective headship. Is this any different for the Primary head? Surely the Primary head is 'leading professional' and is also 'chief executive' of his–her enterprise. The total number of adults and pupils to be 'managed' will vary, but the essential needs are the same – to establish curricular aims; to translate these into plans for action; to marshall and manage the resources to deliver the plans; to communicate the school's aims to parents and governors; to enthuse and encourage staff; to monitor and evaluate achievement of the aims; and so on. A few years ago I asked several Primary heads to assess the relevance to their job at the 'POST' project analyses of the Secondary head's tasks. There was universal agreement that the Primary head's job is no less complex than that of his/her Secondary school colleague, even if it is different in scale!

My first expectation is that the Primary head as employee should fulfil the tasks and the responsibilities outlined below:

School pastoral and curricular organisation

1 Identifying and determining, in consultation with all interested parties, overall school aims and objectives.
2 Determining a curriculum relevant to the academic abilities and needs of all pupils, and allocating curricular responsibilities to staff.
3 Evaluating standards of teaching and learning through appropriate criteria and instruments.
4 Determining a policy and organisation for pupils' pastoral care.
5 Determining the norms of behaviour and discipline for pupils and staff.

6 Arranging for the appointment of suitable staff.
7 Establishing the approval of governors and of the LEA, to the number and grade of post above scale 1.
8 Allocating and controlling the LEA budget and other school funds.

General administration

1 Determining procedures for school policy-making, including the delegated responsibilities of the senior management team.
2 Coordinating the school's work with that of feeder schools and of further and higher education institutes.
3 Defining staff tasks and producing job descriptions.
4 Completing returns and keeping records required by the LEA.
5 Establishing sound procedures for supervision, security and maintenance of buildings and grounds.

Leadership and human relations

1 Motivating pupils and staff by personal influence and concern for individual needs.
2 Developing and implementing policy for staff development and support.
3 Solving problems and resolving conflict by applying skills of chairmanship, arbitration and reconciliation.
4 Establishing and using effective channels of communication with pupils, staff, governors, parents, and the community at large.

External accountability and community relations

1 Attending and reporting to Governors' meetings and liaising with them in matters of school policy.
2 Working in accordance with LEA policy and liaising with LEA officers and advisers.
3 Determining a policy to achieve the support and involvement of parents in school activities.
4 Presenting the school to the local community and taking into account its expectations.
5 Establishing communication with employers and linking the school within supporting external agencies.

This 'POST' Project job description will need some amendment but it essentially confirms the importance of the head as leading professional and chief executive. Recognition of the scope of the head's responsibilities is vital. LEAs and governors have to trust the headteacher and provide space for him/her to operate effectively. It would be regrettable for LEA restrictions to be replaced by pettyfogging rules invented by governing bodies fearful of their new responsibilities.

Performing the tasks is one thing; performing them effectively is quite another. I am pleased that the Local Management of Schools will encourage LEAs to delegate responsibility as far as possible. But what makes for effective headship? How can this be measured or assessed? In my involvement with the International School Improvement Project of the OECD, I have come across a surprising concensus of views about effective headship across a variety of educational systems. One mark of effective headship is to operate as a team leader.

The power and responsibility of the British headteacher has no parallel in the rest of thw world. His position was set in tradition of the great public school heads before education authorities assumed control of the local system. Jones, (1980).

Roy Jones goes on to examine the myth of autonomy, however, and to identify constraints on the full use of autonomy. In these days of participation, the head has to learn to work co-operatively with staff, with governors (including teacher and parent governors) and with parents and other voluntary helpers who can enhance the work of the school. The movement to a National Curriculum, the Local Management of Schools and a systematic system of monitoring school, teacher and pupil performance and the exposure of schools to 'market forces' will emphasise the need for effective participative styles of management will be essential in the post ERA world of education. The constraints are clearly to be seen in the National Curriculum and other legislative requirements but they do provide a clearer and more consistent framework within which the effective head can operate. The ability to lead a professional team in the local situation and gain the full confidence of governors, parents and the local community will be the hallmark of an effective head. Effective headship has been examined in the USA by a number of researchers. The National Association of Secondary School Principals has prepared a research summary which gives easy access to some of this research, (NASSP, 1982). One of the research papers by Persell and Cookson outlines some of the 'behaviours' characteristic of effective headship:

Demonstrating commitments to academic goals.Effective heads have a clear vision of long term goals for their school. In their own understanding and teaching they serve as hardworking examples, and display a strong desire to achieve curriculum aims. Their attitude encourages teachers to give more willingly of their time.

Creating a climate of high expectations. Effective heads do not let teachers write-off students as non-learners because of race or social class. The effective head does a great deal to set 'a tone of respect for teachers and students'. One of my greatest concerns as a CEO and as a Consultant to schools arises from visits to some schools where expectations are low. This is often a reflection of low parental and community expectations.

Functioning as instructional leaders. The English head has traditionally taught and provided an example of others of what can be done. The effective head also involves teachers in discussion and development of teaching strategies.

Being a forceful and dynamic leader This is one mark of effective headship where the different social settings of the USA and the UK must be considered. I have seen forceful and dynamic leadership exercised in the UK by all kinds of people – not only the loud extroverts!

Consulting effectively with others Many of the local crises that make their way into the in-tray of the CEO are failures to consult and communicate. Even good ideas and dynamism fail if the head cannot build 'coalitions of support'.

Creating order and discipline. Effective heads serve as facilitators of other people's actions, either by minimising factors that may disrupt the learning process, or by obtaining support and materials. The higher achieving schools set general discipline standards for the whole school' (Rutter et al, 1979).

Marshalling resources When resoources are limited, the effective head actively influences activities in school as a 'resource and reward allocator'.

Using time well The more effective heads 'get out of the office' and into classrooms.

Evaluating results Effective heads evaluate student progress and visit classrooms to give useful feedback to pupils and teachers.

In summary, the effective head is seen in classrooms on a regular basis, announces his or her expectations and serves as a model for others, while at the same time buffering the school from outside interference.

It can be said that similar characteristics of effective leadership should be observed in CEOs! The CEO as employer has a duty to help the employee (in this case the Primary head) to be aware of expectations in terms of the job description and the preferred style of management and behaviour. In various contexts the job might look the same, but be very different in practice. In Western Australia the head may be expected to 'deliver' the instructions of the State Education Department, and may have less flexibility than in England. In the Netherlands there is not a strong model of assertive headship in Primary schools, and in parts of Switzerland the head may be seen as the teacher amongst other teachers who is the link with the Authorities in little more than 'postbox' terms.

The Education Reform Act (1988) is in place to 'raise standards'. School improvement is not delivered by means of decrees from the CEO, the LEA or the Secretary of State. It is achieved through the willing and active involvement of heads and teachers in each school.

The CEO represents the LEA and provides guidelines to the Governors as employers. It is essential that an effective and continuing dialogue between the CEO and heads is maintained. This will enable the CEO to issue sensible guidelines and will help to build up a strong professional input into LEA policies. There are a number of ways in which the CEO and head teachers can devlop their work together. There are many ways in which heads and CEOs can build up effective employer/employee relationships. The CEO is an employee as well – employed to provide a vision of long term goals; a climate of high expectatioons; effective consultation; effective marshalling of resources; useful 'feedback to heads and some protection from outside interference. All these are characteristic 'behaviours'. There are many ways in which CEO/head teacher relationships can be developed.

The employer: some aspects of right conditions for development of the (relatively) autonomous school

I am conscious that much that is done by the CEO can only serve to further complicate the life of the Primary head. There is a good example in the many attempts by LEAs to delegate further responsibility to heads prior to the Education Reform Act. As soon as something is delegated, various people find compelling reasons for increasing the administrative burdens on schools. This is counterproductive in terms of the LEA's own objective in achieving better schooling. This is because 'successful principles are not bogged down in administratism'. (Rosenblum and Jastrzab, 1980). Every-time the treasurer seeks one more signature than necessary, or the maintenance man produces three more monitoring forms for remedial work on the drains, then the head's attention is further distracted and his or her blood pressure further increased.

I have not yet achieved the checklist that follows. It represents some of the ways in which a CEO might improve the employee's chance of behaving as an effective head.

A clear job description for the head

This should be available to selectors involved in the selection of a head, to school governors, to all senior advisors and administrators and especially to the head.

Provision of a 'personnel specification' for the job

If the LEA and school governors want heads to be proactive, to develop teamwork and do all the other 'effective' things needed to aid school improvement, then such a statement of 'preferred behaviour' could help.

Governors benefit from a clear statement of the style of manage-ment required for success and can be encouraged to establish freedom and flexibility for the head within the global budget and broad curriculum policy guidelines. The committees and working parties established by governors will then be able to provide help and support to professional effort. The possibility of bringing other people on to such working parties may provide the head with some valuable professional and managerial allies prepared to speak up for the freedom to manage required by the schools' 'Managing Director'.

Delegation to the head

With delegation comes accountability and the responsibility to con-sult staff, governors and parents. Consultation will enable the head to secure:

- Decisions on the numbers of teaching and non-teaching staff within an overall staffing budget.
- Freedom to approve expenditure and exercise virement within the total budget without constant reference back to the governors.

Delegation of such decisions should help heads to deploy resources towards curriculum aims and improved pupil achievements.

Lessening of the administrative load

LEAs should now be reviewing and simplifying administrative procedures. They should also be creating 'user friendly' returns for schools to complete as part of the accountability to deliver the National Curriculum. This will be possible only if the DES simplify their own information requirements and their demands on the LEAs as monitoring and reporting agencies. Undue administrative burdens can only serve to distract the energies of the head who has to manage an over-burgeoning administrative infrastructure. New technology should help! So will clear and simple handbooks on LEA rules and procedures.

Governors

Clear Articles of Government and guidence to governors on their duties are required. The CEO may also be able to help the head faced with a governing body which is reluctant to give the head freedom to manage the school.

Procedures

Clear procedures for the occasional crises in employer/employee relationships will help the head and the CEO:

For example the aim of a disciplinary procedure is to improve performance. It provides a formal framework within which an individual employee knows the specific improvements required; it provides a timetable for review and provides various levels of response. It replaces the furtive, underhand methods still used in some schools, where everyone except Mr X of Miss Y are aware that X and Y are considered to be failures! Grievance Procedures solve nothing, but provide a proper framework for serious grievances to be heard by independent adjudication.

Appraisal

Appraisal is now to become a requirement. There is urgent need for proper appraisal procedure for heads. It should be positive and should answer several questions for the employee – not least:

- How am I doing?
- How can I improve?
- What am I doing well?
- What are you going to do to help me do better? (resources? – training?
- pastoral support?)

A Support 'Network'

In 1982 I invited some foreign observers to look at headteacher training in England as part of the OECD 'International School Improvement Project'. One visitor was Mats Eckhom, one of the leaders of the compulsory headteacher training programme in Sweden. He visited a scheme which did a great deal to analyse headteacher needs before training, and which provided a systematic opportunity for heads to meet each other residentially and non-residentially. Part of the course was a chance to discuss problems in one's own school and to seek the help of other heads in the same study group. Heads on the course told Eckholm that the most valuable part of training was getting together. 'Then why don't LEAs spend time and effort on creating networks?' he asked.

In 1980 I visited training courses for heads in 5 European countries (Esp 1980). Many times the most valued outcome of the training (or, in some cases, a deliberate part of the training) was a network of heads who met regularly to share experiences and support each other. Many heads find such support in their professional association, or in ad hoc groups set up as a result of a reorganisation or some other stimulus. In my view the LEA as employer has a duty to provide a regular contact group for mutual support for every headteacher. Where LEAs fail to provide effective networks heads will be seeking other ways of meeting to achieve mutual support. Developments such as TVEI have encouraged many LEAs to develop 'clusters' or consortia of schools and there should not be many LEAs unaware of the benefits of networking.

Professional development

The LEA Training Grant Scheme is encouraging a more systematic training and development programme for headteachers. The national review already indicates that there is still much work to be done on the preparation of proper induction arrangements for new heads. Some LEAs have developed aspects of headteacher training, but the total national effort still seems small in comparison with the investment in training provided in the private sector for senior staff. Training Provision for Primary headteachers has been overshadowed by the more obvious needs in Secondary schools.

Special contracts for headteachers?

The Swedish authorities have established a separate contract for heads, incorporating a 10-session week, training provision and shorter holidays than those enjoyed by teachers. Amongst other things, because there is no great salary differential between heads and other teachers, there are still recruitment problems. The issue of pay relativities and career 'routes' within the education system as a whole needs attention and may be the proper subject for a systematic review of 'management' careers in education. It could be a retrograde step however if teachers, advisers and education officers were placed on the other side of a great contractural divide from the rest of the teaching profession.

For CEOs and heads and Education Reform Act has triggered new approaches such as the emergence of the fixed term contract.

The proactive employee

The 'thinking school' needs a headteacher who is prepared to help the development of the National and LEA policies and programmes which influence his work. The CEO suffers from the handicap of all who find themselves based at headquarters, whether in the public sector or the private sector. It has always been fair game to comment on the faults of 'them at HQ'. Indeed, HQ actions have often justified criticism. Sometimes these actions may have been justified by circumstances unknown to those at the 'chalk face'. But often, HQ has not fully realised the impact of a seemingly minor change on the school. HQ's are all more effective if they include people who have present or immediate past experience as a head. The trouble is that present career patterns make transition from school to advisory service or administration a one-way traffic. There are a few people who manage to make re-entry from an advisory or administrative career. Immediate past experience is soon out-dated after a short period, and LEAs have to seek other ways of tapping into the experience and ideas of headteachers. It is a special feature of the English system that it is rare to get transfer between the national civil service and local government, between 'admin' and advisory work, between schools and the education office. Some other countries seem to achieve a more flexible response to the needs of the service. A Danish 'HMI' will be seconded to the Ministry, but will retain a day-a-week teaching load in school. A Netherlands administrator, working on policies to meet unemployment, may move to local government in order to implement the measures he helped to devise. I think it was John Sayer who observed that CEOs, heads and further education college principals shout to each other from summit to summit across the mountain peaks. Fundamentally flexibility must therefore await a review of the administration and management of education. There are signs of change. More LEAs are keeping a smaller 'core' of permanent staff at HQ and are making greater and more flexible use of people with immediate experience at the 'chalk' face. There are now some signs that heads of schools and principals of FE Colleges can seek and secure appointment as CEO.

There are a number of formal mechanisms which can be used to engage the active participation of heads in policy development and review. The professional associations provide an opportunity for some people to take part in discussions of policy issues with LEA members and officers. Heads may also have the opportunity to serve on education committees as added members. Short secondments, membership of working parties and other devices can engage the active participation of heads. Secondments give a useful opportunity to look at the system from another perspective and obtain some understanding of life at County or Town Hall and the overall problems of managing the service. Equally, the CEO and his senior colleagues will gain a great deal from injections of people with immediate experience of problems in the schools. Such opportunities can only engage a small number of heads at any one time. It would be difficult to find such opportunities for all heads of Primary schools in most LEAs.

It is vital, therefore, that the CEO is exposed to 'feedback' and suggestions from heads. Regular meetings on an area basis can provide some feedback, and if the CEO can make regular visits to some schools each term, he can 'have his ear bent' by those who care to pass on their assessment of school needs.

The effective head will be engaged in evaluation of the effectiveness of the school, and will hold a great deal of information that can be of help to policy makers. CEOs write numerous circulars and instructions to schools. We have yet to learn the opportunities to be gained from an active encouragement of headteacher comments on the effectiveness of LEA provision. Without a regular and systematic invitation to participate in policy review, the CEO is deprived of valid and immediate evidence of the LEAs performance as a provider of effective education. Generally the only feedback will be partial and sporadic. HMI have undertaken 'audits' of LEA provision, but it could take beyond the end of the 20th century for them to complete the review of all LEAs. Each LEA needs to devise its own systematic reviews and assessments of policy. Such assessments will gain greatly from the active involvement of heads. This is particularly important as LEAs and schools implement the plethora of new developments arising from the Education Reform Act. The CEO has his own 'eyes and ears' through the work of the advisory service and the education officers. The work of all these people is also enhanced if there can be a more systematic approach to policy review which involves the active interest of all head-teachers.

The CEO has special difficulties when he tries to maintain personal contact with Primary headteachers. I know that some Primary heads feel that Secondary heads get more opportunities to meet the CEO. This is partly because the many 'high profile' issues affecting Secondary schools bring the CEO into more frequent contact with Secondary heads. It is also because Secondary heads come in more manageable numbers if meetings are to be arranged. In a previous LEA I benefitted greatly from an annual residential training session where Secondary heads, further education college principals and all senior education administrators and advisors were required to attend. Those sessions stimulated that group of people to propose and develop some significant policy changes. It is important to find ways of engaging Primary heads in such opportunities. However, if they have the opportunity of working alongside the CEO and others in this way, the impact on the CEOs diary and the education budget would be noticeable. In my own case, even Secondary heads came in numbers too large for such an exercise to be fully effective. For a maximum of 30-40 heads each year at a 'think tank' training session. I developed regular meetings in a medium sized County LEA. It was not feasible to develop these meetings further without consuming more time than would be acceptable to elected members. Such developments would have taken 15 per cent of the CEO's available working time in a year. But perhaps the service would gain?

This chapter has put emphasis upon the informal and personal links between employer and employee because the success of the education service depends upon people. The 1977 HMI paper on good schools observed that the most important single factor is the quality of leadership of the head. HMI saw heads of good schools as having:

> qualities of imagination and vision, tempered by realism which enabled them to sum up not only their present situations, but also attainable future goals.

They appreciated the need for specific educational aims, both social and intellectual, and had:

> the capacity to communicate these to staff, pupils and parents, to win their assent and to put their own policies into practice. Their sympathetic understanding of staff and pupils, their accessibility, good humour and sense of proportion, and their dedication to their task had won them the respect of parents, teachers and pupils.

This description reminded me of my very early readings about management and leadership. In conclusion it might be helpful to remember that CEOs and heads have the responsibility to pursue the task, maintain the group, (eg the 'morale' of those they work with), and to be aware of individual needs. The head's pursuit of the task is helped if the CEO can 'deliver' a clear policy steer as well as the necessary resources. The various people involved need to have a clear understanding of their role – hence the need for job descriptions, personnel specifications and handbooks for heads and governors. The Education Reform Act produces demands on the education service which should encourage the development of effective informal cooperation.

The morale of the head is greatly affected by the degree to which he or she is given an opportunity to break out of isolation, meet other colleagues, contribute to policy change and review, and meet the CEO regularly to engage in a positive exchange of views on matters affecting the 'delivery' of a sound education service. If heads' morale is maintained, they stand a better chance of maintaining teacher morale.

Individual needs will be served by proper disciplinary and grievance procedures in the context of a challenging but supportive and participative management 'style'.

Finally, however, it is worth remembering that the CEO and the head do not operate in a vacuum. A chance statement by a local or national politician can make morale rise or plummet in a moment. Nevertheless a responsive service has to listen to criticism and rspond positively. Increasingly, schools are subject to all kinds of pressure groups and the 'hidden agendas' of individuals and factions. This is inevitable as public participation in schools increases. The CEO cannot wave a magic wand and make these trends disappear. He can develop communications between employer and employee to the extent that the service can draw on 'best evidence' as it responds to change. At the time when the Seebohm report prompted the development of Social Services Departments, it was said that education was no longer the only tiger in the Local Authority jungle. More recently, an American educationist, Professor Dick Schmuck, has described schools as 'wild' organisations living in a jungle. If our working environment is as wild as any jungle, then the CEO and the primary head need to learn the art of jungle warfare together!

References

Audit Commission (1985), *Good Management in Local Government*, Local Government Training Board.
DES (1985) *Better Schools* (Cmnd 9469), HMSO.

Esp, D (1980) 'Headteacher Training and Selection' in *Learing from Europe*. Councils and Education Press.

Jones, R (1980), *Primary School Management*. David and Charles.

NASSP (1982), *The Effective Principal*, National Association of Secondary School Principals.

Rosenblum, S and Jastrzab, J (1980), *The Role of the Principal in Change* Abt Associates.

Rutter, M, Maughan, B, Mortimore, P, and Ouston, J (1979), *Fifteen Thousand Hours: Secondary Schools and their Effects on Children*, Open Books.

Contributors

Robert Balchin is Chairman of the Grant Maintained Schools Trust and Director-General of the St John Ambulance. He is a former independent school headteacher and a county councillor.

Michael Brunt is Assistant Director of Education for Solihull having previously been Assistant Education Officer responsible for Primary Education for Walsall.

Barbara Bullivant is Secretary (and founder) of the National Association of Governors and Managers (NAGM), and Secretary of the Home and School Council. She is also a magistrate, and serves on the South Yorkshire Police Committee.

Ciaran Clerkin is a primary headteacher in Newham and secretary of the South East branch of the British Educational Management and Administration Society (BEMAS).

Rick Collet is Inspector for Multi-Cultural Education, Kent. He was previously Director of the Bedfordshire Multi-Racial Education Resources Centre. He has taught at the University of Wales (for three years) and in Bulgaria (for six years).

Ian Craig is Senior County Inspector for Primary and Middle School Education, Kent. He was previously a primary inspector in Croydon and a primary headteacher.

Elsa Davies is the Education Liaison Manager at the British Institute of Management. She was formerly a primary headteacher. She is a National Council member of BEMAS and the Advisory Centre for Education (ACE), and a member of the National Curriculum Design and Technology Working Group.

Brenda Ebbs is head of Stanshawes Court Junior School, Avon, her second headship. She is currently tutor of a Primary School Management course at Bristol University School of Education.

Derek Esp is an education consultant who was until 1988 the Director of Education for Lincolnshire. He is a member of the Council of the European Forum on Educational Administration and of the Foundation for International Co-operation in School Improvement.

Charles Frisby is head of Riverside Middle School, Suffolk, having previously been headteacher of two Junior schools in Coventry, and Director of the Tri-University Project in Elementary Education at the University of Nebraska, USA.

Ann Mason was formerly the head of an ILEA primary school, and then a lecturer at the University of Durham. She has recently taken on the headship of a new primary school in the London docklands.

John Pease is now retired from primary headship. Until recently he was Secretary of the Berkshire branch of the National Association of Head Teachers (NAHT).

Calvin Pike is Inspector for In-Service Development, London Borough of Bromley. He has taught in Primary, Secondary and Special schools, and in Adult Education, both in the UK and in Italy.

Ian Sandbrook is an Inspector for Primary Education, Hampshire, having previously worked with the ILEA as a primary inspector and as a headteacher. Part of his teaching career was spent in New Jersey USA.

Brian Smith is Senior Adviser for Leeds. He was previously an Adviser in Berkshire and was President of the National Association of Inspectors and Educational Advisers (NAIEA), 1984/85.

Eric Spear is head of Staplehurst Primary School, Kent, his second headship in the UK. He was before these a headteacher in Swaziland. In 1984 he was one of the first headteachers to attend an 'OTTO' management course, and since then has himself regularly contributed to school management training courses.

Audrey Stenner is head of Buckden CE School, Cambridgeshire, and currently seconded to the Authority's LMS team. She began her career in secondary schools and was a co-opted member of the Cambridgeshire Education Committee for twelve years.

Hazel Taylor is Senior Adviser, London Borough of Enfield, and was previously Adviser for Equal Opportunities, London Borough of Brent. Her teaching experience ranges from nursery to secondary.

John Thorp is a Senior Lecturer in Education at North Riding College, Scarborough. He was previously a primary headteacher in North Yorkshire and before that taught in the Midlands. Work in both rural and urban contexts has contributed to his interest and research in community education.

Derek Waters is Visiting Fellow, University of London Institute of Education. For twelve years he was Director of the ILEA Primary Management Studies Centre, and before that an Adviser with ILEA, and the head of a Primary school.

Pat Williams is Senior Adviser for Primary Education, Berkshire. She has been headteacher of two primary schools, first in Berkshire, then in Hampshire.

Index